What a gift of hope to parents agonizing over a rebellious son or daughter! The fast-paced narrative style shifts scenes from Karilee, praying mother, to her rebellious wild-child, Wendi, whose life is spiraling downward in rebellion. It is a wonderful story of hope—Wendi's return to God is a triumph of redemption!

Keith Drury
Associate Professor of Religion
Indiana Wesleyan University

This book is real—real people, real issues, real answers. This story of restoration and hope is sure to speak to parents and prodigals alike.

Dan Seaborn
Founder of Winning at Home, Inc.
Speaker and Author

Nothing—and I mean nothing—can hurt as much as a wayward child. However, the story does not end there. Closely associated with the painful term "prodigal" is the comforting phrase "came home." And such is the case in Karilee and Wendi's book with the heartrending title *Wild Child, Waiting Mom.* Candidly, I began reading the book with the ominous sense of encroaching wounding. But the subtitle—*Finding Hope in the Midst of Heartache*—evoked the immediate opposite reaction. Read the book—not because it will be easy—but because there is hope . . . hope for every hurting parent.

Dr. Jim Garlow
Senior Pastor
Skyline Wesleyan Church, San Diego

WILD CHILD + WAITING MOM

wild child + waiting mom

FINDING *hope* IN THE MIDST OF HEARTACHE

KARILEE HAYDEN
WENDI HAYDEN ENGLISH

Tyndale House Publishers, Inc., Carol Stream, Illinois

Wild Child, Waiting Mom

A Focus on the Family book published by
Tyndale House Publishers, Carol Stream, Illinois 60188

People's names and certain details of their stories have been changed to protect the privacy of the individuals involved. However, the facts of what happened and the underlying principles have been conveyed as accurately as possible.

Editor: Marianne Hering
Cover design by Jennifer Lund

Printed in the United States of America
1 2 3 4 5 6 7 8 9 / 12 11 10 09 08 07 06

Library of Congress Cataloging-in-Publication Data

Hayden, Karilee, 1941-
Wild child, waiting mom : finding hope in the midst of heartache / by Karilee Hayden and Wendi Hayden English.-- 1st ed.
p. cm.
Includes bibliographical references.
ISBN-13: 978-1-58997-355-8
ISBN-10: 1-58997-355-0

1. English, Wendi Hayden, 1968- 2. Christian biography--United States. 3. Problem youth--United States--Biography. 4. Mothers and daughters--Religious aspects--Christianity. 5. Hayden, Karilee, 1941- I. English, Wendi Hayden, 1968- II. Title.
BR1725.E525H39 2006
277.3'08250922--dc22

2005029216

Dedication

This book is dedicated in overwhelming joy to our Savior and Lord, whose unfailing faithfulness brought us victoriously through each difficulty and whose persistent love drew this prodigal home.

And, to Dan—
Our deeply loved husband and father—
a man of courage, strength, and steadfastness
during our family's prodigal experience—
You always brought us back to the hope
found only in Christ.
You are our personal inspiration and example
of what a godly man should be.
Thank you . . . thank you! We love you dearly.

Table of Contents

PART THREE—*The Long Journey Home*

Acknowledgments

To those who faithfully upheld our family in *prayer* through the difficult years—we thank God for you. You not only uplifted our souls, but we are confident that your prayers wrought mighty spiritual victories on our behalf (James 5:16).

To our friends and family who *stood by us* in love, support, and encouragement—you brought light into our dark times and helped us discover moments of joy and laughter even in the tough times (Galatians 6:2). We love and appreciate each one of you.

To Duane and Eunie Mathews. We truly count ourselves blessed through the years as the Lord directed our families into ministry together—twice! *You listened. You cared. You prayed*, through this entire story. We remain friends always—even across the miles.

To my husband (Wendi's), Mike, who graciously let me spend the many long hours needed to complete this book. I know the details of my story were difficult to hear, but your standing by me has been so encouraging. Your love has strengthened me. Thank you.

To Kristen Wisen and Renee Gentzler, who *mentored me* (Wendi) for the first two years after I came back to the Savior, and to the Sola Scriptura staff and their families who *lived out the Christian life* in a way that drew me lovingly to Christ (Matthew 5:16). You have blessed my life and set me on the right path. Thank you!

Larry Weeden, editor. You graciously received our first-draft manuscript, looking beyond its mechanical weaknesses to the power of God in our story. Your invaluable editing advice offered encouragements and suggestions as to how to better tell the story. We thank you from the depth of our hearts.

Lissa Halls Johnson, editor. When our manuscript landed on your desk, your enthusiastic response filled our hearts with great joy. We realize your energetic efforts on our behalf made the publishing of this book possible as you led us through the process. We are eternally grateful.

Marianne Hering, editor. Your editing expertise helped us maintain clarity and purpose in the writing of our story, and your hard work, diligence, and insightful guidance brought improvement and continuity to this emotionally difficult chronicle. We know that God selected you to help us fulfill our desire to communicate hope to prodigals and their families. Thank you!

Preface

Karilee:

THE AGONY A PARENT experiences while watching a beloved child spiral downward is all-consuming. When our daughter's wayward behavior stretched into months and then years, my husband and I faced a wide range of challenges and deep trials.

Emotions became raw, feelings intense. One day we would feel hope—the next day, despair. Fears and frustrations interwove with the joys of birthdays, weddings, newborn babies, and answered prayers. In an instant, months of Wendi's progress could be reversed by a single foolish action or choice.

For my husband, Dan, and me, learning to trust the Lord when things deteriorated, or sensing His direction in parenting, or practicing the discipline of earnest, effectual, fervent prayer—these were hard and painful lessons.

In this story, as we move step by step through our prodigal's journey, I will describe as openly and honestly as I can the many heartaches and constant soul-searching we experienced. Guilt, questioning our parenting abilities, and second-guessing were uninvited companions on our journey. In retrospect, our failures and inabilities were many. But I can honestly say we did the best we could at the time—prayerfully seeking God's path for each of our two children.

One child stumbled and fell, one did not.

My side of the story—the mother's side—offers great hope for the parent of a much-loved wayward child. Dan and I can affirm that God hears the prayers of the broken-hearted—the middle-of-the-night pleas of mothers and fathers. *He heard ours.*

Our Lord knows the deep-felt anguish of parents, and He answers the cries of helplessness. *He answered ours.*

God gave us strength when ours was gone. When our faith wavered, His faithfulness was unwavering. When I complained or whined or accused Him of not caring, God tenderly bore my grief-filled accusations, readily forgave my confessed inadequacies and sins, and patiently restored my soul through His love and sweet fellowship.

"And lo, I am with you always" (Matthew 28:20).

Wendi:

It is with deep thankfulness and a humble spirit that I share my side of this story—the story of my rebellion—for it is filled with God's grace amidst much darkness. You'll see how Satan reigned in my life for many years. You'll see alcoholism and drug addiction from the view of a user. It's a story of parties, rock 'n' roll, life on the edge, and relationships built around physical abuse.

I am not proud of my poor choices during those 20 years of wild living. I wasted so much of my life by my selfishness and recklessness. I can only express great sorrow and regret to all those I've hurt—especially my family.

But throughout my prodigal years as I wallowed in the pigpen of waywardness, God pursued me with His love. Though I consciously closed my heart to Him year after year, I saw glimpses of His grace here and there as He touched my life through the love of His people around me.

I am convinced that the prayers of my parents kept me from ultimate disaster. For that I am filled with gratitude and thanksgiving.

I pray that my story will shout a strong warning to the preadolescent who "innocently" seeks the wilder side of life. And I hope that in spite of the darkness of the story, a bright ray of forgiveness will shine to those angry or despairing teens who feel they have gone too far to be restored.

May this story also bring hope to despairing parents, who have lost all hope for their prodigal child.

Parents do not give up on your rebellious child. Love them in spite of their actions. Pray daily for them, and *don't lose hope*, for God is in the business of restoring broken lives.

> The righteous cry, and the LORD hears
> And delivers them out of all their troubles.
> The LORD is near to the brokenhearted
> And saves those who are crushed in spirit. . . .
> And none of those who take refuge in Him will
> be condemned. (Psalm 34:17-18, 22)

PART ONE

Rebellion

The heart is deceitful above all things,
and desperately wicked:
Who can know it?

—Jeremiah 17:9 (KJV)

CHAPTER ONE

Life Unravels

Karilee:

LITTLE SNAGS. LOOSE THREADS. They don't seem like much until something (or someone) grabs hold with a hard yank. Then a garment can unravel in a moment.

A snag in our family garment began unraveling quickly one November afternoon in 1985 as I was clattering dishes at the kitchen sink. I gazed out the window in front of me—caught up in the ever-changing scene of the Wisconsin River gurgling past our front yard. How I loved it here!

Often on our five-acre lot we could spot deer, raccoon, fox, and rabbits foraging in plain view, seemingly unafraid as they chomped on various tidbits. Otters and beavers cavorted right outside our front door. Eagles, hawks, and ospreys swooped gracefully overhead while songbirds trilled, twitted, and warbled a soothing symphony.

My husband, Dan, and I had lived four years on this

restful property with our two children—Rob, who had recently left home for his first year in college, and Wendi, now a senior in high school. We had come to the north woods when Dan joined the staff as pastor and teacher at Fort Wilderness, a nearby Christian camp, set in 80 wooded acres and surrounded on three sides by another forty thousand acres of state forest. Situated on a sparkling lake, the camp offered a full gamut of summer and winter programs.

Today, just a week and a half away from Thanksgiving, beams of sunlight warmed my face as I reflected on last month's fall-leaf splendor. The colors had been spectacular: bold splashes of crimson, gold, and fiery oranges lit up the riverbanks. Today held a beauty all its own—brilliant deep blue skies lightly dusted with delicate wisps of clouds. Crystal-clear air.

A ringing phone broke into my tranquil reverie.

Dan, who was engrossed in studies at the kitchen table, glanced at me, saw my hands immersed in soapy water, and reached for the phone. I listened absently at first.

As the call lengthened, I sighed. Most likely a school official or teacher was expressing concern about Wendi's falling grades—a follow-up to our parent-teacher conferences. A deepening concern had been growing in us, too, as we noticed her losing interest in school and extracurricular activities. She had detached herself from many things she previously enjoyed, including our family.

I dried my hands, pulling a chair next to Dan as his face clouded. His tone changed, his voice growing stronger as he grabbed a pen and scribbled on a yellow pad. "What was that? . . . She's *where*? . . . No, I can't believe that's right. . . . What is your name again? . . . May I speak to the supervisor? . . . Oh. . . . All right. . . . We'll be there as soon as we can."

My husband hung up the phone and stood, shoulders stooped, gathering himself. When he turned around, his face was pale and expressionless.

"Was that about Wendi?" I asked, knowing full well it was.

"Yes, honey." Reaching across the table, he grabbed both my hands. "Something incredible has happened," he said, choosing his words carefully, "and I'm not sure just what to make of it."

"What's wrong? Was that the school? . . . Is Wendi hurt?"

"No, that wasn't the school—it was the county Social Services. Karilee, she's been put into a foster home! We can't contact her unless she requests it." Dan shook his head in disbelief. "Just like that! She's been taken from us. . . . How can this be? Why would Social Services feel such an action is warranted? Can this be legal? She's *our* child!"

I felt as if someone had taken a baseball bat and walloped me in the chest. I couldn't breathe. This couldn't be happening to *us*. We were a loving, well-balanced family! Yes, we knew Wendi was having teenage difficulties, but weren't we handling them as well as most other parents facing similar challenges? Rob had breezed through his high school years—one out of two teens was bound to be difficult—right? Rebellious teens were as common as weeds in a garden.

"How can they take her away without consulting us first?" I squeaked.

Dan shook his head again. "I don't know . . ."

Flashbacks

They say that when you're drowning, your life flashes through your mind. Right then I felt as if I were going under. Instantly, snapshots of Wendi's life flashed through my mind:

as a toddler—bubbly, outgoing, fun-loving, rosy-faced smiles. Grammar school—inventive, creative, artistic, always laughing, pigtail-waggling cheerleader. Junior high—lithe gymnast, gifted vocalist, imaginative, fun . . . Bam! Like a cannon shot, darker pictures invaded my thoughts: High school—smooth start but with increasingly difficult struggles, then detachment, irritability, self-absorption, moodiness. What had happened?

One incident from Wendi's sophomore year pushed into my thoughts. That dismaying time had also begun with a phone call informing us that Wendi and a girlfriend had started on a weekend hitchhiking "adventure" from Wisconsin to Iowa. Seven hours into their escapade, they were picked up by a sheriff and held until all parents arrived. Two 14-year-old girls hitchhiking alone on the road—it had given us the shivers! But this horrifying episode had faded somewhat when Wendi finished her sophomore year without further incident.

At the beginning of Wendi's junior year, however, not-so-subtle changes emerged. She dropped all extracurricular activities: no music, no sports, no other outside interests. She began to withdraw from us, and try as we might, we couldn't draw her out. Our loving concern was interpreted as nosiness. She wanted to be left alone.

Our approaches toward communication usually turned into arguments—generally centering on five basic issues: a messy room, her shabby attire, our suspicion of a smoking habit, her demeanor, and falling grades.

Issue number one—a messy room—had been a struggle since childhood. When she was young, Wendi's initial high enthusiasm for star charts and rewards fell flat after the newness wore off. In her junior high years, we removed privileges if her room was messy, but that hadn't worked either. Our last approach was to let Wendi live in her pigpen, hoping that she would tire of climbing over the debris. But the clutter didn't bother her at all.

Issue number two—grungy attire—triggered constant arguments. Before high school, Wendi had dressed neatly in coordinated, clean, nice-looking clothes. Midway into her freshman year, however, things changed. Dressing down became cool. Dirty jeans with knees torn out, camouflage pants and army jackets, baggy T-shirts, and filthy shoes were first-choice picks. It was a constant sore spot with me especially.

Issue number three—our suspicion that she smoked—started in Wendi's freshman year, and she was extremely clever at hiding this habit. I often found myself questioning her like a district attorney. "Mom," she'd answer, "you know a lot of my friends smoke, and the smell just gets into my clothes." The confrontations were regular. I would search her room and ask pointed questions; she would volley them with lies.

Issue number four—personality change—was a slippery and subtle problem. Who can say whether or not a daughter's mood changes are hormonal? Or a result of fatigue? Or just due to the normal stresses of school? When Dan or I felt it necessary to approach Wendi about her demeanor, a full-fledged outburst of anger often erupted: "Just leave me alone!" We never knew what to expect from day to day—would she be settled, moody, or volatile?

Issue number five—falling grades—showed up on Wendi's report card her sophomore year when *all* her grades began to slip. I extended my help, tried to encourage and cajole, and sometimes offered rewards for good grades. Mostly Wendi listened quietly and then did nothing. She didn't care about her grades. Or her academic future.

But I cared!

I cared that she was disintegrating before my very eyes and I could do nothing about it. I cared because she had so much promise—so much going for her, and she was wasting it all. Wendi was pretty, intelligent, and gifted. I ached for her—feared for her—and prayed that she wouldn't get sucked up into a situation with consequences like addiction to hard drugs.

Many times I found myself looking at her, wondering, *Who is this child? Can this be* my *child . . . the one I once held in my arms while weaving lofty dreams for her?* The carefree, happy little girl I used to know had changed so much! I hardly knew her now, and the pain was almost unbearable. I wrote this poem to express my feelings.

This "Stranger" Child

Who is this child?
—This troubled, angry silent teen
who cringes when she's seen with me—
Is this the same my heart yearned for,
(with lofty dreams and hopes galore),
when newly wed so long ago?
I do not know . . .
I do not know.

• • •

Who is this child?
—Part child, part woman—sullen still!
She lives in secrets, filled with angst—
Is this my soft-cheeked toddler who
with outstretched arms would run to you,

a chatterbox with face aglow?
Where did *she* go?
Where did *she* go?

• • •

Who is this child?
—Withdrawn from family, drawn by peers,
she knows no boundaries seeking thrills—
This cannot be mine, once so sweet,
now drawn to darkness and deceit!
What happened? What has changed her so?
I want to know!
I want to know!

• • •

Who is this child?
—I know naught of this "stranger-girl,"
yet stranger still, I know her well—
Now trembling for her future years,
with aching heart, I pray through tears.
Releasing her, to God I go.
He loves her so . . .
He loves her so!

Deep Troubles

By her senior year Wendi had a new set of friends, many of whom used drugs. Dan and I talked with her so many times that we sounded like a broken record, even to ourselves. The conversations were mostly one-way. As we tried to root out the problems, we sensed and feared that she was using drugs. We also realized that she was lying to and manipulating us.

The more we tightened the rules at home, the surlier Wendi became.

Daily I found myself nagging Wendi about her poor grades, grungy clothes, disrespectful attitude, or the dangers of cigarettes and drugs and her association with kids using drugs. *She* had changed, but so had *I*. And I didn't like what I was becoming—a worrying, critical, nagging mother. So I made a conscious effort to pull back and asked Dan to take on some of these "confrontational" times. He readily agreed and helped smooth over some of the rough edges of home-life.

In fact, the morning of our phone call from Social Services we had experienced an explosive confrontation with Wendi, who was increasingly hard to wake up on school mornings.

This morning when she hadn't climbed out of bed after several calls and knocks on the door, I had gone into her room, sat on the edge of her bed, and pulled her into a sitting position.

Arms flailing, she screamed at me, "Leave me alone! I'm not going to school today!" As I tried to sit her up, she lashed out at me, rudely yelling harsh, insolent words.

Shaken, I left the room and asked Dan to intervene. Entering her room, he reached down to the bed and strong-armed her to her feet. "Do not *ever* speak to your mother like that again!" he growled. "You *are* going to school. Now get dressed, and I'll drive you." He left the room, staying in the hallway until he heard her thumping around the room and slamming drawers.

"I'll drive myself," she raged, thundering down the stairs, long hair flying, while buttoning her shirt. She strode out the door without eating, climbed into her dark blue Pinto, and slammed the car door. We watched out the kitchen window as she floored the car, scattering a dust cloud down the driveway.

Could that early morning wrestling match have been the trigger that caused Wendi to seek Social Services? we now wondered. *Had she falsely reported Dan had physically hurt her?* (He hadn't, of course.) Recently she had told us that several of her friends were in foster homes. It was common knowledge, she informed us, that it was easy to get out of your home if you didn't like your parents. *Had she been planning something like this all along?* We recalled her statement that "all my friends had to do was to tell Social Services that they were thinking of running away or contemplating suicide. Then they are taken out of their homes and put into foster care."

Did Wendi hate us that much? Was she that desperate to get out of our home? How had we miscalculated this, if it was so?

I wept. We prayed. I wept some more. *Are we unfit parents?* The thought was humbling and horrifying.

Numbly we gathered up some of her belongings as requested by the faceless voice on the phone. Wendi would need a week's worth of clothing. "Please bring the clothes and toiletries by as soon as you can today," the social worker had requested.

Stepping into the Unknown

The ride into town, usually an enjoyable 20-minute scenic drive, seemed to take forever. Each of us lost in private thoughts, Dan and I spoke few words. As we drove out of our driveway it felt as if we were being pulled by an unknown force to an unknown place. Soon we found ourselves in a parking lot in front of a bleak, gray cement building. We fumbled for the worn duffel bag and walked like zombies into this strange territory.

A matronly woman at the front desk led us into a small

room sparsely furnished with a gray metal desk and several metal-armed office chairs. Another stranger, a petite, dark-haired woman with half-glasses balancing midway down her nose, sat behind the metal desk. My eyes, darting hopefully around the room for Wendi, landed on an empty, colorless, overstuffed chair.

"Wendi has been put in a foster home because she needs some time away from the home situation," the counselor informed us passionlessly. Just another day at the office for her. "Please don't try to contact her during this period. This is for your benefit as well as hers." Her eyes glanced down to an open file as she continued in a monotone, "We'll be working together through some problems Wendi feels have developed."

Problems? What home problems had Wendi shared with this woman? What in the world were we doing here with a stranger mediating between us and our daughter? I closed my eyes, wondering what she had said to Social Services that had landed her here. *Had she threatened to run away? . . . or God forbid, to commit suicide?*

All our questions were put on hold. "We cannot," the counselor emphatically announced, "discuss anything further until our next meeting." There. There at last was *some* emotion from this woman. But it wasn't compassion. It was firmness—a warning in her eyes as she lifted them above her glasses. She was in full control here.

"Some time is needed," she continued. "Try to be patient. This is only a temporary arrangement, and we will do all we can to evaluate and help you both during these next few weeks. We are not creating a case file on Wendi; we're not putting her in the system because we expect this separation to be temporary."

A plastic smile tugged at her lips, not making it to her eyes. "Please give this a bit of time. We'll call you soon—in a week or so." She stood up, hand extended. The meeting was done.

We handed over the battered duffel. It felt as if we were symbolically transferring our parenting rights along with the bag, that we were being coerced into relinquishing our responsibilities. *We are not giving her to strangers!* my heart screamed. I stumbled out of the room with Dan's supportive arms around me.

An endless week dragged by, hour after hour, minute after minute. Our empty nest cried out the fact that it was not a "natural" empty nest. One child had left for college; the other had been snatched from us like a bird of prey plucking an unsuspecting rabbit from its burrow. We had heard nothing from Social Services. Perhaps there was a misunderstanding. Had they forgotten to set up our meeting? I called the office inquiring, *Could we be given any word about our daughter? Was she all right?*

No, they had not forgotten. They will call soon. Please be patient.

We felt so helpless. In our helplessness, we brought the situation to a respected Christian counselor in the area. He made a few calls and advised us to hang tight. Since Social Services was not creating a file for Wendi's case, he felt it was indeed a temporary situation, and that we should wait until we had our face-to-face meeting with the authorities.

Thanksgiving came and went. For many years we had joined our extended family of 30-some people for traditional Thanksgiving dinner. We always rotated homes and had hosted it ourselves in years past. This year, although we could have made the four-hour trip to Madison for the festivities, somehow we just didn't feel festive. We encouraged Rob to attend, but we ate our Thanksgiving dinner—just the two of us—at a Holiday Inn buffet.

I wasn't hungry. The food seemed to stick in my throat. *What is Wendi doing now? It's Thanksgiving—is she missing us? Is she glad to be away from us?*

A third week began, and finally—a meeting was scheduled. But the day before the meeting, Dan came home from an errand in town and announced, "Karilee, I've had a chance to talk with Wendi." I turned off the iron and threw the blouse over the ironing board, holding my breath.

Dan explained that she had called him, with Social Service's permission, at his camp work number. Dan was asked to come alone to talk with Wendi at a local restaurant.

Sadly I realized her need to exclude me, the confrontational parent. Dan would be the buffer. This realization stung like a scorpion, and a deep sadness washed over me as I listened in anticipation mingled with dread. Would I now find out what was happening?

"She wants to come home now," he explained, looking at me tenderly. He put his arm around me and walked me into the living room. "Social Services is releasing her, and it's up to us not to condemn her. We need to give her all the love possible." Putting a hand under my chin, he raised my face to look directly into his. "Wendi really needs to know that we love her and will accept her—*and* her baby."

Wendi:

"Sweet" Sixteen

The plan had been set. My best friend, Cassie, and I walked into the cluttered dime store in need of only one item to confirm my suspicion that I was pregnant. Heading down the main aisle, then off to the left and around the corner—there it was. I picked it up as Cassie kept a trained eye open. A second later we headed for the front door and out to the parking lot. Tucked safely inside my jacket was the test I needed to confirm the blatant facts.

"Now, promise me you'll wait till school tomorrow," reminded Cassie, effervescent as usual.

"I will, don't worry," I replied with mounting anxiety.

The next morning came with a heavy nausea. I blundered my way down to our little farmhouse bathroom with my stolen pregnancy test in tow. I had all but memorized the instructions but reread them again just to be sure. Carefully I administered the test and shook the test tube. Then I gave it one last look and tucked it safely into the front pocket of my flannel shirt.

The results would be complete by the time I got to school. Fearful thoughts swirled inside my head and jumbled my emotions into near hysteria.

Tired, scared, nauseated, and with thudding heart, I headed to the student smoking area at the back of the school. Cassie's eyes caught mine, and off we went. We wound down the back hallway toward the shop wing, then along the long stretch past the swimming pool, arriving at the end of the corridor by the back door.

I reached for the little vial in my pocket. This was it—I held the tube in my hand and we looked. Pink. Positive. I was pregnant.

Cassie jumped and squealed with delight. "Oh, we're going to take such good care of this baby. I'll help you, you know that."

My mind spun out of control. There I was—a 16-year-old

senior in high school. Summer had just ended, and now my life as well, or so it seemed. One thing was for sure, I was not about to tell my parents. If they had a hard time with the other things I had done, this one would be the worst of all.

My compulsions, my need to live life on the edge even though I knew my actions were wrong, had slammed me full force into a brick wall. Wanting freedom, I had purposely chosen friends who had no parental restraints on their actions, adapted their lifestyle, and ended up in a huge mess. What would I do now?

I spent the next few days trying to come up with a game plan. I had broken up with my boyfriend, so my only confidants were my friends. I did get an offer from a friend's mother to help me get an abortion. What should I do—what *could* I do?

The morning sickness persisted with a vengeance. Each day it became harder and harder to get out of bed. I couldn't think! So I turned my frustrations about my predicament into anger toward my parents.

One morning Mom was going through the exasperating routine of trying to get me up for school and I lunged at her, calling her some names. I saw the shock in her eyes as she left my room. I had gone way over the line.

Within seconds my father was in my room, and was he angry! The words flew as I ranted from exhaustion and he protected my mother.

That day I drove to school and went straight to my guidance counselor. Storming into the office, I slammed the door and lit up a cigarette. "If I'm not placed in a foster home by the end of the school day," I threatened coldly to Mr. B, "I'm gone! Nobody will ever see me again!"

What an attitude! Scared inside, I was playing the tough

girl, as I shot out my demands one after another. Mr. B promised to get the results I wanted, so off to class I went.

By the end of the school day, I had been placed in a local foster home. I soon discovered that there were no restrictions on me, other than a curfew at night. I now had the freedoms I so desperately wanted. I was out in the world and away from all restrictions—and all religion—and I was completely out of control.

The following days were filled with cigarettes, marijuana, and shoplifting. I was doing what I wanted, when, where, and however I pleased. But the feeling of loneliness was overwhelming.

Yes, I was free—but still in a loveless vacuum.

Free?

I was pregnant . . . how was I ever going to take care of a baby? Who was I kidding?

After a couple of weeks, I realized that this total freedom did not bring any satisfaction. In fact, after my little rampage of self-absorption, I felt even worse. I dreaded going home. I could just hear Mom saying, "I told you so," but I also knew both parents would be so disappointed with me. What a mess!

I called my dad, who asked me to lunch. I knew Dad loved me and would listen to me even though I had broken his heart. So I went. I sat there at Hardee's an angry, sullen, and guilt-ridden kid whose body was bearing adult responsibility. I was in way over my head. That much I knew. We talked, and he asked probing questions to help me decide my future. Weighing the options before me, I chose to go back home to think them over.

CHAPTER
TWO

Sugar 'n' Spice

Wendi:

IT'S NOT JUST OLD age that causes memory lapses and fuzzy recollections. Frying your brain with drugs and pickling it with alcohol has much the same effect. For that reason, although my mind was clear during early childhood, 20 years of using drugs and consuming alcohol have made many of my early childhood memories vague.

I do remember being a secure and happy little girl with few worries or insecurities. And I wasn't lacking in spiritual upbringing. Attending church was an integral part of my little world. I spent many hours of my free time at the church building because Dad was pastor and it felt like a second home—comfortable.

Additionally, my mother and father took care to tell me about Jesus, reading and telling interesting and exciting Bible stories. Early on, at about six years of age, I knelt with my mother beside my bed and prayed a childlike prayer to receive Jesus into my heart.

I knew Mom loved me without reserve. I can still feel the tender touch of her hand as I laid my head on her lap while she tickled my face (this was a soothing church service pastime). When I was sick, Mom always stayed by my side. She worked tirelessly to make things special for my brother and me: awesome made-to-order birthday dinners and parties, Halloween outfits a hundred times better than the ones from the store, creative science project ideas, and homemade after-school treats. She did it all . . . smiling and with love.

I knew I was loved unconditionally—and that was true even when I made mistakes.

For example, once when I was young I carefully picked a huge bowlful of peony buds from our soon-to-be-blossoming bushes. Proudly, I presented my gift of love to Mom. "Look, Mommy! Look what I picked for you!"

Her look of interest quickly turned to dismay. She knelt down, touching the metal mixing bowl, and looked gently into my eyes. "Oh sweetie, although you thought you were doing something nice just for me, you forgot to ask permission. And because of that, these pretty buds you picked can't grow into beautiful flowers, as God designed them to do. Do you understand what I'm saying, sweetheart?"

"I think so, Mommy. Did I do bad?"

"You weren't trying to be bad. I know that," Mom answered. "It's just that you forgot to ask Mommy or Daddy first. Even when our other flowers are fully grown—and they will be blossoming pretty soon—even then, you need to ask permission first before you pick. Okay?"

"Okay. I'm sorry, Mommy. Can we put them back on?"

A chuckle and a hug accompanied the explanation. No, they could not be put back on. I learned the lesson of flower picking. And I learned that lesson couched in love. Yes, I knew I was still loved, even when I made mistakes.

Karilee:

From infancy through grammar school Wendi had been a sheer joy to us because of her outgoing, bubbly, and nonargumentative nature. Rarely did Dan or I have to raise a voice in correction. She sought to please others and was considerate, obedient, and friendly. Wendi was fun-loving, creative, and musically talented—a jabber box, full of energy! Mischievous hazel eyes twinkled in delight from morning until she flopped into bed at night. She stole teachers' hearts, collected friends with ease, and squeezed into every minute of life a zest and vitality hard to rival. Our only daughter was one of a kind and deeply loved.

Wendi:

My dad? I have always adored my dad—a man of love without limits, enthusiasm, and charisma. Warmhearted, charming, silly . . . Dad was a blast! His was a love you could feel, and it warmed the whole house. Seeing his car pull in the drive at the end of a long day always brought a sense of excitement. Dad loved to tickle and wrestle with my brother and me. We built human pyramids. His contagious energy and laughter filled our hearts with passion and delight. And when he needed to punish my brother or me, Dad's loving eyes displayed a sorrow that told us his heart was breaking.

All these qualities wrapped up in one man made him

the perfect pastor and my personal hero. I recall the many hours I stood quietly by his side as he greeted the people after church, proudly sharing him with the church members. But I got to take him home with me! I was proud to be his little girl and I knew he felt proud of me, too. It was great!

Karilee:

Wendi is not overstating her assessment of my husband, Dan, whom I met when I was a senior in high school. Sitting in the church choir loft in Wheaton, Illinois, I first spotted Dan in the auditorium among the Wheaton College incoming freshmen who were visiting our church on the first Sunday of the school year. When my eyes fell on him I was immediately intrigued. This sandy-haired guy with flashing hazel eyes was so cute—and, as I soon discovered, without an ounce of self-absorption. Unpretentious *and* handsome . . . I wanted to get to know him better. We dated steadily for a year, broke up for a year, then resumed dating through our graduations. Five years after our first introduction we stood hand in hand at the altar to pledge our love and commitment.

Indeed, Dan was (and is) the bedrock of our home. A man devoted to God and His Word, Dan possesses great strength and a tender heart—a heart so giving that sometimes he runs himself ragged helping others.

Many times his church work drew him away from home and interfered with special family occasions. But we all knew his heart—he *wanted* to be with us. And for that we adored him.

Wendi:

As I grew, I was free to be me. Me—the little tomboy. Being faster than most of the boys, and tougher too, gave me a sense of great satisfaction. Mud puddles, frogs, and snakes made for a great day's fun. I always felt up to a challenge, taking any dare—any time, any place. No dresses for me! And I despised the "girlie" color pink.

This rough-and-ready exterior, however, housed a tender and compassionate soul. I always rooted for the underdog and considered it a sin to intentionally kill an ant. Taking care of every stray animal became a personal mission.

The makeup of my being could be described by two words: passion and compassion. I sought adventure and liked to save the oppressed—both good qualities. But either quality can be dangerous for the immature.

TEMPTATION

And I was immature. Because my birthday fell precisely at the break for the required school-entrance age, I began kindergarten at age 4. Eager, excited, and raring to go, I was thrilled to attend early, but now I wonder if the need to always prove myself to the world—the need to display my toughness and resiliency—stemmed from being smaller than my peers.

At the age of 8, I was exposed to something new—something I innately sensed was wrong. It was my first encounter with temptation, and I failed the test.

That summer my best friend, Teri, and I were playing at a large sand quarry on the outskirts of Middleton, Wisconsin, when a boy from school appeared on his bike. He stood watching us for a few minutes then dropped the bike and sauntered our way.

"Guess what I've got?" he boasted. "You're probably too young, but have you ever seen naked ladies?" He shoved the pages into our hands. There, standing in our ragtag outfits, we gazed at several pictures of naked centerfolds. We were speechless. And we were curious. No, we hadn't seen such a thing. We looked and looked in wonderment.

After a few minutes our visitor grabbed the pages, stuffed them back into his pocket, and hopped on his bike without another word.

Well! We giggled and whispered a bit, and went back to our adventures. But it wasn't many days before we found ourselves wondering what it would be like to be beautiful like those women. And soon our playtime took a different turn. We sure didn't want to be naked, but maybe we could do stuff to look grown-up . . . and beautiful!

So we began sneaking into Teri's siblings' rooms to steal "adult" things like makeup, sensuous adult clothing items, and some cigarettes that we pretended to smoke. We felt so regal and alluring—so grown up! My mom had warned me about the dangers of cigarettes, but since we weren't actually inhaling, I didn't feel too guilty about it. But the first step toward smoking had been taken.

The following spring my dad told me we would be moving. And that was the end of that.

Upheaval

When Dad resigned from the church and took a job at a Christian camp a few hours north of our current residence, I felt saddened because I knew I would miss my friends and the security of the town where I had lived since an infant.

But those feelings didn't last long. With so much to do at the camp, my days were spent playing hard—swimming, horseback riding, canoeing, arts and crafts, helping out in the canteen, exploring the woods, and meeting new friends.

Accompanying all this fun was our family's personal traveling ministry—"Family Four." During my fourth-grade year we traveled the Midwest presenting the gospel message through goofy yet lively puppet shows and magic tricks (some that included live doves). We sang family songs in four-part harmony—all carefully arranged by my mother and accompanied by professionally taped backgrounds or Dad's guitar. I thought I had found my niche . . . what a wonderful life I had.

And then—it happened. We had to move again!

Just *one short year* after arriving, we were heading off into the wild blue yonder—this time a world away from all I knew. This time it was no mere four-hour jaunt across the state. We were heading from northern Wisconsin all the way to Dallas, Texas.

What a horrifying thought! I hated it.

Karilee:

We sat the children down to explain the reason behind this move, but it was especially hard for them. Dan had decided to seek his doctorate degree, a degree that would greatly enhance a new and innovative program that he and another camp leader were developing. The board felt this added degree would be valuable toward accrediting the program, and the best time to obtain it would be now. Our family planned to return to Wisconsin and the camp upon Dan's graduation. We tried to encourage the children with this explanation but both of them remained brokenhearted.

Wendi:

With a withered heart and falling dreams I left "paradise" to head south—the threat of entering a new school looming on the horizon.

I entered school timidly and with dread. And my fears soon became reality—I became a laughingstock, a freak of nature. My classmates' smooth Texan drawls seemed like a foreign language to me, while in turn my nasally northern accent became the brunt of jokes by them.

"Say maiouze," the kids would request in amusement.

"Mouse," I would reply . . . then the class would erupt in laughter. Not "we're laughing with you" kind of laughter, but a humiliating, scoffing laughter.

Another time, the teacher called on students for spelling. This fair-skinned, middle-aged lady with a soft brown pixie haircut looked frail, but her spunky spirit made us all want to please her. One by one each student would stand as she called out words to be spelled correctly. When she came to me, she drawled, "Spell 'flo.'"

Puzzled, I thought for a moment before answering, "F-l-o-w, flow."

"No, you don't understand," she repeated, giving me another chance. "Spell 'flo.'" I repeated my answer. In exasperation, she almost shouted at me—"No, I mean the flo' you're standing on!"

The entire class broke out in laughter. Mortified, I spelled, "F-l-o-o-r, floor." Instances like these filled each school day. The pain was immeasurable. I hated being a freak.

It only took one girl to start a class-wide campaign against me. Months and months dragged by as I was totally ignored. Every day after school I ran the block and a half home so I could weep in private. I despised it there!

Every morning I walked to school carrying a leaden weight.

Finally, one day my bottled up feelings all came flooding out. The teacher had left the room, and a surge of valiant courage swept through my heart. I rose from my little desk and there, before the entire class, I opened my pain for all to see. With blazing resolve I poured out my heart and shared my loneliness and the longing to have just one friend.

As I looked around the room I noticed many red and teary eyes. Those kids who had been so merciless were seeing me differently for the first time. One by one the girls came over and reached out in friendship.

The remainder of that semester was far less painful. It seemed as though survival was now an option. And then . . . my parents dropped another bomb: *We were moving—again!* I had worked so hard to make friends at this school—and now I would have to start all over again in a new place. Although devastated, I had no tears to offer with this move.

Karilee:

Dan and I were deeply disappointed when he was forced to drop out of seminary due to several events that made attending graduate school financially impossible. To make ends meet, Dan carried two meager-paying jobs. At night he worked at a meat-packing company as security guard, making hourly rounds before returning to a cubicle the size of an interstate toll booth. Afternoons Dan donned a hideous "zoot suit" to work as a doorman at a prestigious apartment complex tower.

Financial problems mounted. The move itself had been expensive, and several months before the move, Dan had undergone back surgery. The medical bills and a large tuition obligation had left us deeply in debt, even with both of us working full schedules and alternating shifts to care for the children. Additionally our car had broken down, which forced Dan to walk or hitchhike 10 miles to classes. We couldn't even afford the daily bus fare.

Then late one evening, having completed the three-hour walk after a day of classes, Dan wearily came home carrying his heavy satchel. He found me on the sofa dabbing a reddened nose, a wastebasket overflowing with Kleenex at my feet. "Karilee, what's wrong?" he asked in alarm.

Dropping his load, he stepped toward me, but I sprang from the chair and dragged him by one arm into the kitchen. "*That's* what's wrong," I wailed, pointing to the ceiling. I had come home around 3:30 from a frenetic day's work at the orthopedic doctors' office to meet the children after school and prepare supper. Upon entering the kitchen I'd found disaster.

It looked as if a bomb had fallen through the ceiling, leaving a huge, gaping hole. Chunks of plaster soaked in oozing water lay piled on the floor. Plaster was everywhere—on the countertops, refrigerator, and stove. Our air conditioner system had frozen up, leaking water through the ceiling for so long, that a huge segment of the ceiling had collapsed. It was a hot and humid day—and tonight would be a hot and humid night—*all* night. And I did *not* do well in heat.

"Look at this mess!" I sobbed. "We've had no car for a couple weeks. Now we have no air conditioning, and it's hot, hot, *hot*. I won't be able to sleep tonight, and I have to be at work tomorrow at 8 A.M. We don't have any money to fix the car *or* the air conditioning." I leaned my back against the kitchen wall and slid to the floor as I continued sobbing. "I just can't take it anymore!"

It was a low point, for sure. Our world had collapsed. We could not pay all our bills, and food was meager. Mentally and physically depleted, I felt as if Dan and I were teetering on the brink of nervous breakdowns.

As we discussed our plight and considered Dan's returning to his job at camp in Wisconsin, we received word that the "Work/Study/Mission" program was being dropped for financial reasons. We couldn't return there.

What in the world was happening to our lives? Where could we turn? We had lived in Dallas less than one year. Continuing at the seminary was out of the question, so what now?

At that precise time of discouragement, out of the blue a church in Orlando, Florida, contacted us. The congregation extended an invitation to Dan for pastoral ministry. In His graciousness, the Lord had intervened and provided for us. Dan answered yes, and we loaded up our belongings yet again, encouraging our bewildered children with exciting tales of beaches and visits to Disney World.

CHAPTER THREE

Disenchantment with God

Wendi:

MY FIRST YEAR AND a half in Orlando passed uneventfully. Slated to enter seventh grade in a new Christian school. I was filled with expectancy and excitement. Junior high! Wow! Unfortunately, the events of that year would become the catalyst that began my disenchantment with Christianity.

I tried out for and made the cheerleading team. On game days, I proudly sported a green-and-white, custom-made cheerleader's uniform while enthusiastically cheering and waving pom-poms. Most fun of all, I got to climb to the top of all the pyramids because I was tiny, agile, and balanced.

Life was wonderful. Feeling light as a cloud I soared in cheerful innocence with the gentle breeze of puberty approaching on the horizon. Then, mid-year, without warning, I fell into a raging burst of adolescence.

As my body reached womanhood, my emotions stretched and snapped like huge rubber bands. Things that I had not previously noticed suddenly became irritating. I cried at insignificant incidents, and easily took offense. Unexpected little turns in life seemed monumental. Life's weight seemed to have landed on me with a heavy thud. Homework became laborious, and life became insufferable.

Satan's Pit

That year I found myself in what I quickly dubbed "Satan's pit"—the second-floor classroom of Mr. Farris. This teacher was an arrogant man who took great pleasure in punishing his pupils. Most days, after class or during recess, any number of young students could be found carefully writing promises of perfect behavior on the blackboard. This mighty hunter enjoyed wounding his innocent prey.

I became one of the wounded.

On this particular day I was sitting in the classroom working away on an assignment when, glancing over, I noticed a classmate nearby unaware that her white satin blouse was gaping open. Several of the pearl buttons had worked loose, and there she was, oblivious, showing her ample bosom and bra. I leaned over and whispered my warning.

Her face turned crimson as she mouthed, "Thank you."

"You're welcome. I thought you'd want to know," I replied, just as Mr. Farris looked my way.

He was up and out of his seat striding toward me like an angry pit bull. "Miss Hayden, I see you feel you have important things to say during our work time. Do you care to share it with the rest of the class?"

I knew better than to try to explain. Besides, I didn't

want to embarrass my friend any further, so I kept quiet.

Mr. Farris, always eager to demean, had only begun. "I thought not. Why is it, Miss Hayden, that you have the need to disregard the rules of my classroom? What, pray tell, did your clever little mind and busy little lips think *so* important—so crucial—that you had to disrupt our study time? Can you tell me that?"

Still I kept quiet. The eyes of the entire room of students were now looking my way.

"I thought not. Well, Miss Hayden, since your busy little lips have gotten so much exercise, I'll give your restless little hands something further to do. You will compose a two-page essay on the subject of talking in class, and you will bring it to me tomorrow." He glanced around the room like a prison guard. All heads turned back to their homework as his heels rat-a-tatted to the front desk.

How I hated that despicable man!

That night I explained my plight to my parents. They understood my frustrations with the unfair treatment and commiserated about the unjustness of being punished when trying to help a friend. But they explained that not completing the assignment would only compound the situation and incur further wrath.

So my parents jumped in to help me compose this impossible paper. We decided to write a summary of the virtue of modesty from a Bill Gothard book called *Character Sketches*, offering a well-developed argument explaining the reasons I had been talking. Mom and Dad worked hard to help me come up with just the right words detailing why, in this case, helping my friend had been the proper thing to do. The words were tactfully and humbly written.

This project took me the entire evening, forcing me,

with the additional mountain of other homework, to stay up extremely late to accomplish everything.

The next day, tired but eager for Mr. Farris to read my justification, I handed in my paper, hoping to find some redemption. Mr. Farris took it from me, lifted a page to see that both pages were full, and tossed it into the trash without a word.

A rush of anger followed my initial incredulity. What a hateful man! God, church, and the Bible had been my entire upbringing. Now here I was under the daily rule of an evil-hearted Pharisee. I grew to loathe Mr. Farris. Anger consumed my heart as I absorbed the daily pounding of this wretched man who presented himself so piously to parents. To me, his soul seemed black with vileness.

Each morning it became harder and harder to get up and go to school. Tears and pleas came shamelessly as I worked to avoid another day in that pit. Emotions, fueled by teen hormones, swept through my 12-year-old body and I felt entirely alone while battling the world.

It was then that I began to reject God, who I felt had abandoned me in my plight. As the months passed and Mr. Farris's persecution toward his students continued, I drifted away from prayer, feeling God wasn't listening, or if He was, He was too busy to care about little Wendi. Frustrated, I consciously turned away from religious people. I saw no point in pursuing Christianity if self-righteousness was to be the outcome. My young heart, churning with angst, was fixated on this man and all I deemed to be wrong at the school.

For whatever reason, I failed to see the many, many Christians who were caring, and good, and righteous—including my own parents.

Closing the Door of My Heart

I allowed Satan's influence to creep into my life and began to close the door to my heart. Soon I discovered rock 'n' roll. A lot of the music pulsated the same anger I was feeling, and the lyrics seemed to give me the answers I wanted.

One particular memory is crystal clear. I was outside in our carport slamming a tennis ball against the side of our house while listening to the radio. No one else was home so I tuned in to a rock station. Pink Floyd's song "The Wall" perked up my ears. "We don't need no education . . ." *That's it!* I thought as the words continued—"All in all you're just another brick in the wall."

I don't know why, but those words caught hold of my heart, and I latched on to them. *Who needs education anyway? Everyone is just a brick in the wall, going nowhere.*

Then and there I made a conscious decision to quit trying at school and to create my own life. I closed the door of my heart to spiritual things—after all, the Christian leaders at my school hadn't brought me anything but grief. *I'm done! No more! If my parents won't take me out of that school, I'll just get myself kicked out.*

I quickly developed a friendship with another angry girl who was one year my senior. Since both of us were fed up with school, it didn't take us long to devise a plan. She came from money and I came from brains, so the plan fell together with ease. We decided to get on a bus, ride to Daytona, and just hang out. That was the entire plan—no thought was given beyond getting there.

This friend began taking chunks of cash from around her house. Within a week she had over a thousand dollars! For several days we put on two layers of clothes in the morning before school, then stowed them away in our gym lockers.

Now we had plenty of duds for the journey.

The morning arrived for our departure. As soon as we got to school, we emptied our schoolbags and filled them with our goods. Quietly we slipped off the campus and through the woods, making our way to the mall just a few blocks away.

In the restrooms we changed into our tattered jeans and T-shirts. We split the money and placed it throughout our persons and bags (so that if by chance some cash was lost, not all would be gone).

We were clever, weren't we?

We proceeded to the Greyhound station and purchased our tickets to Daytona. Then, while awaiting our departure, we went to a small cafe in the mall.

Busted!

Suddenly, out of nowhere, there she was—the enormously mean Mrs. Haight from our school. She had spotted us! The rumbles of anger welling up inside turned my stomach into a tight fist as the blood drained from me.

We were hauled back to the school office and placed in separate rooms for interrogation. I slumped into a proffered chair and sat with crossed arms waiting for all hell to break loose.

My mental gun was loaded as I looked with taunting eyes at the enemy. Perched in a perfect row along the side of Mrs. Haight's desk were the "spanking boards." One of them resembled a paint stirrer, another was sizably larger, and the last was a mammoth board with holes drilled in it. I hoped they knew that it would take a tranquilizer gun to subdue me!

Enter my father.

He looked bewildered and concerned. *Now I had everybody's attention.* Words, bottled up for so long, shot out from my tongue. Mrs. Haight heard, in no short terms, exactly what I thought of her and her hypocritical staff. I even made the threat to my father that I couldn't guarantee what I would do if I were not removed immediately from this place of inhumane torture.

It was done. I was out.

I walked away without looking back, taking with me an enormous chip on my shoulder. My plan to leave that school had succeeded. And as an added bonus, I had escaped with a rather large chunk of cash that I had not returned.

I never again saw that girl who was to be my companion on the road. When the dust settled, I withdrew even further into my solitary world. Music became my escape as I sat alone in my room covertly listening to AC/DC, Black Sabbath, Pink Floyd, Kiss, and all the ear-tickling music the radio had to offer. I had fallen for Satan's lure of seeking fulfillment in the world, and swallowed it hook, line, and sinker.

Karilee:

Wendi had been showing increasing distaste toward attending school. Since it's normal for kids to want to stay home to avoid work and study, Dan and I constantly asked ourselves, *What part of her behavior stems from just being 12 and complaining about school, and what part is a result of a truly unhealthy environment?*

Wendi was hiding the depth of her emotional pain. At first all we saw was a girl trying to avoid going to school. Each morning with various feigned sicknesses and copious tears she begged to stay home. "Unless you have a fever or are vomiting, you need to go," we'd reiterate time and time again.

Several weeks before this incident, however, we began to realize something was wrong—very, very wrong. Wendi's emotional and physical distress on school mornings turned into severe stomachaches or headaches or unusual fatigue. Was she simply being dramatic or were her complaints valid? We needed to find out.

We began talking with other parents, teachers, and even students, and discovered a heavy-handed legalism combined with some huge inconsistencies. When we asked Rob, who was attending this same school, to share his feelings with us, he admitted that he found it hard to enjoy the classes, too, because of the severe legalism.

"Mom, it's really pretty bad," he confided. "Boys' haircuts are inspected (hair must be off the collar) and girls' dress lengths measured almost every day (yes, dresses were required). Teachers and kids stand around with clipboards writing down every infraction they see. Some of the 'perfect' kids are always tattling on one another. And lots of the time things are really unfair."

"Tell me some of the unfair things," I urged.

"Well, for one thing, the teachers' and staff's kids get away with murder. They're never disciplined. Then other kids—ones who the teachers may not like—get into trouble every day. I know one boy who never gets to go to recess because he's always writing on the blackboard, usually for nothing really bad. And one girl got sent home for wearing a dress with spaghetti straps even though she wore a cardigan sweater on top.

"In fact," Rob continued, "just last week David and I got pulled out of chapel into Mrs. Haight's office and paddled with one of her paddle boards—for nothing. During chapel

David had drummed his fingers on the pew ahead of him, and she said we were being disruptive. Mom, we were doing absolutely nothing wrong."

I knew that David was one of the sweetest, most gentle kids I had met. He would not be one to act up or disrupt. Both kids had protested their innocence, but they were paddled anyway. Rob shared several other incidences he had witnessed. We didn't like what we were hearing.

As a matter of fact, Dan and I had been on the verge of pulling the children out of this school when Wendi's terrible occurrence took place. Our decision was immediate. Both children were struggling there; we pulled them out that very day.

Wendi and Rob were glad to be out of the oppressive atmosphere. Unable to find another Christian school with an opening for our children, we enrolled them in the Orlando public school system—not our first choice—for their second semester.

We made a point of having several heart-to-heart conversations with Wendi, but antagonism toward spiritual things continued to fester in her heart. While prayerfully keeping a sharper eye on things, we tried to monitor her comings and goings. So when she attached herself to a neighborhood friend who sought the wild side of life, we became even more concerned.

Wendi:

The first few weeks in my new public school passed smoothly as I silently observed the environment and the students around me. A girl from church was in my class, and she persuaded me to join the track team.

It didn't take long, however, for me to grow weary of this endeavor. I was becoming restless and found myself yearning for some kind of thrill. Running hurdles, sprints, and long jumps were certainly no big thrill.

Still angry at life, I went looking for the troubled kids. I had made a conscious choice to shun spiritual things, and a restless agitation consumed me.

I started skipping out on track practice after finding a freewheeling girlfriend, and within a few weeks of meeting her, I dropped out of track completely.

After school, Diedre and I would look for things to do. With no supervision, we started causing trouble and experimenting with smoking.

The first time I smoked pot I was in the bedroom of a kid from school. When Diedre and I had stopped by to visit, we found a small group of kids passing around a bong from one to the next and then around again. We eagerly joined in.

It was the best feeling I had ever known! My seething anger lifted. I never laughed so hard in my life. I loved the huge emotional high. Nothing mattered, nothing at all. I could only explain that feeling to others by the term "psychedelic rapture." With that first high, at the age of 12, I was instantly addicted. I wanted more—*forever.*

Although that habit would be temporarily put aside within a few months' time, I would never forget how ecstatic marijuana made me feel. The next 19 years of my life would be spent in rigorous pursuit of this feeling. The insatiable desire was always lying in wait just below the surface of my mind.

For reasons unknown to me at the time, my father resigned from the church he had been pastoring and accepted a position as the Director of Spiritual Ministries back up at the camp in northern Wisconsin. We were moving back to a familiar place.

Three eventful years had passed since we had left that area. The walls of resentment that were under construction in my life were not impenetrable yet. A longing to have a good life—an anger-free life—still existed within me, but there was a lot of reconstruction to do.

Karilee:

This was the first and only time we made a cross-country move based upon our children's needs. Wendi was in over her head with harmful relationships and pressing hard for more. Even our son encountered a situation that could have involved the police. The big-city life of Orlando was swallowing up our children's lives, and we felt swept up in a torrent of detrimental circumstances.

With burdened hearts we prayed earnestly—intently—for God's wisdom in determining guidance for our children's hearts and future. Within a week a door had opened to return to ministry at the camp in Wisconsin; Dan then shared his heart with the deacons of our flourishing church, explaining our need to move. A few weeks later Dan read his resignation to a sorrowful congregation, who expressed their heartfelt love through tearful good-byes.

We felt we had no other choice.

CHAPTER
FOUR

Caught in the Act

Wendi:

"WE HAVE A SURPRISE for you, Wendi," Dad said one evening soon after we had settled into our Wisconsin home the summer before eighth grade. "We know that things were tough in Orlando, so Mom and I decided to do something special as a sort of 'Welcome-back-to-Wisconsin' and 'We-hope-you-really-like-it-here' gift." I was intrigued. What in the world could it be?

Dad and Mom had me follow them out to our detached garage. "Now close your eyes," they instructed as they led me through the garage door. "Okay, now you can open them."

There it was—a royal blue 1967 Suzuki 90! It was the best present I had ever received. I hugged and thanked them both, immediately threw a leg over the seat, and sat grinning from ear to ear as I gripped the handlebars. Then Dad got busy teaching me how to ride my new motorcycle.

What a sight we must have been! He would hold on to the back of the bike and run along behind me so that I wouldn't tip over as I learned how to balance the heavy bike while shifting the gears. I loved it! The feel of the air in my face sent me head-over-heels in love with biking. The greatest part was that my friend Jill, whom I had left behind after fourth grade, was still there—and she also had a motorcycle. We had a blast!

(By the way, my brother received a beautiful compound hunting bow with arrows. But I only had eyes for my Suzuki.)

That summer, camp was in full swing, providing me with adventures galore. Jill and I took up sailing on the camp lake. With the one-man boats on their sides and the sails dipping into the water, we enthusiastically rode the wind, even mastering the stunt of jumping on to each other's boats while passing.

Horseback riding was another love of mine. I rode hard and within a few months was competing in the rodeo barrel races. I felt relaxed, free, and happy. The family move had pulled me out of the destructive path I had been on, and the tough stance I had taken against my parents (and authority in general) began to wane. At the same time my need for thrills was being met; in truth, everything was "smooth sailing."

Karilee:

Dan and I felt that the move up north had paid off. We were very grateful to the Lord, and our hearts were full of joy. Wendi was happy and compliant, and Rob was showing great spiritual growth and responsibility. We all seemed to have found contentment and fulfillment.

In the midst of this tranquil period, however, my older brother, Jim, was declining rapidly in a battle with cancer. For several years Jim had undergone chemotherapy and radium implants to quell the advance of a malignant brain tumor. Sadly, on October 21, 1981, my wonderful 43-year-old brother died, leaving a wife and three children, as well as a poignant testimony of faith in God.

Jim had been my buddy. In my early tomboy years, we wrestled together, climbed trees, and loved the outdoors. I greatly admired my big brother, and would miss him immensely.

Wendi

Eighth grade came and went without a glitch. I joined the gymnastics team and excelled in the floor exercises. The days of smoking and petty crime had been left behind in Florida.

Life on our five-acre oasis was dreamy, and I was allowed to bring home many of the stray animals I found. Within a year we had 12 cats, two dogs, three rabbits, a hamster, and a pinto pony. A sense of contentment had come into my troubled heart, and it felt good. However, some scars of my past hurts remained as I cautiously watched the people around me and hoped that they would not let me down.

The rest of the summer I spent working various jobs at the camp: I "did time" in the kitchen (peeling hundreds of potatoes), helped out in the canteen, tended to the horses at the stables, and worked as a baby-sitter during family camps. It was good, hard work, and really quite satisfying.

Turbulence (Freshman–Early Sophomore Years)

My freshman year started well. I was excited to be a high-school student. I felt so mature—grown up!

An additional bonus came by way of a wonderful new friendship with my Christian cousin Amy, who had moved to Wisconsin from Oregon. Her zany sense of humor and bubbly spirit were contagious. We spent endless hours creatively enjoying our newfound friendship.

My life was heading off in the right direction. School was tolerable, although my tendency to daydream left me behind in the classroom sometimes.

My downfall started toward the end of my freshman year when I met a new friend—a neighbor who lived in the country quite close to our house. This friend and I were not so good for one another. Dara came from a loosely run home and was allowed to venture into mischief without much supervision. Together we started taking cigarette butts from her parents' ashtrays, smoking the little bits of butts and redepositing them in the trays.

Just like that the yearning to smoke grabbed me by the throat.

"Let's see if we can buy a pack on our own," I suggested one day. Mine was the lesser-known face in town, and showing an ID was not required back then. We picked up our pack of smokes with no questions asked.

"Well, that was easy," I said, proudly thinking I must have looked really grown-up to the clerk. Dara and I laughed together as if it were the biggest joke in the world.

Karilee:

The summer between Wendi's freshman and sophomore year a new friendship with Dara sprang up. But although Wendi spent some time with Dara, more of her time was spent at camp and having fun with her Christian friends Amy and Jill. Because of the busyness of camp life and the involvement with the campers, summer flew by quickly.

Soon fall arrived, and the excitement of school activities took hold. Rob was involved in studies and football practices, and Wendi seemed favorably caught up in her sophomore classes and friendships. The fabric of our family life seemed intact—until we received an afternoon phone call from one of Wendi's classmates.

"Mrs. Hayden?" a girl with a soft voice had begun tentatively.

"Yes."

"Are you Wendi Hayden's mother?"

"Yes I am."

"Well, uh . . . I'm a friend of Wendi's and uh . . . um . . . she asked me to call you at four o'clock to tell you she left you a note. . . . She said she put it inside the zipper of her beanbag chair."

"A note? Excuse me, what did you say your name was?" I searched the junk drawer for a pencil and tore a scrap of paper from a nearby tablet.

"I didn't. I'm just a friend, and Wendi just told me today to call this number and tell you where she left the note."

"What kind of note are you talking about?" I was stalling, trying to figure out what was happening. "Do you mean she left a note *to* us? Or something she forgot to take to school?" *Why didn't she just leave it on her dresser? The beanbag chair?*

"Just a note. That's all I know. She said she put a note in the zipper of her beanbag in her room. That's all she told me. So, um . . . I gotta go. Bye!" The phone went dead.

Bewildered, and somewhat troubled, I took the stairs two at a time and headed straight for Wendi's mint-green plastic beanbag. Yanking the zipper open, I pulled out a neatly folded paper torn from a lined spiral notebook and quickly unfolded it. My eyes fell on her carefully rounded handwriting:

> Mom and Dad
> Me and Dara are going somewhere for a few days. Don't worry. We'll be fine. i'll call you Saturday or Sunday.
> Love, Wendi.

"They're WHAT? We'll see about that," I muttered as I began dialing the number of one of her friends. "Hello, Jill? This is Mrs. Hayden. I'm calling to see if you might know where Wendi is right now."

"No, I don't know where she is. She wasn't in school today, so I thought she was sick." She seemed genuinely unaware of her whereabouts.

"No, Jill. She wasn't sick today," I replied, "but I *do* need to find out where she is. It's important."

"Sorry. I don't know."

"Well, if you hear from her, or find out where she is from one of your friends, please call me, okay?"

"I will."

"Thanks, Jill." I hung up, perplexed. *She wasn't in school today?* I had driven her to school myself. I had watched her amble nonchalantly through the glass doors, backpack slung carelessly over one shoulder, right on time for classes.

Pulling out the thin local phonebook, my fingers began searching through the last names of the few classmates' parents that I knew. I called one or two others, receiving the same response. Wendi had cut classes. No one had seen her, but someone had heard that she and Dara were going somewhere out of town. *Out of town!* I immediately dialed Dan.

I recounted what I knew. As I gave him the facts, my mouth began to feel dry and sticky. "A lot of their friends said they weren't at school *all day*," I added. "Dan, it's already four-thirty, and it's starting to get dark. . . ." *They have been gone since morning!* Now my heart was racing. "I've tried phoning Dara's home, but no one is answering. . . ."

"I'll be right home. Keep trying Dara's house," Dan replied.

For the next 15 minutes I repeatedly dialed Dara's home, and between the unanswered calls I tried several other phone numbers of friends. Each time someone answered, I received the same response. No one had seen either of the girls.

And that was strange, because almost everyone showed up at school on homecoming Friday, a day of pep rallies and festivities—a school day generally considered a freebie, a goof-off day. The big homecoming game was tonight. *Nobody* missed that.

Rob arrived home right after I hung up the phone with Dan. I casually asked if he had seen her, fed him a quick sandwich, and sent him on his way to suit up for the football game. I didn't want to needlessly worry him or distract him from the game by telling him about Wendi's disappearance. There was nothing he could do, and I wanted him to play his best. I couldn't imagine Wendi missing this game—Rob was the star running back. Oh, how I hoped she'd be there!

Dan walked in the door around five o'clock as dusk slipped in quietly.

The approaching darkness brought a sense of fear that crept into my stomach as we sat down together at the kitchen table. We bowed our heads, asking the Lord to give us discernment and guidance. We prayed for Wendi and Dara's safety—for the Lord's protection (hoping they hadn't done anything really stupid). Were they simply in town at someone else's house? Or had they truly gone out of town, as their friends had suggested?

What if they had been lured by strangers into something over their heads? We knew drugs were rampant in our small town—had even heard names of town officials who were supposedly involved in supplying drugs. My mind began conjuring up several more frightening scenarios, and I breathed another prayer, this time for myself. *Please Lord, be merciful. Please take away my fears and settle me down. Give Dan and me sound minds, reasonable thinking, and a peace that only You can give.*

It was a few minutes after five P.M. We decided to wait one more hour to free up the phone in case a friend—or Wendi—called. By now if she *was* still in town she might realize how worried we would be. Perhaps she would come to her senses and phone home to put us at ease.

We decided that if we had heard nothing by six o'clock we would contact the police; but we also knew that the police waited 24 hours before acting on a runaway case.

We sat by the phone volleying ideas. Then one of us would jump up to make another short call. Again, we would sit and wait. Minutes dragged by. I could not sit, so I reached for a sponge and began scrubbing the kitchen countertops. Then the stove. That done, I grabbed the broom and began jabbing it under the round oak table and chairs as my mind tumbled through options.

Should I stay by the phone while Dan attended tonight's game?... Maybe Wendi would show up at the game with friends... so Dan should *probably go to the game. Besides, Rob needed his dad there to watch as he played.... But if we called the police, one of us would most likely be asked to fill out forms downtown.... Who, then, would stay by the phone if Dan was at the game?... Maybe Dan should go to the police station first, and then to the game.... I would stay by the phone.... Someone always should stay by the phone...*

At ten minutes to six the phone rang. Dan answered, "Hello. Dan speaking."

"Is this Daniel Hayden?" a man with an assertive voice had inquired.

"Yes it is."

I stood next to Dan as he listened for a moment. Suddenly he raised his eyebrows before replying, "Wisconsin Rapids?"

I leaned in, trying to hear the authoritative voice resonating through the receiver but I couldn't make out the words. Dan whispered to me, "It's the Wood County Police. They have Wendi."

The police? Wisconsin Rapids? Neither girl could drive. What were they doing so far away? Had they been in some kind of accident?

"Is everything all right?" Dan responded.

My mind leaped to action on hearing his side of the conversation. *Wisconsin Rapids was over one hundred miles away! And why would the police call? Had the girls gotten into trouble? Or hurt? They hadn't been arrested, had they?*

A creeping fear started at the back of my neck with a tingle and spread through my body as I processed fragments of conversation. At last Dan hung up the phone.

"We have to leave now," he explained as he walked to

the entryway, taking my elbow and guiding me along. He lifted a jacket from the entryway hook. "The police picked up Wendi and Dara hitchhiking along a highway. They're both okay, but we need to go pick up Wendi as soon as we can get there."

I grabbed a jacket too and started out the door with Dan. "Did the girls get into trouble—what happened?"

"The police said they'd discuss things more fully when we get to the station. A truck driver spotted them carrying backpacks along the road, noticed how young they were, and called in their location to police headquarters. Karilee, they were on their way to Des Moines, Iowa!"

The officer had stressed that the girls were lucky that the truck driver had taken the time to call in. "Many wouldn't have," he had said to Dan. "You sure can thank that truck driver, Mr. Hayden."

We sure could! And in our hearts, we surely did. Just as surely, in overwhelming relief, we thanked our heavenly Father. After leaving a message for Rob, we set out to retrieve our daughter.

Relief . . . frustration . . . incredulity . . . anger . . . deep thankfulness. Every emotion played through our hearts as we began the two-hour road trip to Wisconsin Rapids. Deep relief and mounting anger bounced back and forth in our hearts the entire trip. Wow! How glad we were the girls were safe—and they had not met up with a predator-type individual. Horrifying things can and *did* happen every day. I trembled at the thought.

I planned on giving Wendi an enormous hug when I saw her. But then—oh, how frustrated I felt! *This act was so very thoughtless. In fact, she didn't think at all. Had she even once considered the dangers? She certainly hadn't considered her brother, or dad, or me, let alone the homecoming game—Rob's biggest game of the year. Boy, I hate to miss that game!*

As we entered the Wisconsin Rapids city police headquarters, we looked across the room through a windowed cubicle and saw Wendi sitting all alone on a metal folding chair.

Upon being picked up by the police, the girls had been immediately separated and quietly questioned. Satisfied that there were no domestic difficulties, the police planned to release Wendi to us, asking only for a signature. Dara's parents had not yet arrived, but we were not allowed to see or talk with her.

An officer led us into the cubicle where Wendi, her long brown hair straggling over her shoulders, sat slumped in faded jeans and jean jacket. Silently acknowledging our entrance, she stood, gathering her backpack. Dan and I *did* give her big hugs. She was safe! And right now, that was what mattered most. After completing a short discussion with the authorities Dan signed a release paper, and off we went.

Conversation came in spurts during the two-hour ride home. "Okay, Wendi," Dan began, "we're not going to yell at you about this, but of course there will be consequences. Right now we need to know just what you were thinking today when you took off for Des Moines. Why were you going there? Whose idea was it—yours or Dara's?"

"I guess it was mine." Wendi didn't seem all that bothered. No big deal. "There wasn't much at school today, so we knew we wouldn't miss anything at classes. We were going to be back by Monday classes," she emphasized, implying she had thought things out and it made perfect sense.

"Wendi, I'm sure you realize that this action was a direct disobedience in several ways. That goes without saying, and we'll discuss the consequences later," Dan continued. "But do you have any idea how far away Des Moines is? Did you know how long it would take you to travel that distance? And hitchhiking! Never, *never*, should young girls be on the road hitchhiking! Didn't you think of the dangers? You never know who might pick you up. There are perverted people out there!"

"Oh, Dad!" Wendi's tone of voice evidenced exasperation toward her overreacting parent. "We were careful! We weren't just standing by with our thumbs out. We only asked nice-looking truck drivers at rest stops. Our first ride was a really nice man."

"Ted Bundy looked like a nice man," I reminded her. "You can't tell the character of a person just by looking at him. You know that. We've talked about that since you were little."

Silence. We were not convincing her of the danger the girls had placed themselves in, and there was much more than the danger to discuss. "Wendi, you had to know that this would make us very upset," Dan eventually said. "How long were you planning this? And why Des Moines?"

Wendi told us she had met a young high-school boy at camp during the summer. She had a crush on him. So she'd decided to bop on over to say hi. No problem. She had talked Dara into the "adventure," and together they had packed a couple of large backpacks with the necessities—clothes, food, toothbrushes, and toilet paper. They would have been fine, thank you very much!

The entire escapade had been a thoughtless, impulsive "adventure." Dan and I strongly expressed our displeasure and tried to convey the fears she had brought to our hearts. Wendi seemed genuinely surprised at the distress she had caused, and apologized—sincerely, we believed.

She would be grounded for at least a month, and then we'd see.

Wendi:

Just Once More

A consuming restlessness settled in. After being grounded I tried to pull myself together, tried to hang out with Christian friends, but it wasn't enough. I felt bored and yearned for a bit of excitement in my life. I felt like a caged animal.

I had started my smoking habit at Dara's house, using her parents' butts; now I had figured out how to purchase them for myself, and began a concerted effort to cover up this habit. It wasn't long before I began to itch for something more. I recalled the ecstasy of my marijuana experience in Orlando and thought fondly of that pleasure.

Don't do it, an inner voice reasoned. *Don't blow it and be a disappointment to Mom and Dad. Think of the trouble you'll be in if you get caught!* I began arguing with myself.... *I just want to try it once more.* Good sense won out for a time—but not forever. The draw was too great. I had to try it—*just once more.*

I gave in.

Finding marijuana was so easy it amazed me. I could easily recognize the troubled kids, so I sought out a girl in choir class who I knew was a smoker. A couple of days' friendship was enough for me to ask, "Hey, you ever tried pot?"

"Sure," was her answer. "You lookin' to get some?"

That was all I needed. I asked her how to get hold of some, and that same day I was introduced to "Smiley," a big, goofy-looking senior, so blond he could have been albino. I produced my two dollars and he handed me a joint. Done deal. I took that little joint home and safely tucked it under my waterbed mattress.

It took Dara and me a couple of weeks to find a good time to smoke it. But we did. One Friday afternoon we took a walk into the woods and got high. What a joke—me thinking I could try it *just once*. They say marijuana is nonaddictive. I disagree. Perhaps it is not a physical addiction, but I was mentally hooked again, and this time it was for keeps.

Karilee:

Suspicious. I always felt suspicious that Wendi was smoking, but her denials were vehement, and her artificial sincerity kept me off balance.

Wendi would walk in the door reeking of smoke. Immediately I'd let her know how bad she smelled. Then I'd follow up with, "You're not smoking, yourself, are you?"

"Don't worry, Mom. A lot of my friends smoke, and their smoke just gets into my clothes and hair." Big sigh.

"I hope you're telling me the truth," I'd lecture, "because smoking is so very bad for your lungs. People who smoke have poor health and often die earlier because of it. Don't even try it, Wendi." After *the look* from her (eyes rolling upward), I'd punctuate my point: "I mean it. I've seen lungs in autopsies black as soot. Lung cancer is a horrible way to die."

Wendi:

Cravings and Cover-Ups

My lies flew like darts and I didn't care about anything except getting my next high. In fact, I dedicated the rest of my high school years to the pursuit of these addictions—cigarettes and marijuana.

How did I get the money for this? First of all, my friend Cassie had plenty of money. Additionally, I had access to Rob's car when he was in after-school practices (football, wrestling, track). So on those rare occasions that Cassie ran out of cash we would look for friends who needed a ride and were willing to give us gas money. Add a second rider, and the money doubled. It's easy to be resourceful when you're desperate.

I worked like mad to keep this habit from my parents. I made a practice of jamming stick after stick of chewing gum and peppermint candies into my mouth to cover up the smell. And just to make sure, I nibbled on food whenever I was around my parents. Peanut butter, nacho-flavored chips, and Tic Tacs served as mouth deodorant.

I was constantly thinking of these habits—craving them and covering them up. This became an all-consuming, full-time job and I gave everything I had to it. Soon studies didn't matter. Family didn't matter. Nothing mattered but my increasing need for nicotine and marijuana.

I was hooked.

CHAPTER FIVE

Sowing Seeds of Destruction

Wendi:

IT WAS ASTOUNDING. MY request for one joint cracked open a door that had been shut. I had merely wanted a peek, but instead a trapdoor flew open, and my cravings yanked me down into the darkness. Two years of marijuana abstinence were wiped out in a moment's time by "just once."

I quickly became a regular in the school smoking area. There I discovered a whole world of drugs I hadn't known before: Kids carried Band-Aid boxes full of joints, assorted tackle boxes of every kind of speed on the market (white crosses, pink hearts, black caddies, robin eggs, etc.), $20 bags of pot, hash, hash oil, hits of acid by the sheet, and hallucinogenic mushrooms—all could be purchased by cash or barter.

I was inside the ring. I guess I enjoyed being part of this group of kids because of a perverse attraction to their wild behavior. Their lives of rebellion seemed exciting to me, a contrast to the norms of society. The rest of that year I did a bit of curious dabbling with a few new substances, landing on speed and hash as my favorites.

New Friends

My new peers not only accepted me, they embraced me. They were more than happy to bring in a new "party friend." I was taken in, and that somehow made me feel important.

It all seemed so inviting to me. These kids, coming mostly from homes of alcoholics and busy parents, had total freedom with their lives. They ran the streets and stayed out all night partying. They were the hard-faced "I dare you to mess with me" kind of kids. My new friends were the ones punching teachers and fighting in the halls; many of them turned up missing at school because they had been thrown into juvenile detention. They stole cars and vandalized at will.

It was a tough world—a scary world—but I didn't even realize that I was in really bad company. It's difficult to articulate, but I felt comfortable with them. At that age, immature as I was, I wasn't thinking beyond the moment. Nothing mattered but having fun.

Karilee:

By Wendi's junior year, Dan and I were definitely aware of her decline in most every area of her life. Withdrawn and secretive, her grades were slipping, and her buoyant spirit had turned sullen. We tightened the reins and curtailed her freedoms. Dan and I regularly offered guidance and tried to advise Wendi, seeking to draw her out by talking things over.

But she had attached herself to a group of friends who

were more important to her than we were. We felt so frustrated that we looked into other schooling possibilities. In those days, however, home schooling was not an option. There were no Christian schools nearby and although we did look into boarding schools, we could not find one that suited our needs and budget.

I prayed continually, and hoped that Wendi would weather this teen storm without permanent damage; all the while, disputes over just about anything occurred almost daily.

Many mornings went something like this—

"You're not going to school like that, are you?" I'd comment as she came down the stairs dressed like a vagabond.

"What's wrong with this?"

"What's *wrong* with it? I'll tell you what's wrong with it. First of all, your shirt is dirty. Second of all, it's ripped on the pocket and there's a button missing. Third of all, it's faded and looks like something someone else threw away. And your jeans . . . can't you wear a pair that doesn't have those big holes in the knees?" She looked terrible! *What in the world will people think of us if she goes out like that?*

Aghast, I would make a suggestion, "How about that cute sweater you got for your birthday? That looks great on you. And it's not 'preppy.' " (She hated preppy.)

"I'm going to be working in shop today. I don't want to wear anything too good. I'd probably get grease on it or something."

"Couldn't you just put an old shirt over the sweater when you're in shop class?" That seemed reasonable to me.

"Ma, all the kids dress like this—it's no big deal. Really."

I knew that all the kids did not dress like that—just her circle of friends. So I'd argue with her, right out the door. The few times I insisted that she change her clothes, she would thump up the stairs belligerently, retreating to her room. Then just at the last minute, when it was "leave now or be late for school," she'd fly down the stairs clad in a change of clothes that looked equally grungy.

As Wendi's personality declined and she withdrew from us, I often found myself approaching her with concern.

"Wendi honey, are you feeling okay?"

"I'm fine."

"You sure? You seem so quiet."

"I'm *fine*."

"But you didn't eat much supper. Are you sick?"

"I . . . *don't* . . . feel sick."

"Well, if something is wrong, I'd love to help out if I can. Is there a problem in your classes or anything?" I was pushing it, but I loved her so much, and it hurt for me to see her this way.

"Mom. Just leave me alone! Please." Now she was agitated. "Everything is fine. I just hate living out here so far from everything. It's boring, boring, b-o-r-ing! I wish we lived in town," she'd lament, heading upstairs to her room.

Wendi never used foul language and never lost control by screaming at us (although both she and I raised our voices when things got heated).

Seeing her demeanor change, Dan and I did suspect drugs. We probed Wendi for information through conversations and checked her belongings when we could—all the while gingerly walking the tightrope of trying not to disrespect or invade her need for privacy, something we knew all teens cherished. We never once found drugs in her room, possessions, or car. Frustration and increasing anxiety daily chipped away at my peace of mind.

Wendi:

In a short time I went from dabbling in drugs to needing a constant high. I couldn't stand the mood swings, the lows of bottoming out when the drugs wore off. It became all consuming just to keep the buzz from dying out.

Even though my parents watched my curfew and monitored my whereabouts carefully, it only took a few minutes to get into a lot of trouble. There were times when I would pack my little Pinto full of kids and we'd roll up the windows and pass around joints until the smoke was so thick we couldn't see out the windows. Then with an altered state of mind I'd drive around town pretending I was in a video game. This seemed so humorous to me—so much fun.

Karilee:

Because the high school was far away from our home, we couldn't afford the gas for two trips to town every day. Rob needed his own car because his schedule was different from Wendi's, so our family needed Wendi to be able to drive herself to school for practical reasons. When Wendi got her license, we laid down strict rules regarding the hours she was allowed to be out with the car. We permitted her to drive to and from school her junior and senior years, and we allowed her to drive to other events when we knew someone we trusted would be with her (our son Rob, or Christian girlfriends).

But where there's a will, there's a way, and Wendi found ways to cover up and use her car to party. I can't explain why she was able to so easily fool us. Perhaps I was not prepared to accept the depth of her deceit, for although I didn't really trust Wendi—*I wanted to*. I found myself believing the illusion that the daughter Dan and I raised and taught so diligently—our beloved, cherished daughter—would not lose sight of her early faith in the Lord.

Wendi:

I was 16 when I got drunk for the first time. Most of my underage friends and I did not have access to alcohol, but one day I found myself in town with friends who had a jug of wine. Not realizing the effect it would have on me, I drank much of the gallon while my friends were busy talking. In a drunken stupor, I somehow wound up at a church youth-group birthday party—just a little group of kids from church at Pizza Haven, with no adults present. I showed up snot-slingin' drunk.

What a pathetic sight I was to those kids—including my own brother, who decided to save me from the consequences of my destructive behavior. He shipped me off with my cousin Amy to a movie, where she filled me with caffeinated soft drinks. Once I was sober enough, she took me home. I received a stern lecture from my brother, and the entire episode was dropped.

After that, I was more careful. It took a lot of energy to plan and carry out my covert operations. I devised blatant lies and intricate schemes so I could tend to the new life I'd discovered—the life of "field parties." Kids would pool money at the arcade, find someone of age to buy a keg of beer (the drinking age was 18 at that time), then off into the woods we'd all go.

As with anything I did, I went full-out with alcohol, drinking until I was oblivious, then passing out in my car or under a tree somewhere. I was out of control, and I now realize that only the prayers of my parents and God's love for me kept me from harm.

All during this time I played the game of leading a double life—hanging out with Christian friends but slipping more and more into the wild scene. I thought I had all the answers. Life seemed to be some kind of "harmless" Russian roulette game. *Yeah, sure, some of my friends have died in accidents. But, hey—that won't happen to me!* I lived only for the moment and felt invincible. I couldn't see far enough ahead to realize that these seeds I was planting now would someday grow into a gnarled bramble of destruction.

Karilee:

Then it happened. I discovered Wendi's smoking habit. One Saturday morning as Wendi slept, her window fan fell to the floor making a racket. I hurried into her room to check out the clatter and discovered an open pack of cigarettes on the floor by her bed. I picked them up while she slept and carried them downstairs to the kitchen table.

When Wendi awoke late in the morning she saw her pack was gone and knew at once that she had been caught at last. As she stumbled into the kitchen, I was waiting. "Are these yours, Wendi?" I asked, pointing to the pack on the table. Still half asleep, she nodded yes.

I knew it! "Oh, Wendi! After all my warnings, how *could* you? . . . How long have you been smoking?"

"I started my freshman year, I guess," she answered, half defiant and half scared.

For two and a half years Wendi had diligently hidden her smoking habit. We had suspected it, but had never once found tangible evidence. Now we knew.

What could we do? We had already placed so many restrictions on her we had nothing left to take away. Dan and I sat her down and talked at length about the dangers of smoking, and after a few days we persuaded her to try to stop. We learned of a physician who had good success in helping people quit smoking. The program would be expensive, but we were willing to pay anything to prevent a lifelong addiction. *Could we help her quit—now—while she was young?*

She begrudgingly agreed to try.

We made an appointment. A few weeks later on a blustery winter afternoon Wendi and I traveled to the physician's building in Minocqua. I pulled the car into an icy parking lot and we scrambled out of our warm car, winter coats gathered at our necks as we hurried through the frigid air to the front door. We spoke little as the elevator took us to the second-floor office.

It wasn't long before a middle-aged, dusty-haired doctor stepped into the waiting room and introduced himself. Clad in a white lab coat, he warmly shook our hands.

The doctor led us into his comfortable office and when we were seated he carefully explained his approach in helping people overcome smoking addiction through relaxation techniques. I was encouraged by his explanation, and also with the high percentage of success rates he demonstrated with a printed sheet of statistics. My hopes were high. Would he be able to help Wendi nip her smoking habit in the bud?

"I'll be taking Wendi into the treatment room in a few minutes," he said after all questions were answered. "The nurse will assist me, and our first session will take only about a half hour. If you'll return to the waiting room, the nurse will bring Wendi back to you there when we're finished."

Wendi silently followed the doctor to a treatment room

for further evaluation while I returned to the waiting room. I filled a Styrofoam cup with coffee from the pot on the corner table, found the most comfortable stuffed chair, and began flipping through magazines.

Thirty minutes passed.

Shortly after the 30-minute mark, a nurse stepped into the waiting room. "Mrs. Hayden, the doctor would like to have a word with you," she said softly. "He's with Wendi in his office."

I gathered my purse and walked down the carpeted hallway to the office. *I thought Wendi was returning to the waiting room. . . .* Puzzled, I stepped through the door.

The doctor sat behind the large desk, his arms stretching across the middle of the desk as he leaned forward in conversation with Wendi. He stood slightly upon my entrance, motioning to the seat immediately in front of his desk. He looked at Wendi, whose chair was positioned at an angle directly to my left, and then at me, cleared his throat, and began speaking directly to me.

"Mrs. Hayden, I've talked more in depth with Wendi, and I've discovered that she is not ready for this treatment. In probing her deeper feelings and thoughts, I've found that she does not really want to quit smoking."

I glanced Wendi's way. Her eyes were fixed on the floor.

"If Wendi doesn't want to quit smoking, there is no way I can help her," he stated.

"Wendi, is this true?" I asked incredulously. "I thought we had talked about this and that you really wanted to stop."

Wendi shrugged. She had no further words. When push came to shove, the desire to quit smoking was not there.

I had been duped—either by Wendi or by my own manufactured false hopes. The treatment wasn't going to work, and I knew it. Chagrined, I paid our substantial bill and left discouraged and frustrated.

High School Senior

Wendi's senior year of school arrived and I held my breath. I hoped that she could get through this final year and then involve herself again with the camp and Christian friends whom she now kept at arm's length. I hung on to the fact that I had seen her drawn back to things of the Lord on two prior occasions—once, upon our return to Fort Wilderness from Orlando, and another time her freshman year at Snow Camp for teens. I prayed earnestly that the Lord would protect her from the evil she was drawn to with her friends at school.

Wendi:

Mom and Dad didn't fully know the terrible depth of my bad behavior. When, for the second time, I turned away from God and gave Satan control of my life, my heart became stone-cold and my eyes became totally blind to spiritual things. I stopped seeing sin for what it was. I only wanted to please myself. If it felt good, I did it. Hard-hearted and depraved—that was me.

I jumped into my senior year full throttle. Then a couple months into the school year my life of wild friends, drugs, alcohol, rock 'n' roll, and parties hit a wall. I couldn't see it coming.

I had given my heart away to a boy—I thought it was love. It felt so right. We were the best of friends, and I longed for this love. We had sex.

Nothing in this physical world can ever give back the sacred purity that God designed to be enjoyed by husband

and wife, and I gave it away to the first guy who asked for it. I gave away God's precious gift to me. You can't take back virginity.

A few months later the nausea of morning sickness hit me like a tidal wave. I was pregnant. Talk about sobering! What do you do when you're a little girl trying to be so big but instead end up finding yourself empty, alone, and scared? I had stopped communicating with my parents years ago. I didn't feel I could go to them. Of course I knew I had failed them and didn't want to face their disappointment. I knew that this pregnancy would break their hearts.

Confusion without any hope clouded my mind, suffocating me. Angry and in a panic, I had myself placed in foster care. My ex-boyfriend learned of my pregnancy, came to me, and offered to mend our relationship. He even said he would be a father to the baby. He was no more responsible than I. That was no way out.

Then, my best friend's mother offered to help me get an abortion. Every option seemed too overwhelming. *How could I ever get out of this mess?*

CHAPTER SIX

Facing the Consequences

Karilee:

WHEN DAN TOLD ME of Wendi's pregnancy—the day he'd just returned from meeting her in town while she was in foster care—the news took me by complete surprise. *A baby!*

Trembling, I sank into the living room sofa. *Our daughter—pregnant!* In all the soul-searching I had done during those months, not once had I considered that she might be pregnant. *Lord, give me strength!*

Tears, which in recent days had always been so near the surface, flooded my face. My mind whirled. All my life I had been reared with and lived by a deep spiritual conviction that sex was reserved for marriage. Even though society was now less critical of teens who became pregnant, the memories from my strict upbringing surged to the forefront of my mind. My worst fear for my youngest child—my only daughter—was a reality!

Oh God, give me grace! Help me show her the love and acceptance that she needs.

Immediately Dan and I knelt together by the sofa while he prayed. My muffled sobs subsided as his prayer drew our hearts and thoughts upward to our only hope and anchor. Dan asked the Lord for His strength . . . His wisdom . . . His grace . . . His mercy . . . His direction. We thanked Him that our daughter was now returning home from foster care; we committed this overwhelming circumstance to His care. Clinging like drowning refugees to Christ, our life preserver, we said "Amen."

We stood together embracing for dear life; then Dan stepped back, keeping both hands on my shoulders. "I'll go pick her up now," he said quietly. "Are you ready to have her come home—to accept her just as she is? Remember, she needs us desperately right now. She needs our unconditional love."

Tears streaming anew, I nodded to Dan and whispered, "Yes. Go pick her up. We *will* work through this—we'll show her that we *do* love her"—my voice broke—"and her baby. Let's bring her back home."

Choices

Our family's normal life-flow instantly shifted. The business of life became disheveled because all thoughts—all energies—all of life's activities flowed toward this trauma like blood rushing to an injury. Wendi's "wound" throbbed inside me, too. My burdened heart literally ached with sorrow.

She now had choices to make. Bad, bad, worse, and unthinkable: those were the answers to the four choices looming like buzzards waiting to consume us all. None of the choices seemed good. Adoption, raise the child alone, marriage, or abortion. What would Wendi choose?

Fears crept into my heart—a deep helplessness—especially in the still darkness of the nighttime hours. *This boy and my daughter are but young children. They're not even in love. Surely marriage isn't the answer. . . . Will Wendi plead for an abortion? Please, God, don't allow her to think in that direction. What about this tiny life developing within her child-womb? Will she fall in love with her unborn child and wish to keep it? Can we help her raise a child should she choose to do so? Would she be able to part with her baby, giving it up for adoption? What is best for the child? What is best for Wendi? What is the best counsel we can give her?*

Dan, my pastor-husband, had counseled many families, had given advice in countless such situations. *But this was* our *daughter. This was to be our first grandchild!* Somehow it felt so different.

Wendi took several days off from school, each day lying listlessly on the living room sofa. She agreed to meet with a renowned counselor-friend who lived nearby and did so without enthusiasm or interest; she remained troubled and distant. The counselor confirmed that her problems reached back to her days of strict legalism at the Christian school in Florida.

Some children thrive in spite of adversity, criticism, or legalism; other children wither or become angry or embittered. Wendi's anger against authority had led her into a wild and rebellious lifestyle. My mind began to play out scenarios of "might have, could have, should have"—*might* we have prevented this? Perhaps we *could have* averted some of the difficulties that lay ahead for Wendi if we had probed more deeply back then. We *should have* been more vigilant . . . we *should have* delved deeper into her difficulties . . . *we should have* been stricter . . . or less strict . . . we *should have . . .*

Lord! We should have recognized the depth of her problems early on. I failed her, dear heavenly Father! Please forgive my ignorance and failure as a parent. Oh, the guilt I felt.

Guilt was an emotional burden I would carry off and on in the years ahead—until I learned much later to roll my inadequacies onto the Lord, to let Him carry the load—"My yoke is easy, and My load is light" (Matthew 11:30). [1]

Wendi:

My mind had shut down. Day after day I curled up on my bed or the sofa, trying not to think. The bad news was out. My parents hadn't killed me; yet I knew they were hurt, disappointed, and frustrated. But I wouldn't let my mind think—I didn't want to deal with anything, just sleep, sleep, sleep. Funny, though, sleep didn't help. *Nothing will help me now*, I thought. *What a loser I am.*

Karilee:

We spoke with family members one by one, relaying news of Wendi's plight and asking for prayer. Rob expressed his sadness, concern, and support, as did the grandparents in Wisconsin and New York. Their words of encouragement and comfort helped steady our hearts as each of them promised to pray earnestly in the days ahead. Then we told close friends and opened our hearts to the small church congregation to whom Dan was currently pastor.

It wasn't long before Wendi assured us that she would not seek an abortion. "I know I'm carrying a life inside of me," she said tearfully. "I couldn't . . . wouldn't take that life."

Relief washed over me. One dilemma solved—so many more issues to go.

We talked to the high school authorities and made arrangements for Wendi's graduation. She would finish the semester, attending school until Christmas break; then, only one course away from completing graduation requirements, she would be allowed to take an elective correspondence course through the University of Wisconsin system. Upon completion of this course Wendi would receive her diploma.

Shame on Us

News travels fast. Good news spreads rapidly, but this bad news spread like a California wildfire. Friends called. People inquired. Still others seemed that they were trying to keep their distance, walking the opposite direction if they saw me approaching.

For the first time in my life I struggled with a self-consciousness that bordered on paranoia. Everywhere I went, it seemed, eyes darted furtively toward me—some curious, some filled with pity, some condemning. I wanted to simply stay indoors away from knowing looks. Oh, how I battled the war of shame! Here we were—pastor and wife, and we couldn't even bring up our child properly. What right had we to remain in the ministry?

This question, in fact, drew us to a passage of Scripture found in 1 Timothy 3:1-7, which lists the qualifications of a pastor. Verses 4 and 5 describe these overseer (pastor) qualifications:

> He must be one who manages his own
> household well, keeping his children under
> control with all dignity (but if a man

> does not know how to manage his own household, how will he take care of the church of God?).

One evening after supper Dan and I sat in the living room with a cup of coffee, each of us deep in thought. "Karilee," Dan said, breaking the silence, "I'm still wrestling with whether or not I can stay in the pastorate. In fact, Warren spoke with me today about this. He used the 1 Timothy passage, and feels strongly that I should step down from the pulpit."

Warren was a respected leader in our church. *If he felt this way, were other people feeling the same?* "Honey, you know that I'll fully support any decision you make, because you'll follow God's leading," I said and then asked, "Do you think it would be wrong for you to remain as pastor? Have you spoken with the deacons? How do they feel?" My mind darted from question to question like a skittish filly.

Dan drained his cup and set it down. "Some of the men aren't sure about it. I think they're looking to me for guidance as to what this passage is really saying. Stan brought up Isaiah 1:2, pointing out that God, the perfect parent, had rebellious children, too. Stan is fine with my staying as pastor. He feels that I am ruling my house in a Christlike manner and that Wendi's wayward behavior is a result of her own choice toward disobedience."

Stan was a retired pastor, and for that reason his wisdom and perspective seemed important to consider.

"I don't know," I said, vacillating between the reasons for staying or for resigning. "I can see both sides. I know a lot of townspeople are aware of what's happening—and they're watching us. We don't want to hinder the church's work in the community. If we stay, it could be an obstacle to our outreach. On the other hand, this mess could be a springboard—a platform—for witness. We'll just have to keep praying that the Lord will give you clear direction."

Because of the small-town setting, and in order to maintain the Christ-honoring reputation of our church, Dan felt led to resign. Upon reaching this conclusion, and without the security of another job lined up, he read his resignation letter several Sundays later.

When we returned home after his resignation Dan told me that Warren had approached him after the service, commending him for his decision. "But what took you so long?" he had asked. The condemnation in Warren's tone and manner had hurt Dan a lot. *What would this man have said if Dan had felt led to stay on as pastor?*

And, oh, how I despised the shame! Over and over the verses from the book of Hebrews bore into my heart, "Looking unto Jesus the author and finisher of our faith; who for the joy that was set before him endured the cross, *despising the shame*, and is set down at the right hand of the throne of God" (Hebrews 12:2, KJV, emphasis added).

Yes, I hated the shame I felt concerning Wendi's pregnancy and my own struggle with personal failure as a mother, but stronger yet was the genuine feeling of sorrow that the name of Jesus Christ was being put to shame.

My stomach seemed always to be in a knot, and I felt as if I wore a scarlet letter around *my* neck.

As I continued to ponder those beautiful verses in Hebrews, my eyes were opened still further to the meaning of the phrase "despising the shame." Studying other authors' comments on the subject of shame, I found that the phrase can also mean "thinking nothing" of the shame, or holding it in low regard.

I purposed right then to look at Jesus—to look beyond my shameful circumstance—to the author and finisher of my faith. Then I deliberately rolled the feelings of shame upon His shoulders, *knowing He had already borne the shame of sin*. He counted it as nothing, and I too could count it as nothing.

The Life Preserver of Others' Prayers

Now that Wendi's pregnancy was out in the open, we began hearing from people who had been watching her wild behavior for many months and, in some cases, several years. We heard stories we really wished we didn't have to hear. Close friends and strangers alike called or pulled Dan or me aside to tell rumors or share "facts" about our daughter. It was horrible. I began dreading going out.

Responding to a scathing letter from the mother of one of Wendi's unsaved friends, I replied to her vitriolic accusations by way of a lengthy letter explaining our faith and asking for forgiveness for the hurt Wendi had brought to her heart and her daughter's life. As best as I could, I shared the fact that Wendi's life was not an example of Christian moral behavior.

It seemed that each day hurtful remarks would blanket my soul with a depression—until the blanket was lifted through the reading of Scripture, prayer, and the Spirit of God. While a few acquaintances showed outright condemnation, most friends were loving and supportive. Many promised to pray for us. Those prayers became a spiritual life preserver, and I gladly clung to it.

Attitude Adjustment

Then God threw me another life preserver. An unexpected one. A personal one. Sometimes as we look back upon painful experiences we can see not only some blessing we missed along the way, but also a bit of humor in the way the Lord worked in our lives.

For example, I struggled emotionally with one woman who had regularly criticized Wendi to her face. (She once claimed to have the "gift of confrontation.") On one occasion she pulled Wendi aside to reprimand her concerning her "worldly socks," which were shocking pink with sparkly gold threads: "Don't you think they're a bit flamboyant for a Christian to wear?" the woman asked. Wendi haughtily replied that these "worldly socks" had been a gift from her godly grandmother, that she adored them, and that she would wear them all she wanted, thank you very much.

I wish this woman would have reached out to Wendi in gestures of genuine, loving concern or positive exhortation instead of seeking to find fault with her. I tried to undo the damage of the petty criticism and other such cutting, thoughtless remarks, but Wendi harbored this woman's constant comments in her soul. Each critical remark was just one more cup of gritty sand thrown into the cement mixer of her hardening heart.

Now for the humorous part. Dan and I possessed a tape of vocal music made by this lady and her husband, and until this particular crisis I hadn't taken time to listen to it. But my soul was currently troubled, and music soothes my soul. So during these excruciatingly difficult days when Wendi was deciding what to do with the baby, I played the cassette. It was wonderful!

One song in particular anchored my thoughts in hope and I played it over and over again because of its analogy of a ship being in stormy, troubled waters. The words confirmed the believer's hope in Christ. "Hang on to the rope," it exhorted. Each time I listened, I sang along, visualizing my drowning self hanging desperately on to the rope of the Lord Jesus Christ.

Right then and there I was able to thank the Lord for this couple's ministry of music in my life, and for the soothing balm the words lent to my battered soul. God used this song to turn my critical spirit into one of thanksgiving toward that couple. Only He can do a work like that! I could almost see Him smiling at my heart's turnabout.

A Hard Choice

Two months passed and Wendi entered her fifth month of pregnancy. We needed to broach the subject with Wendi: What would she do with her baby? She couldn't put off her decision forever. Our counselor friend advised that the decision must come from Wendi. "You don't want to be the cause of possible regrets and misplaced blame," he pointed out. "Guide her—but let her make that final decision. You have to treat her like an adult now."

It was Wendi who opened the door of conversation. Dan and I were sitting in the living room in front of our stone fireplace one chilly evening, appreciating the warmth and delicious smell of a crackling fire, when Wendi walked in quietly and sat down Indian-style on the carpet. The flickering fire reflected on her face while, entranced, she gazed for several silent minutes. Then hesitantly, she spoke softly. "Mom and Dad," she began, "I'm not sure what I should do about the baby. What do you think about it?"

We both put down our reading material, turning our heads toward her. "Honey, let's do what I often do when I'm making a big decision," Dan offered. "Let's get a piece of paper and list out the pros and cons of each option."

Wendi eyed him quietly as he reached for a yellow pad and drew a line from top to bottom, making two columns. On the left side Dan wrote "Keep the baby." On the right column he printed the heading "Adoption." These two categories were separated once more into the subtitles "Pros" and "Cons." We were ready to go.

"Now," Dan continued, "I'll write things down. You do the thinking. What would you say are the pluses of keeping your baby, Wendi? Let's begin there."

"I'd get to hold it and watch it grow," Wendi began.

Dan scribbled this down. "What else?"

"Well, the baby would know its mother . . ." A frown fell on her face. " 'Mother' —being called 'Mom' . . . that sounds *weird*," Wendi murmured. "How can I be a *mother?* I haven't even graduated from high school."

"Let's put that on the side under 'Cons,' " Dan suggested. "You *are* young. And you're struggling with your own problems right now. I guess we can also add *that* to the 'Cons.' But can you think of any more keeping-the-baby 'Pros'?"

Wendi thought a while. "I guess not, other than not having to give my baby away to strangers. I can't think of any more good reasons that I should keep it—I can only think of the reasons not to. Where would I get the money to raise a kid? Where would I live? I'd probably have to live with you guys . . . I don't . . . I can't . . ."

"Wendi," I ventured, "raising a child *is* a big responsibility—in fact, it's a huge undertaking. It's not all coos and giggles. It's changing diapers, it's staying up nights with fevers and colic, and it's doctors' bills, and baby food, and clothes to buy. It's teaching the child as it grows. But besides all of that, a mother has to . . . that is, *you* as a single mother have to realize the fact that everywhere you go the child goes with you or needs a baby-sitter. It won't be just your own life to consider. It's another life to care for, too. Are you ready for that?"

"I don't know. I just don't feel old enough to be a mother."

"Well, we can come back to add to our first list," Dan said, "but let's jump to the second side and see what the pros and cons of adoption would be."

"If I adopt out my baby," Wendi began, "I would never see it again. That would be hard . . ."

"What else?" we both prodded.

"Maybe the baby would grow to hate me because I gave it up. I don't want it to hate me."

"There are open adoptions now," I explained, "that allow the natural mother to stay in contact with the adoptive parents. We could look into that."

The discussion went on, with the lists growing. When we were finally done, Dan handed the yellow pad to Wendi. Overwhelmingly, the pros of adoption—what would be best for the child—outweighed the pros of keeping the baby, and the cons of adoption were mainly Wendi's feelings.

Dan ripped the page off. "Take this list, Wendi, and read it over again—even add things you didn't think about just now. Mom and I will be praying for you. It's important that *you* decide; but your decision should be based on reasoned thinking and prayer—so review what's on that list."

My heart simply broke watching our 17-year-old child weigh such an immensely important decision. She was so young; she looked so vulnerable just now. And this mother-to-be had so much growing up to do. I glanced at her thickening tummy. Our first grandchild was being formed within her. Would we ever see this baby? Would we be asked to assist Wendi in raising her child? The whole situation was so overwhelmingly sad . . . and frightening. What would she choose?

Within the week, Wendi came to us with her decision. She knew that she was not ready to undertake the raising of a child and also realized that her baby needed a secure upbringing. She had chosen adoption.

Based on Wendi's present situation, the decision felt right to us. We would help her (through a lawyer) to find a Christian couple looking for an adoptive child. But it was heart wrenching to realize that we would never know . . . or cuddle . . . or play with . . . or read to . . . our first grandchild! We had witnessed the profound joy of our friends' first grandchildren, had happily listened to their exultant boastings; we would never experience those feelings with our very first grandchild.

Oh, how empty that left me—how deeply sorrowful.

Wendi finished her high-school classes through the first semester and completed her requirements of graduation by a correspondence course from the University of Wisconsin.

Many details still lay ahead. As much as possible, we helped gather information as to how to go about the process of adoption. At last we all decided that Wendi would travel to California, where my sister lived, have the baby there, and use the help of a well-known Christian organization to find a home for this child. This would also keep Wendi away from the friends who had been a bad influence.

We couldn't afford airfare, so Wendi and I chose to drive to Santa Maria, California, to use a Christian lawyer through a program Chuck Swindoll offered to unwed mothers. We would set out in Rob's old rust-colored Dodge Dart (dubbed "Bessie").

Lord, have mercy . . .

CHAPTER SEVEN

Empty

Karilee:

THE WEEKLONG JOURNEY TO California was God ordained—tenderly overseen by His love. As the miles rolled by, I became so glad Wendi and I hadn't jumped on a plane, because sitting in the car together hour after hour brought us so much closer. We talked. We enjoyed spectacular scenery while crossing the heartlands, mountains, and desert. We talked some more. Fragile strands of friendship and appreciation for one another tentatively emerged. We even managed some laughter.

Along the way two friends (in Nebraska and Arizona) opened their homes for us to stay overnight, and I hoped that their warm, unconditional love would reach into Wendi's heart. Open communication between Wendi and me blossomed during that long journey. Perhaps this was the healthy beginning of a renewed mother-daughter relationship.

A few mishaps dotted our way. Mt. Vesuvius erupted from Bessie's radiator and it had to be replaced. The small-town repairman was a middle-aged Christian man who put in a new radiator for next to nothing and sent us on our way with hugs and a "God bless you."

The next day, when a front tire went flat during a deluge along an interstate highway, Wendi and I were forced to wait out the torrent of rain. Both of us knew how to change a tire—but the pouring rain wasn't letting up. We decided to sit tight.

Twenty minutes later a knock on the window alerted us to a policeman clad in a plastic rain parka, leaning toward us with a pleasant smile in the downpour. "May I help you ladies?" he offered, glancing at the flattened wheel. Of course we said yes. The added evidence of the Lord's watch care over us was the fact that the lug nuts were corroded and nearly immoveable. If the policeman struggled with them, Wendi or I certainly wouldn't have been able to break them loose. *Thank You, Lord.*

Within a week we arrived safely at our destination. I planned to stay for two weeks to help Wendi settle in and establish contact with the lawyer and physician.

Leaving My Heart Behind

My two weeks flew by. It was time for me to leave—and I found it heart wrenching! As I boarded the plane in Los Angeles, a tune played through my mind. I couldn't get it out—the town and circumstance were different, but the pathos of the San Francisco–based song was fitting as the plane rose steadily: "I left my heart . . . in . . . Santa Maria."

Soon the plane soared above the clouds and my soul turned heavenward. I put the seat back, closed my welling eyes, and drew from the comfort of the Spirit of God. My child would soon be bearing a child. Alone. There was nothing further that I could do. "Thy will be done," I breathed.

Wendi:

I was now 17 years old. I had left school halfway through my senior year and moved across the country to my Aunt Judy's home in California.

It all seemed so strange to me as the baby kicked and moved inside my belly. The joy and excitement that most mothers feel about a baby-to-be just wasn't there for me. Carrying a baby was a thing of shame. Everyone who mattered to me knew I wasn't married.

Realizing that I would never personally know this child, I tried to mentally detach myself—tried not to allow myself to actually *think*. My cousin Mark offered me a job at a Christian bookstore, and I accepted. I poured my energies into the new job. Days quickly sped by.

Choosing Parents

I began a search for a couple who could care for my child in a way I was unable to. It wasn't long before Aunt Judy drove me to the Christian lawyer's office to choose adoptive parents for my baby. There, I was handed six files of résumés to leaf through—files of couples hoping to adopt. Stapled to each file was a color photo and personal biography of introduction. One picture grabbed my attention instantly. I read the biographies through once, and came back to this particular couple's résumé. They looked happy, positive, and loving.

"I think this is the couple I want," I told the lawyer. He offered to bring in another group of files so that I could be sure about my decision, but my heart was totally satisfied. I wanted to meet them.

We met at a small park—a quiet, restful setting—and there we sat and talked. I fell in love with them. She looked beautiful, with shining, long, golden-brown hair swept up behind her ears. Her demeanor was serene. A warm and natural smile was confirmed by her eyes. She was real. But I really liked the husband, too—handsome and charming as he shared his love for music with me. Both were relaxed as we all chatted, and I connected with them because they seemed so genuine. Not phonies. I liked that in people.

I wanted them to be my child's parents, and told them so. They accepted with excitement.

"Our" Pregnancy

Together we enjoyed the last couple of months of "our" pregnancy. We went to Lamaze classes together. I'll never forget looking over at them as they watched my belly ripple with activity as "their baby" moved around inside me.

When the contractions came I called my baby's mom-to-be and we met at the hospital. I don't know who was more nervous—she or me. During the next seven and a half hours, she held my hand and cried with me. I gave birth to a beautiful little boy. She wept.

The next day, they took him home while I was wheeled out of the hospital—alone and empty.

Karilee:

Of course, back at home, Dan and I prayed, and prayed, and prayed some more. We knew that we would not see nor hold our first grandchild. And although my mind had accepted this fact, it was excruciatingly painful for me.

In the meantime, God had directed Dan's and my path to another part of the country. After resigning from the pastorate at our camp church in Wisconsin, Dan had received an unsolicited phone call from our former church in Orlando, Florida. The leadership of the church offered an invitation to Dan: Would he consider returning? The pastor who followed us at the church had recently resigned. Even after learning of our present circumstances, the church issued a call to Dan.

God's mercy was upon our lives, and we made the move to Orlando in late spring, about six weeks before Wendi's baby was due to be delivered. Our friends in this loving body of Christ prayed faithfully for Wendi. Truly I sensed the Lord's strength and grace in our lives and hers as the time grew near.

Special Delivery

I hated being so far away when our daughter would face the pain of labor without a husband, and I was beginning to lather up a full-fledged anxiety as her due date approached. How could I not be concerned? But God knew my longings, heard my fearful prayers, and in spite of my feeble faith, orchestrated events through His abundant mercy and compassion by allowing Wendi a trouble-free delivery.

In late June our daughter—our teenage daughter—delivered her baby, a healthy son.

During her labor, the Lord was so wonderfully gracious to me—the long-distance grandma-to-be. Wendi went into labor while Dan and I were on a cross-country flight to a speaking engagement. We were in the air when my sister tried to reach us with this news, and I was blissfully unaware that the several-hour window of flight time protected me entirely from worry. Upon arriving at our destination, we learned that Wendi had safely given birth.

I was incredibly thankful—and humbled at the goodness of the Lord. And there was a double blessing that day, for the child was born on the exact date of my dear mother's birthday. Although we wouldn't know our first grandson personally, he would always be remembered by us in the celebration of Mom's birthday. Maybe one day we would be privileged enough to meet him.

Wendi:

Now that the delivery was behind me, I began preparations to return to Orlando to live with my parents (temporarily!) until I could earn enough money to be on my own. First, I would remain in California for a month after delivery to recuperate.

I had recently brought a new life into this world; now a couple weeks later the adoptive parents were allowing me a last visit before I left the state.

I entered their house, my eyes drinking in the surroundings of my son's—*their* son's—home. On this afternoon of farewell, I held my baby—*their* baby—closely. I touched his soft, rounded cheeks with my fingers, tenderly circling his face with my hand. Delicate little fingers with perfect fingernails wrapped around my index finger. He was so very tiny! He was warm and soft and sweet smelling. *What in the world have I done? How will I be able to live without my baby?*

"Please forgive me," I whispered to him. "I'm doing this because I love you. Please, please know that. And please don't hate me. Above all, please don't hate me." I kissed his forehead—his cheeks—his tiny hand strongly grasping mine. That was the last time I touched him.

Allured by the Lure

Yes, I had given my son to this caring couple because I loved him too much to deprive him of a stable home. But I also knew that I was totally incapable of thinking of anyone else but myself. No way could I have raised a son. Not a chance. Even as I walked away from his new home, I was on the edge of exploding as my body tried to balance hormonal upheavals and a sudden, frightening pull toward my past.

Like a jack-in-the-box, my past cravings inexplicably popped into my mind, fixating on a huge yearning for some emotion-soothing marijuana. I knew my parents were praying for me—they constantly told me so. "But," I rationalized, as I rested in California's sunshine, "I have just survived a mega emotional and physical hurdle. I've *really* been through so much!"

Soon I had talked myself into believing that I needed just one more adventure before heading to Orlando. *After all I've gone through, I deserve a little fun. I'll take a quick visit to my Wisconsin friends before facing the rest of my life.* Once that idea entered my mind it grew like cancer, invading every waking thought. I'm not sure that I could have turned back from that pull even if I had changed my mind.

I spent some of the money saved from my job in California to purchase airfare and some "party favors" for my return. *One big party—one celebration of making it past this hurdle, and that's it.* I hadn't learned anything.

I purchased some marijuana, a few hits of acid, a little bit of cocaine, and a sampling of crystal meth. Carefully, I packaged all my goodies inside some fragrance bottles and sealed them up in a Ziploc bag, tucking them into my suitcase. I checked my bag at the Los Angeles airport and boarded the plane.

What in the world was I thinking? I'll tell you. *Who cares what happens to me?* That's what I was thinking. *I've been through a lot. I deserve this, and I'm going to do it. Come and get me, world—I dare you!*

Wouldn't my new son have been proud of his birth mother?

Back at the old haunts in Wisconsin I was a smash hit. I spent two weeks partying hard with my friends. Then I was off to Florida. I thought I was in control of my life, but the pull of drugs had me firmly hooked.

Karilee:

We were now grandparents! And we couldn't brag about it to anyone. A deep sorrow settled into a corner of our hearts—an empty space that has remained there to this day. A part of our flesh and blood lived a world away. *Take good care of him,* I breathed to his adoptive parents. *Dear Lord, protect him and draw him to Yourself,* I prayed. *If he becomes a believer, at least I will see him in heaven.* I would pray to that end. . . . I committed in my heart to regularly pray for this innocent, sweet, first grandson whom we could not know.

Dan and I were thankful that this part of the ordeal was over. In two weeks Wendi would arrive in Orlando to live. Soon she would have the opportunity to begin again. At the time, we had no inkling of her drug habits and that she was springboarding full throttle back into her past mistakes.

Our thoughts were full of hope for her future. *Would this be a new beginning for us all?*

PART TWO

Wild Living

Do not be deceived: God is not mocked,
for whatever one sows, that will he also reap.
For the one who sows to his own flesh will
from the flesh reap corruption.

—Galatians 6:7-8 (esv)

CHAPTER EIGHT

New Beginnings, Old Ways

Karilee:

"WELCOME HOME!"

A large, hand-painted tagboard sign caught our eyes as Dan and I pulled up to the parsonage—a tan, three-bedroom cement-block ranch trimmed in dark brown. Fastened to the door amid multicolored balloons, the sign welcomed us like a warm, vigorous handshake. An even more spectacular display, though, brought a big lump to my throat. Huge yellow ribbons tied around the giant live oak trees in the front yard greeted us—the same welcome given to soldiers returning from battle. How apt! How good of God to sprinkle our difficult ordeal with this splash of joy. The congregation loved us. Wanted us, welcomed us. A deep peace settled into my soul.

Coming to Orlando, life felt fresh and new as we picked up the pieces and settled into the ministry while awaiting Wendi's arrival. Rob, who had transferred from the University of Wisconsin–Stevens Point to the University of Central Florida, quickly began rigorous football practices and was making new friends and enjoying the renewal of previous friendships.

Dan and I jumped into the church work, so thankful for the warm and loving welcome we received upon our return. A pastor is rarely called to the same church twice, and we felt honored and optimistic as we embarked upon the rebuilding of this disheartened church body.

Wendi returned from California in late summer looking tan, rested, and happy. Both of our children now lived at home with us this first year back in Orlando—what a blessing! I felt as happy as a school kid on the first day of summer break.

Our joy was tempered, however, by the realization that Wendi needed much restoration. We held our breath during her transition back to Orlando. Every single day we prayed for Wendi: "Oh God, please reach into her heart and help her see her need for You in her life. We so long for her to follow You—to learn of Your peace and joy. We pray that she will find good friendships in the young-adult group. Create in her a desire for You, dear Father."

I hoped her brother's presence at home would influence her in a positive way. Perhaps Rob, a vibrant Christian young man with a strong sense of leadership and love for others, would draw her into spiritual things. Perhaps his Christian friends, who often hung out at our house, would have a positive influence on her. Perhaps the warmth and love of our church body would soften her heart.

Perhaps . . . perhaps . . . perhaps . . .

This habit—looking over difficult circumstances, figuring out my own solutions, and then telling God how to go about bringing my desired results—was one that I drifted into effortlessly. But it wasn't a healthy practice.

Over and over I did this. I'd figure a way God could use this person or that person, or this circumstance or that circumstance. I'd tell God of my plan, pinning my hopes on the "solution" and then wilt with disappointment when things didn't work out the way I had it figured. It was at this juncture of Wendi's life journey that I started to hone my "skill" to perfection, and I'm embarrassed to relate that I continued to exercise this fault for several years.

The book of Isaiah says:

> "For My thoughts are not your thoughts, nor
> are your ways My ways," declares the LORD.
> "For as the heavens are higher than the earth,
> So are My ways higher than your ways
> And My thoughts than your thoughts."
> (55:8-9)

It took me *way* too long to discover this, to apply these verses to *my own* heart, to *my own* situation. When Wendi joined us in Florida, I found myself constantly placing false hopes in my self-made solutions. Then when things didn't go my way I'd question God's mercy and sovereign grace. Trying to devise preconceived results by my own means always led to disappointment, and many times it produced frustration, anger, and sometimes even a bitter spirit. I struggled with all of these feelings at various times until a couple of years later God taught me how to overcome this tendency.

Meanwhile, before I finally understood that I could not manipulate Wendi's turnabout—that only God could accomplish that—I continued my self-efforts. Behind the scenes I made sure others always invited Wendi to gatherings for the college-age adults. I tried to invite "suitable" friends to our house for any occasion I could conjure up.

But Wendi's interest in church activities and the college/career group never took hold. She attended several get-togethers, but often slept in on Sunday mornings, missing her age-group's Sunday-school class as she dragged in late for the morning worship service. "After all, Mom, I have to work late Saturday nights to close up the store." Usually it was long after midnight when she climbed into bed.

Wendi:

My parents lived in the same parsonage that had been ours while I was in the fifth and sixth grades. Here I was, a little girl "all grown up," returning to her tiny bedroom of years gone by.

I had to get out of there!

When I spent those two weeks in Wisconsin fully re-immersing myself into the drug scene, I had pulled the stopper on my bottled-up desire for drugs and alcohol, and there was no turning back. Now, back in Orlando, I contacted my childhood friend Diedre—my seventh-grade friend with whom I first discovered pot—but our interests were no longer the same. We had grown apart.

I soon found a job at a frozen yogurt shop and started the process of earning some cash. There I met Tracy, the manager of the store. She invited me to hang out with her and her friends. I accepted.

Drug Disaster

On the way to her place in a run-down "red neck" neighborhood, we pooled our money and purchased a bottle of Southern Comfort. Her small group of friends ranged in age from 14 to 21. They had all known each other for many years and lived within a three-block area.

These were to become my new close friends. Not much was going on with them other than a lot of drinking and pot smoking. But that was enough to keep drawing me back.

When Halloween arrived, one of the gang scored some acid. I popped a hit in my mouth, ready for some fun. We polished off a bottle of Southern Comfort and then decided to hang out at the pool near apartments just down the road. This was a favorite hangout spot because of the old 10-foot wooden fence surrounding the pool. It assured us privacy to party all night long. By the time we got there, we were in full swing of the acid trip and feeling the alcohol in our systems.

As we rounded the wooden fence, we spotted a horrifying sight! An unmoving man was draped over the edge of the pool. Clad only in swimming trunks, his large body lay facedown on the cement, his legs dangling in the water.

I walked over to the body and leaned over. *No breath! Wow! Is this real?* I bent over within inches of his face. Sure enough, this was real. *This isn't supposed to happen to people on acid,* I thought, turning to my friends to see their reactions. They were gone!

What had started for me as a routine party night had suddenly turned into a horror trip. Quelling my panic, I tried to use logic to guide my actions, fighting through my jumbled, skittering thoughts. *Call for an ambulance*. Finding a nearby pay phone, I dialed *O* for an operator. She patched me through to the local hospital. I was informed that it would be about 45 minutes before someone could get there.

I hung up the phone and stood all alone in an altered state of mind, both palms pressed against my temples. *What now?*

I knew I had to dial 911. I have no idea what my blown-out brain caused my tongue to scream into the phone, but within moments I heard sirens approaching from every direction.

Lights flashed madly and walkie-talkies punctuated the balmy air as police officers stepped out of their cars and hurried over to the guy hanging partway into the pool. I stood on the sidelines, seemingly invisible to the police as they knelt over the body. An officer started to turn him over, lifting the man's left shoulder about six inches from the cement. But the dead weight of the body caused the corpse to slip from the officer's hands, and when he flopped back down to the cement, a gush of blood oozed from his mouth.

That was it for me. I turned and ran. I ran . . . and ran . . . and ran.

The madness in my head was like nothing I had ever experienced before in drug use. My psyche had exploded into billions of jagged, menacing pieces and a feeling of sheer evil pierced me to the core. It was menacingly psychedelic—it was terrifying!

The experience scared me to death. I never touched acid again.

Karilee:

Unsuspecting

Dan and I still had no suspicion of the reckless, drug-filled life Wendi was living. She was adept at covering up her wild behavior. To all appearances she seemed to be working hard at her job, showing responsibility by earning money, helping with household chores, and attending church—with prodding on our part. We were aware of her smoking habit, but certainly didn't realize the depth of dangerous activities that she had so quickly jumped into.

Fall came and went without fanfare. No array of fall leaves in Florida–just a bit of relief from the sweltering humidity.

Swept up into the frenzy of life, we attended the regular church meetings (Sunday morning and evening services and mid-week prayer service), held our enjoyable weeklong fall missionary conference, and helped with the church's Thanksgiving dinner. We celebrated Wendi's 18th birthday in November. These activities were sandwiched between the UCF home football games, and Christmas was just around the corner.

Music in our church was unusually good; this year's Christmas music promised to be exceptional. Our choir director was putting together an elegant musical evening for Christmas Eve. Rob and I had joined the choir, but Wendi, the music lover, wasn't interested—with her work, she "didn't have time."

It always seemed that Dan and I struggled with how much to push and how much to pull back. Do we nag or ignore? Should we offer counsel or hold our tongues? Our hopes were so high, our desires so great for Wendi to find the peace of God and His direction for her life, that I often found myself trying to orchestrate Wendi's participation in church activities or functions.

She most often politely refused.

New Year, Old Lifestyle

Before we knew it, the New Year had rolled around. The hubbub of the holidays was over, and when we came up for air, we started looking more closely at Wendi's newfound friend from work. Tracy was a pleasant enough girl–but definitely one running with a wilder crowd. Wendi had begun attending get-togethers with that gang and was hanging out with them most evenings when she got off work.

I didn't like what was happening, and I certainly told the Lord about it. (Note the attitude! I was still trying to be in charge.) I also enlisted close friends to pray and stood back waiting for a miracle.

With both children at home with us, along with my parents who had arrived from Wisconsin for a couple months' winter stay, we found ourselves appreciating the comfortable feeling of being with family while savoring a near-perfect Florida climate.

An Unforgettable Valentine's Day

When Valentine's Day arrived, Wendi dressed up in a cute white skirt and peach blouse, her long hair painstakingly curled. She really did look stunning when she put herself into it.

"Mom and Dad," she explained, "I'm going to Tracy's house after work for a Valentine's party. We're just going to hang out there with some of her friends, have some wings and pizza, and watch TV. She'll take me to work tomorrow afternoon. I'll be home after work tomorrow night."

And she kept her promise. Dan and I were in bed reading when she returned, bouncing into our room to say good night. All smiles, she said she had something to tell us—but she'd tell us about it in the morning. It was too late that night. With an upbeat "good night," she was off to her room.

"What was that all about?" Dan wondered aloud.

I closed my book and placed it on the nightstand. "I don't know, but it can't be all that bad, can it? She was smiling—in fact she was grinning from ear to ear. If it was bad news, we'd know by her demeanor, wouldn't we?"

"Probably so."

"Maybe she's being promoted at work, since her friend is the manager there," I suggested, speculating on some of the possibilities. "Or maybe she's deciding to go to college. Whatever it is—it looks like something good has happened."

"Well," Dan added as he turned out the light, "we'll know in the morning, won't we?"

Of course we both got up early, our curiosity pulling us up ahead of our usual schedule. Rob had already gone off to early morning classes when Wendi sauntered up to the breakfast table cheery-faced and sparkling as she tossed an official looking piece of paper on the table.

I can't remember the exact words—who said what first—but I remember her blissful, proud look when she informed us that yesterday she had *not* gone to a party with friends in her nice white and peach outfit. Yesterday she had eloped with a "nice" guy named Jeff. She was married!

This time the news didn't hit me like a baseball bat in the chest. *This time* I felt like I was a colorful piñata that had been walloped with a sledgehammer, and all the candies—my sweet hopes and dreams for my daughter—were lying scattered on the ground with fragments of the piñata—me—splattered helter-skelter all around the room.

We had never met Jeff. In fact, we hadn't even realized Wendi was seeing one particular guy.

We didn't even know our own daughter's last name!

At some point she told us he wasn't a Christian. "But Mom and Dad," she said, "he's the first guy I've met that can appreciate a sunset. He seems so sensitive."

I can't recall the particulars of what followed. I think Wendi went off to work. I remember Dan calling the church office and telling his secretary that an emergency had arisen and we would be gone for the day. I remember both of us getting into the car and driving . . . and driving . . . and driving.

I'm sure we talked and talked, but I cannot recall the words or thoughts. I remember getting out of the car at a mall and walking around and around . . . while Dan and I talked some more. By accident we ran into my parents at the same mall and told them the news. *This horrifying news.*

At last we made our way home. Emotionally exhausted, I collapsed on my knees before God, tearfully crying out, "Why? Why?"—the question a good Christian, and certainly a pastor's wife, would never ask if she truly trusted God's promise to work all things together for good (Romans 8:28). In that moment of despair I felt God had let me down.

I had such hopes, Lord. And I've prayed so much for Wendi. Why did You let this happen? So recently we experienced the birth of a grandson we'll never hold and will probably never know. Now we have a son-in-law we've never met.

Why, Lord? I'll never get to help her plan her wedding. I'll never get to attend *my daughter's wedding! What kind of a wedding is getting married by a justice of the peace? Wendi's married to an unbeliever. Oh, why, dear Lord? . . . Why?*

Wendi:

"I Do?"

After my acid scare I decided enough really was enough. I had frightened myself pretty badly. I needed to rethink my life, needed to be more careful. And I needed to get out of my parents' house, but I knew I couldn't make it on my own. What about marriage?

I wonder what it would be like to settle down. I really have had some grand adventures, you know. So, why not get married? I thought. *After all, I'm 18, and marriage may be a grand adventure in and of itself.*

A guy from my new group of friends seemed to like me, and I liked him, too. Again, I thought it was love—whatever love was. So I started talking to him about us getting a place of our own. "Hey—and while we're at it," I suggested, "let's get married!" *It can't hurt, right?*

Wrong!

In less than three months after turning 18 years old—and only five months after meeting Jeff—we got married. It was Valentine's Day, and I was going to give my life to the domestic pursuits of being a wife. Daydreamer that I was, I envisioned living out a fantasy—my storybook marriage.

So we eloped, just the two of us. Out in the crummy little backyard of the justice of the peace we said our vows and went off to our "honeymoon," which consisted of a one-night stay in a two-bit motel on "the Trail"—the drug section of downtown Orlando.

The next day I returned home after working the evening shift to break the news to my parents. I had decided I'd stay overnight at home that night. (Wasn't it considerate of me to allow them a good night's sleep before dropping the bomb?)

At breakfast the next morning I told my parents, nonchalantly tossing the marriage certificate in front of them. *I am now 18. I am an adult. I can make my own decisions—I just did. Look, Mom and Dad, I'm all grown up!*

With foolish, in-your-face confidence, I let my parents know I'd be just fine. I gathered a bag of clothes, and off I went to experience wedded bliss.

CHAPTER NINE

Roller Coaster Ride

Karilee:

I LOVE ROLLER COASTERS. I love 'em fast, and I love 'em steep. I love the twists and I love the loops. Roller coasters are thrilling and exhilarating—and I'll drag anyone along who'll consent to ride with me.

But I now found myself beginning a four-and-a-half-year roller-coaster ride I did not like at all. It was called "The Heartbreaker," and I wanted off. This roller coaster was breaking *my* heart—and I sensed it would also one day break Wendi's heart. I hated every minute of it!

The ups of this horrendous ride were sporadic. The downs pervaded my daily thoughts, often taking my stomach away. I found myself seeking the Lord's mercy and strength constantly.

From the day of Wendi's marriage union until the sad day of divorce, I immersed myself in the Psalms. The Bible—*God's book to His children*—is chock-full of instruction, encouragement, and exhortations. But oh, the Psalms! These poetic chapters flow from the heart of *humankind to God*. They are heart-cries expressing deep emotion: distress and praise and sorrow and affirmation and fear and joy.

My heart to the heart of God. In this way, the Psalms came alive for me.

Through them I poured out my anguished soul. Through them I gained strength, hope, and great comfort. Each time a verse met a particular day's heart-cry, I penned in the date with a notation of the specific need. Through the years my Bible—especially the Psalms—became an unofficial log of this roller coaster ride as I discovered tremendous solace and encouragement to my unsettled soul. "I wait for the LORD, my soul does wait, And *in His word do I hope*" (Psalm 130:5, emphasis added).

After the initial shock of Wendi's marriage wore off, Dan and I committed to support and nurture this union. They *were* married—husband and wife in man's eyes and God's. Maybe we could lead Jeff to the Lord and Wendi's heart would be drawn back also. It was possible that this union could instill a sense of responsibility in Wendi's life.

These were our hopes, but the marriage seemed doomed from the beginning.

Besides being young and immature, Wendi and Jeff had known each other for only a few months and in many ways they were so very different. Wendi loved being around people. Jeff was quiet, inward, and extremely shy. Wendi was artistic and creative. She loved new experiences and adventure. Jeff liked to sit home and watch TV or spend long hours fishing. He enjoyed motorcycling, hard liquor, smoking, and beer parties at home with his buddies.

We hoped that with Wendi's biblically oriented upbringing and the spiritual input in her early years, she might experience at least *some* conviction from the Holy Spirit as she sought fulfillment in life. At least we prayed so.

Reaching Out

In the meantime Dan and I reached out to Jeff in every way we knew how, including him in all we could. We made big over Jeff's birthdays, carefully choosing gifts Wendi assured us he'd like: "Mom and Dad, all his life—every single birthday of his life—Jeff's mother gave him socks and underwear. He never received anything personal or fun."

"So, what can we get him for his birrhday that he would personally enjoy?" we'd ask. We wanted him to feel we cared about him as a person.

The first year we purchased an airbrush and paints—a hobby he always wanted to pursue but could not afford. The following year we found a used pinball machine in excellent condition. We worked hard to accept Jeff and show Christ's love to him. We tried to build bridges of trust, sharing our faith in deeds first, and then in words.

He showed no interest. Our relationship as in-laws was uncomfortable all the way around.

The church people were also warm, loving, and caring—all the things Christians should be toward believers and unbelievers alike. A photographer offered to take professional pictures as a keepsake of the marriage, and some lovely scenic "wedding photos" were taken and given to them gratis.

A lady from church hosted a bridal shower at which time Wendi received a mountain of wonderful, thoughtful, and useful gifts. It was a spectacular shower, complete with music, delicious hors d'oeuvres and sandwiches, a miniature wedding-type cake and punch, and importantly—an encouraging devotional. Wendi looked so very happy, and I know she was touched by the warmth and love the church friends showed her.

For a while things looked promising as we continued to pray for Jeff's salvation, taking life one day at a time. As the months rolled by though, Wendi became more somber, and we saw disenchantment on her face. But whatever she was feeling, she kept to herself.

Marriage problems usually are not one-sided, so we remained supportive, positive, and uncritical of Jeff. But the more we watched the two of them, the more we grew concerned. Both Jeff and Wendi were working full-time jobs, and the few times I ventured over to their apartment, I saw complete upheaval: dirty laundry strewn all around, fast-food containers and pizza boxes, food dried on unwashed dishes, filthy floors, an unmade bed, and very little cupboard supplies.

This was Wendi's sloppy high-school bedroom, times five rooms and two people.

On one occasion I offered to wash up the dishes piled precariously in the kitchen sink. "Fine," Wendi agreed, "you're more than welcome to wash the dishes." As I began to scrape the mound of pans and plates filled with leftovers I almost gagged—wiggling in the middle of a saucepan of food was a mass of writhing maggots!

Wendi and Jeff's place *was* always a disheveled mess, but I knew this was also true of their lives. They needed counseling in their marriage. We offered to pay for the counseling, but our gesture went unwelcomed and unaccepted.

It's painful for me, even now, to look back on those four-plus years. Wendi flitted from minimum-wage job to minimum-wage job. Both of them put what little money they earned first into cartons of cigarettes and bottles of alcohol. Unable to pay their bills, it seemed like eviction notices arrived at their door as often as junk mail.

Several times a week I would find myself wide awake in the stillness of night. Filled with overwhelming sorrow and an impression from God to pray, I'd quietly slip out of bed, pulling on a robe as I padded into the living room with my Bible in hand to curl up on the sofa by a soft-lit lamp.

Tears running down my cheeks, I would seek God's face through His Word until He quieted my fears with a verse or a passage. Then I'd begin to pray—pouring out a mother's anguish for her child. Many times I found myself praying the exact words from a psalm, asking for God's mercy and grace upon my daughter and pleading for His protection from evil. Always, and with great passion, I asked that Wendi's heart be turned toward Him.

Many times early dawn was slipping in as I climbed back into bed.

More and more Jeff emotionally pulled away from us and from Wendi. One summer Wendi stood up as a bridesmaid in her cousin Amy's wedding in Minnesota. Filled with anticipation and eagerness to see our extended family, we made the trip in two separate cars from Orlando to Minneapolis. The wedding was lovely and Wendi looked gorgeous in her stylish turquoise dress. Jeff, however, hated meeting "strangers" and did not attend the ceremony. Then, in a funk he refused to let Wendi join the others in a full-dinner reception. Wendi and Jeff headed home in stormy silence.

Who's in Control?

In all of this turmoil, I continued my efforts to micromanage God's affairs until the light of His love pierced my clouded thinking. Instantly a basic truth shone into my soul with new, enlightening brilliance.

The setup for this lesson came when I again attempted to fix things all by myself. Dan and I had invited Wendi and Jeff to accompany us to an André Kole magic show. My hopes soared when they agreed to come to this event because I knew the gospel would be clearly presented. And it was. But Jeff did not respond, and so my spirits drooped as I plummeted swiftly into another down. *Here I was, giving God a perfectly good opportunity to bring things together, and He didn't do it!* I truly didn't realize how utterly ridiculous it was for me to try to instruct God.

The fault lay not in the fact that Dan and I felt a burden for Jeff's salvation. And there was certainly nothing wrong in arranging a nonthreatening occasion for the gospel to be presented. Opening another door of witness was, indeed, a good thing for us to do; we knew that God can, and does, reach lost people through planning for and following through on witnessing opportunities.

What *was* wrong was my attitude of "I'll do it myself." And I didn't even recognize my faulty thinking at the time. I had been putting my hopes in my own contrived *results* instead of the *person* of Jesus Christ. It was good and right to bring my hopes, dreams, and requests to God; in fact, it is a command found in Philippians 4:6-7. But my hope had been anchored to *my own plan* and not upon *God Himself* and in His sovereign and perfect plan for Wendi and me.

I knew that God reaches out in love and tender provision to His children in times of need, but I had to come to grips with the fact that sometimes God's plan includes pain and heartache. Sometimes it includes waiting. Sometimes His answer is no. That is how He fulfills His multifaceted purpose in our lives. That is how He grows us. That is how we become conformed to His image. And that is how we become beautiful vessels to be used to His honor and glory.

I needed to allow God complete and unquestioning control, looking to Him alone and not to the result I had envisioned.

Letting Go

I can recall the exact moment I learned to "let go, and let God" during those roller coaster years. I was walking through the living room as Dan listened to a tape series by a great theologian named S. Lewis Johnson. My mind was drawn to Dr. Johnson's voice proclaiming the sovereignty of God. I halted my steps and listened.

Like a surgeon wielding his scalpel, God delicately sliced open my heart and poured in the soothing oil of truth. It was almost as if a voice said, "Karilee, Wendi's salvation is not your responsibility! That is My business. It is a work of the Holy Spirit, and all the planning, persuasion, and arguing you could do in a lifetime will avail *nothing* if I, your God, am not in it. Let go!"

Of course I had known this truth for many years. It was all head knowledge, however. Now all of a sudden it was heart knowledge. It was personal! And this truth affected my life and how I viewed Wendi's life like never before.

I look back upon that defining moment as a milestone for which I am still deeply thankful. From that moment on, any time I picked up the burden of fear, or worry, or anxiety, or frustration concerning Wendi, I immediately gave her back to the Lord. I had done this before, but I had always continued to carry my "burden," too.

But now each time Wendi's life took another downward spiral—and there were plenty of hard times ahead—I consciously gave her life, her spiritual welfare, right back to Him. As I released her well-being to God's providence, I finally understood it wasn't my job anymore.

"O Lord! I cannot bring about the needed heart-change in Wendi's life. You alone can change her life, for she is Your creation. I believe she is Your child—she professed faith many years ago. But only You saw her soul when as a child she prayed to receive Christ as Savior—only You knew her heart, Lord. Wendi's behavior shows no evidence that she is born-again. Take her, dear Lord. I give her back to You."

Now I fully understood: *If Wendi's welfare is God's responsibility alone, I don't have to carry that heavy burden anymore. I don't have to figure everything out! God—not Karilee—is the CEO of Wendi's future.*

From then on, my soul found peace even though I was aware that I might enter heaven's gates without seeing Wendi open her heart to the Lord. *I had to be willing to relinquish her destiny to His hands, even if that meant I never would witness her turnabout.*

I cannot express strongly enough what a weight that truth lifted from my shoulders! Never, from that point on, did I bear the burden of her eternal destiny. Never did I lie awake in bed wondering, *What can* I *do?* There were heartaches aplenty ahead. But the responsibility was God's, not mine! He was not just a Friend sharing my heavy load—this Friend lifted it, carrying the entire load. And along with the load of Wendi's struggles and failures, He carried my own failures and weaknesses.

Wendi:

LOOKING FOR "LOVE"

Jeff and I never did find love. Days turned into weeks, which turned into years. We moved from this apartment to that apartment, from this house to that house, to my parents' house, to Tennessee and back to my parents' house, to his sister's house, and then into our own house. And *never* did we find love. We looked. He looked in a bottle, and I looked in a bag of pot.

I withdrew even further. Life held no joy for me. My friends were the people on my soap operas; my best friend—Karen Carpenter (the singer). I loved her songs. They were so sad and hopeless. I identified completely. "Good-bye to Love" became my theme song in life.

Restless, restless, restless. I went through job after job: grocery-store clerk, gas-station clerk, pet-store clerk, department-store clerk, pizza-delivery girl, lawn-care associate—you name it. I didn't care what I did. Minimum-wage jobs were a dime a dozen. Only a few things mattered—my cats and my marijuana.

By the time I hit 20, my respiratory system was in trouble. I started having frequent asthma attacks, which landed me in the emergency room. The doctors told me my lungs were being damaged by the cigarettes and strongly advised me to stop.

I looked at my options and decided that I could live without cigarettes. I quit cold turkey (although I still hung on to my pot). Somewhere I had heard that menthol cigarettes cause infertility, and in my case it seemed to be true because I became pregnant soon after I quit smoking. I was elated!

I wanted this baby so much—and I needed it. I was so very lonely, and I could hardly wait to have someone to love.

Karilee:

Good News—Bad News

Jeff and Wendi's marriage was still stormy when she casually announced, "Guess what, Mom? I'm going to have a baby."

That's wonderful, my mind responded. *That's frightening,* my heart screamed. My mouth uttered something like, "Congratulations. I'm happy for you—that is, if you are happy about it."

"Mom, I'm really glad. I'm ready for this baby. I think I can care for a baby this time . . . I *know* I can."

As a mother, I knew that this was a big event in Wendi's life. She carried the vacant spot in her heart that giving up her firstborn to adoption had left. Of course she was thrilled to be having a child she could keep and call her own. But I also knew that bringing an innocent child into a tumultuous home could result in further upheaval. As a pastor's wife I had seen too many children suffering in dysfunctional families.

The news of Wendi's pregnancy was a mixed bag of tidings for me.

By this time Wendi and Jeff had been able to purchase a small home of their own. Wendi invited me to help prepare the nursery, and together we painted Garfield figures on the walls and decorated in the Garfield theme.

Eight months offered opportunities to talk about all that parenting entails—the joys and the responsibilities, the challenges and blessings. I observed Wendi's eager happiness and savored sparks of joy I had not seen in her life for quite some time. I hoped that *this* might be the occasion that would trigger a turnaround, but *this time* I left that hope in God's hands and didn't try to orchestrate it myself.

Shower of Blessing

Also during this time, Rob fell in love with a wonderful Christian girl he had met at Bible college in Pennsylvania, where he had transferred the previous year. Learning of their burgeoning affection was all part of the roller coaster ups and downs that we experienced simultaneously.

We were overjoyed with Rob and Rhinda's love. Early that fall, Rob elaborately and creatively "popped the question" to his beloved and she said yes! They were both coming to Florida from Pennsylvania for Thanksgiving, so I got busy planning a bridal shower for Rhinda. Almost every lady in the church planned to attend the shower, which was slated for late November.

Wendi gave birth to a daughter, Gracie. This exquisite little sweetheart was born the week before the shower. Wendi was able to attend with her three-day-old treasure, helping out with games, food, and general hostess responsibilities.

For me, the evening of the shower was the peak experience of my four-and-a-half-year roller coaster ride. I had my daughter, new granddaughter, and daughter-in-law-to-be all together celebrating in joy. What a cherished, enjoyable, totally wonderful evening! What a blessing from the Savior. It became a remembrance to be held in my heart's joyous memory bank for weeks, months, and years to come.

In Our Very Own Arms

Holding our granddaughter in our very own arms was an unbelievable delight—a special grandparent pleasure previously snatched from us. Our hearts nearly exploded from the sheer love we felt for her. She was so beautiful—so delicate—with chocolate eyes and tulip-shaped mouth. We offered to baby-sit every chance we could.

We savored every moment with her, watching her grow into an adorable, loving toddler. We did the grandma-grandpa thing with relish!

All the while we knew that other "things" were happening in that marriage and in that home that scared us silly. Alcohol flowed freely and unsavory people came and went—some of whom we felt were unsafe to have around a small child—*our grandchild*! We were especially concerned when Wendi told us about one young adult man who liked to torture critters—poking eyes out of fish while they were still alive, pulling legs off insects, slowly mutilating them, or maliciously teasing kittens. Might he do something harmful to our granddaughter?

Wendi:

Lifeline

My newborn daughter was absolutely perfect! She now embodied the only reason for me to live. Gracie's smile was my lifeline. Filled with satisfaction I held her in my arms while dancing to my favorite Karen Carpenter songs. She gave me a glimmer of hope that life may indeed have more to offer than sadness and heartbreak. With that seed of hope planted in my mind, I started looking at life differently.

But my loveless marriage grew even colder.

I had begun to keep our house clean because of our new child, but Jeff and his cronies hung around our living room TV most evenings, littering the entire L-shaped area (kitchen, dinette, and living room) with dirty plates, empty bags of snacks, piles of beer cans and whisky bottles, and overflowing ashtrays. Whenever I entered their domain, malicious laughter interspersed with caustic sarcasm and criticism flew my way.

I retreated each night to my bedroom, banished like the town idiot. This became my life until months later I could take no more. I wanted something much better for myself and my six-month-old little girl. But I didn't know how to go about it—where should I start?

Karilee:

It was six months after our granddaughter's birth when Wendi showed up at our doorstep with Gracie. She had moved into our home while we were on a few days' vacation. She had left Jeff, and she was not going back.

CHAPTER TEN

Bad Decisions

Wendi:

THE FIRST 22 YEARS of my life were now gone forever. Because my marriage had failed, I felt like a failure, too. Even though I was surrounded by the ones who loved me more than any others, I still withdrew into deep loneliness. In my parents' home I lingered through each day waiting and watching for some little glimmer of life to sparkle up over the blackened horizon before me.

Who was I? A scared little girl with a broken heart, or an angry woman with a vendetta to settle? Probably both. A thickening layer of callousness covered my heart, preventing the light of God's love to enter my darkness. I sat blind and alone in this darkness. What now?

> **JOURNAL ENTRY:** August 29, 1991—Where do I go from here? What is my purpose? I

have done things recently to greatly change my life. Tonight my emotions are down. I seem to have gotten a spoonful of my own medicine. Time away is proving good for him [Jeff]. I am lonely for my friends, which sadly I may not have. I am trapped in this house by my dearest love—my daughter. I am finding no comfort. The days come and go. They are all the same. Great are my thoughts, yet I am so indecisive. I have so many dreams. Where do I go from here? I will begin a search down a dark and winding road. The shadows are so fierce. The woods can be deceptive, yet they are luring because of their mystery. I have a friend inside myself—my best friend. We will conquer this world hand in hand. Today has been a day full of emotion. I have started to cry many times. I never have been able to release my sorrow. Jeff has told me he is beginning to enjoy his freedom. I no longer have the option of going back to him. That is good. He has shoved me on my way. I have felt lonely today. My parents have left on a two-day vacation. My little girl went to sleep early. Jeff was very insulting on the phone. I suppose it makes him feel better—power perhaps? I have been feeling the need to talk to a friend. Funny how no one is home sometimes—not even the ones I would settle with speaking to. I watched *Sleeping with the Enemy* tonight. The romantic men in the movies are sometimes depressing. If they

> really exist, where are they? I've run out of words . . . good night, cruel world!

In this melancholy state of mind I found myself drawn to the hurting lost souls around me. One such soul was Donna. (She is gone now—alcoholism took her life.) She was my friend. We had met four years earlier because her backyard touched corners with the church parsonage.

Donna was a desperate alcoholic whose run-down home was like a people's Humane Society. A constant assortment of bedraggled souls came and went from her dilapidated four-room house—the rent they paid was Donna's way of supporting her drinking. A bedroom went for 75 dollars a week, the couch cost only 15 dollars a week, and for a mere 10 dollars the recliner was yours for the taking.

I can scarcely describe the people I had the privilege to meet inside those cement block walls. I use the word "privilege" because mingling with these broken "throw away" people allowed me to more fully understand their desperation. Lost, lonely, worn out, hopeless, sickly, gaunt, you know—the kind Christ was drawn to.

At Donna's house I encountered a street hooker, a vagabond, a "will work for food" sign-holding street person, and severe addicts whose minds had literally been blown. I mingled with them all.

I hung around there, unfortunately unable to offer any help at all because I had so many problems of my own. Although I pitied those poor individuals, and grew to love them in my own way, I was part of the mission field, too. I got high with them and listened to their funny bar stories or their heartbreaking tales. I felt their pain. I could identify with their feelings. There was camaraderie to be found among those pathetic, suffering souls.

The pull to be with them became stronger as I looked for an escape from my own reality. I could sit and enjoy a cigarette or get high and then just jump the fence and be back to my parents' house.

Run for Your Life!

One day a stranger appeared. I don't know where Donna found this one, but I was intrigued. He was funny, charming, witty, outgoing, dashing . . . and just paroled from prison.

Do you see it coming? Are you sitting there right now shouting, "RUN, RUN FOR YOUR LIFE!"? Wouldn't a person with one functioning brain cell be hearing common sense yell, "*Head for the hills*"? Yes, I suppose someone would run . . . if she could have seen or chosen to see the dangers ahead.

But I saw . . . attention. I felt . . . important—even a bit pretty. This Southern con was a whiz at charming people. He fanned the embers of my sorrowful heart, and the flicker of life I had been waiting for burst into an unbridled blaze.

With reckless abandonment we painted the town together. We drank to complete oblivion. A new passion for life burst out, and with the compulsion to experience life full throttle, I was game for anything. Yes, anything. Bring it on!

Enter violence.

Karilee:

Mudslide

Wendi was caught in a mudslide in which she could not find her footing—a mudslide that gathered momentum, bringing with it the debris of unclear thinking and the inability to reason things out.

Things got grimier, and her life became dirtier and uglier.

After her arrival to our home, Wendi spent most of her energies in day-to-day care of Gracie—playing with her, pushing the stroller around, feeding her, and so on. But in general, she kept to herself.

The youth director or friends from church often invited her to events and parties. "We're having a cookout and pool party at the Monn's home," Dana or Debbie or Fawn would say. "There'll be swimming, volleyball, and tons to eat. Why don't you let me pick you up? . . . I think we're going to watch a video later on, too. It'll really be a fun time of hanging out." Wendi invariably declined.

Perhaps her renewed smoking habit that she had to conceal made socializing with Christians uncomfortable for Wendi. Or more likely, it was because she once again functioned in a totally different zone—the domain of sin called "the world, the flesh, and the devil." But she always had an excuse to say no.

Now a stay-at-home mom, with Gracie as her main companion, Wendi found life becoming boring. She did need friends, but the college/career group at church must have been wearing "leper" signs, because she always kept her distance.

Instead she let herself be inexorably drawn to the down-and-outers—she could not keep away from daily visits to Donna's house, leaving Gracie with me.

Dan and I did not mince words as we warned Wendi of the inherent dangers at that house. "Wendi, we know what's going on there," we'd say over dinner or lunch. "People coming in and out of that place have prison records and dangerous drug dealings."

In fact, it was a regular occurrence to see a squad car parked in the driveway—and police officers dragging out someone in handcuffs. "You could find yourself caught up in a drug deal gone bad or some kind of brawl that would endanger you. Think of your daughter. She needs you to stay away from those kinds of dangers."

"I'm not there late at night," Wendi would reply. "Not much goes on during the day, and I feel sorry for Donna. She needs a friend—and I am that friend right now. Don't worry. If anything starts to look bad, I'll just leave."

Right.

Meeting Trouble

Soon Wendi was seeing another man. This relationship was worse than the previous one. And she was still married! The mudslide gained even more momentum.

Karl was smooth talking and good looking. But he also had two huge drawbacks: He was very controlling and a violently abusive alcoholic. At first he was so nice to her—someone with whom she could share "all her problems." He listened. He smiled. He sympathized. He spent money on her and lavished attention on her—something she hadn't experienced for years.

But Dan and I knew that Karl was nothing but trouble waiting to happen. What kind of person would be reduced to living in that flophouse behind us, with the constantly changing drug- and alcohol-using vagabonds who hung out there? He would not be living in such a place if he had regular income or, for that matter, a direction in life.

We knew Donna and the living conditions of her home very well—we had conversed with some of her "tenants" and had witnessed to her often, including one visit to jail when she prayed to receive Christ. It was the only time we talked with her when she was sober. But as soon as she was released from jail, her alcoholism took over. We had taken her young preteen son under our wing—feeding him, bringing him to church, and putting clothes on his back. Yes, we knew Donna well.

"Please take time to think about what you're doing," we pleaded with Wendi. "You are still married to Jeff. Now you are seeing another man—one who's going absolutely nowhere. You're turning your back on what you know the Bible teaches about marriage and relationships, Wendi. You are endangering yourself and your child in ignoring what the Lord says. Please—stop seeing this man. Pray to the Savior, who loves you so much, and ask Him for help. He can give to you the fulfillment and happiness you're seeking."

During our talks with Wendi, she dug in her heels and would not face up to her problems or wrongdoings. In fact, in one of these talks she blamed Dan for her previous marriage problems: "If I hadn't felt that you would have condemned me, I would have just moved in with Jeff. I wouldn't have married him. But I knew you would frown on that, so I married him because of you!" That was her in-your-face excuse—her marriage failure had been Dan's fault.

Dan and I were in a quandary. Should we exercise "tough love" and kick her out of our house now? If we did that, what would happen to our precious granddaughter? She was less than a year old. What would she be exposed to? We could not put this innocent grandchild out on the streets.

What *could* we do?

Again, we shared our hearts with close friends and family, prayed daily, and committed the situation to the Savior.

Wendi:

I couldn't see it. I looked at my parents' lives and couldn't see much fun in going to church and reading the Bible. *I'm still young. I made a mistake in my marriage, but I'm still not done looking for thrills.* I made the conscious choice to do my own thing—I wanted laughter, to get high, and I wanted no rules. Karl wanted the same thing.

Talk about two self-centered, immature people.

A Dark Side

The first sign of Karl's violent nature came with a drunken escapade. Karl and I had been to a bar drinking with Donna and a few of the others from her house when he decided he was done partying and it was time to leave.

"Let'sh get out of here," he slurred. "There's nothin' happening here."

"Come on, let's stay a little longer," I coaxed. I was just starting to enjoy myself. The music was cranking up and a lot of people were laughing and having fun. I was not ready to leave.

He grabbed my arm, yanking me around to face him. "I'm the one who's been buyin' the drinks, and I said it'sh time to leave."

But I wasn't ready to go—and I was the driver. I told him as much.

Leaning down to me nose to nose, his menacing eyes bored into mine as his fingers tightened around my arm with alarming strength. "B . . . .!" he snarled. "If you don't get your butt into the car now, you'll wish you had." With that he shoved me toward the door with such force that I half landed on my knees.

In an attempt to shut him up, I faked our departure. We got into my Escort, and I drove back to Donna's house and pulled into the drive. As he climbed out, I shoved the gears into reverse and peeled out, leaving him standing alone in the driveway. Feeling pretty smart, I returned to the bar, finished up my evening, and fell into bed at my folks' house.

The next morning Donna phoned to inform me that Karl had punched out every single mirror in her house. I can now look back and see a deeply disturbed 20-something guy with seething anger; but I wouldn't let myself see it then.

Those were not the last mirrors he would break.

The next few months brought a wild new world of life to me. I was running from reality, but I also thought I was running into great excitement. I was running fast—to nowhere, as my drinking became excessive. On one occasion Karl had to push me home for two miles while I lay in a shopping cart because I could not stand up by myself.

My excessive partying also led to extremely poor decisions.

One evening Karl decided to take me to his sister's house because I was too drunk to return to my parents' house. I didn't want to go there and yelled at him to stop, as I tried to punch his shoulder. I missed and cold-cocked him in the eye. "Enough, I want out!" I opened the car door and kicked my feet out onto the pavement as my feet scraped along the road at 45 miles an hour.

He stopped, leaving the car in the middle of the six-lane road. We struggled as he tried to recapture me. Just then a car pulled up, and the driver asked if everything was okay.

"No, take me with you!" I screamed.

Off I went with three total strangers—a careless, non-thinking decision. They dropped me off in the church parking lot, and I staggered up to the front door of our house next door. I fumbled for the keys—but to no avail. I couldn't focus enough to get the key in the lock. So I lay down and went to sleep right there on my parents' porch.

Karl rolled in with my car shortly thereafter, and opened the front door for me. I stumbled down the hall to my bed and passed out cold.

Drinking is not glamorous. Like the prodigal son living in the pig's sty, I was doing incredibly stupid and embarrassing things—and I wasn't even divorced from Jeff. Totally blind to my sinful ways, I told myself I didn't care. I was having fun. Wasn't I?

Poor Decisions

Then, nausea . . . one poor decision multiplied by each reactive decision brought the dominoes crashing down. *Pregnant? No way!* I knew the drill, so I drove myself to the health clinic and had the test administered. *Positive. Positive? Oh my . . . positive!* My head spun.

Why in the world would God allow someone as messed up as I was to bring another child into this world? (Somehow, this was God's fault! I had to blame others for my mistakes.) I drove my mom's car back home and headed for Donna's so I could do some thinking.

Karl took me from Donna's to his mother's apartment, and they set themselves to explaining my one and only option—abortion. Karl and I were two of the most irresponsible people alive, I knew that. In my desperation I agreed. My heart broke all over again. It shattered into a billion shards—each one piercing my soul with indescribable pain.

But God was listening to my parents' constant prayers. In spite of my rebellion, and in spite of my poor judgment, He interceded with divine sovereignty and compassion.

In my haste to get away, I had gotten sloppy and left the cold, hard evidence of my predicament in plain view. I had run off and left behind that little piece of paper given to me by the health clinic, the one with the box next to "positive" checked. It was right there in the front seat of my mother's car; she discovered it, and that was that.

A wave of relief quelled my agony of being talked into an abortion. Now that Mom and Dad knew of my pregnancy, I found strength through them to tell Karl and his mother no to their offer. In desperation I had agreed to an abortion. Could I have killed my baby? I honestly don't think so.

(Thank You so much, God.)

I now had crossed off the option of abortion. Yes, I was still a failure and a disappointment to my family, but I felt such relief that I would be keeping this baby. It was God who interceded and prevented me from succumbing to that terrible decision.

Karilee:

This New Horror

This new horror struck our lives with landslide force. The mud of adultery had brought with it the likely consequence: Wendi was pregnant again—this time with Karl as the father. Who could have ever imagined that she would be so careless in her relationships? Had she learned nothing?

I was numb. I felt like one of the Three Stooges, being slapped around—one side of my face and then the other—as I stood still taking whap after whap.

Paradoxically though, it was as if I were anesthetized—as if someone with a giant needle had deadened all my nerves with Novocain. Oh, I don't mean that I didn't experience that shame again. I was mortified! I was at a loss to try to explain Wendi's situation to friends and family . . . and our church family. My entire being was filled with a horror too keen to put into words. But it was a *numb* horror.

My whole system went into automatic pilot, and I carried on life like a robot programmed to accomplish various tasks—buy groceries, make breakfast, make lunch, make dinner. Pick up around the house. Do the laundry. Do the dishes. Go to church meetings . . . buy more groceries.

Where Is God?

It was also during this period that my prayer life was severely challenged. Deep inside I began to wonder if God had abandoned me. I continued to pray for Wendi daily, but I secretly harbored the thought that God had turned His back on our situation–for whatever reason. *Why didn't He answer my heart-cries to Him? Why was He allowing Wendi to go deeper into sin? Didn't He care? How long, oh Lord, how long*?

But in this period of time, while feeling near to despair, never did I lose hope in God Himself; I clung to Him desperately, reading countless books and poring through His Word. *Where was God?* Charles Spurgeon answered my question this way: "As sure as ever God puts His children in the furnace He will be in the furnace with them."[1]

God was right there with me, sharing my pain.

I began looking at Wendi as if she were some poor soul we found on the streets who needed not only guidance but extensive therapy. She was like a mangy stray dog snarling at us as we tried to help.

Was she beyond help?

Our hearts were sorely tested by this question, yet our

heads told us that to God nothing is impossible—*nothing*! (Luke 1:37).

Dan sat Wendi down one night and explained again the simple, basic truths of the gospel. To us, she could have been the "prodigal daughter," a wayward child running from the Father (Luke 15:11-32)—but she also might be a "goat among the sheep" (*not* born-again)—spoken of in a parable in Matthew 25:32-34, which describes the Lord separating the saved from the unsaved at the end of the age. Only God knew her heart, and only He knew if her childhood conversion was genuine. Only He knew if she was one of His children.

We assumed nothing. Wendi sat at the dinette table—a wall of stony silence enveloping her—and allowed Dan to lovingly offer the *only* answer to her shattering life.

"I know you don't want to hear this from your preacher-dad," Dan began, "but I cannot just sit by and watch you destroy the rest of your life. Wendi, I don't know if you really *are* born-again. Only God knows that. Only God (and you) knows where your heart is. But Wendi—and this is important—if your childhood conversion was not genuine or if you did not really understand God's offer of salvation when you prayed to Him at six years of age, then perhaps you are *not* saved. If that's the case, Wendi, you are in grave jeopardy of being eternally lost. It breaks my heart and your mom's to think that you might not be in heaven with us someday."

Dan opened his Bible and continued. "The Bible asks the question, 'What good does it do for a person if that person gains the whole world—has everything the world has to offer—but at the end, loses his or her own soul?' Honey, you think you are having 'fun,' but in the end—when it's all over—you lose. When you die there are no second chances."

Shifting in his chair, Dan leaned toward Wendi, looking directly into her eyes. "Look where you are now, Wendi. You're carrying another man's child. Can't you see that whenever you've tried to 'go it on your own,' you always find yourself in a mess? Mom and I love you too much, Wendi, to let you go another step without making sure you understand God's offer to you. It's an offer of His great love to you personally."

He slid a small booklet across the table, opened it to the first page, and began to review the gospel message with her, taking her step by step through Campus Crusade's *Four Spiritual Laws:* "(1) God loves you, Wendi, and offers a wonderful plan for your life; (2) we *all* are sinful creatures and separated from God, making it impossible to experience His plan for us due to our sin; (3) Jesus is God's only provision for our sin through His death and resurrection, making a bridge over the chasm that separates us from God; (4) all we have to do is ask His forgiveness for our sins and receive Him as Savior and Lord. He promises so much to His children: total forgiveness, direction and purpose in life, and eternal life in heaven."[2]

But there was no response at all. No interest. No tears. She had no needs as far as she was concerned. She did not even show anger. Just nothing.

Resetting Boundaries

During this chapter in Wendi's life we had to make some strict rules at our home while she was living with us. Although she was expecting another man's child, we again reminded her she was still married to Jeff. She must honor and abide by her married status; she must stop seeing Karl.

Like a punch-drunk boxer reeling from the many blows

she had taken from her life situation, she reacted by fighting back. Staggering from her "injuries" (most of them self-inflicted) she responded in self-preservation mode. There was no reasoning with her. There was no logic to be explored.

Her response was to move out of our house with Gracie, and into a trailer in a low-income area. Then Karl moved in with her.

Could things get any worse?

CHAPTER ELEVEN

Caught in the Web of Adultery

Wendi:

PICTURE THE SHAME I inflicted on everyone who loved me. I was still married to my daughter's father while moving in with the father of my unborn baby. Oh, what a wretched web I had woven with the sticky threads of adultery; I was thoroughly entangled in the web.

Was I thinking of the pain and heartbreak I was causing my family? No. I was thinking only of Wendi.

I had stepped purposefully into this web, and I was bound and determined to take care of things myself. So the three of us—Karl, Gracie, and I—moved into a tiny single-wide trailer just outside the Orlando city limits. We set up house and tried our hand at being a "family."

Within a few weeks the newness of "playing house" with Karl was gone. Because of my pregnancy I had stopped drinking, but Karl had just been getting warmed up. His alcoholism was in full swing. Many nights I awoke in a pool of his urine as he lay passed out from drinking.

It's hard to keep from sinking in the quicksand when you have cut off all the branches that once reached out to you. I had made my choice. I had cut myself off not only from my parents and few friends I had made at church, but also from God. I was on my own now, and sinking fast, but I sucked it up—until one night Karl crossed the line.

We were at a party with Karl's sister and her neighbors, and he blatantly flirted with another girl—right in front of me! I was infuriated! I knew that it was pointless to try talking rationally with a drunk, so I gathered Gracie and drove the three of us back to the little trailer, all the while biting my tongue.

Gladiator and Lion

Once Gracie was asleep, I came out of her room just in time to see him kick my dainty little black angora kitty across the room. I blew!

"You idiot! Keep away from my kitten! Who do you think you are? You tell me you love me, and then I see you hitting on any girl who comes your way. Well, I won't put up with your flirting with other girls, and I won't put up with your touching my kitten!"

With my finger pointing into his face I continued to verbally let him have it. I was ranting and raving when he stepped back and punched me square in the face. Blood spurted everywhere. (I later learned my nose was broken.)

The blow to my face unleashed 14 years of pent up anger. That narcissistic drunk and I fought like a gladiator and lion. I punched and he punched. I swung with all my might as he swung back with many connecting blows. My adrenaline surged with a vengeance.

When the physical battle was over, the yelling continued. It didn't take great insight to realize we couldn't spend this night under the same roof. We both agreed on that. Thankfully Gracie was small enough to have slept through the whole thing. I lifted her from her bed, put her in the car seat, and drove Karl back to his sister's house.

All the way over he apologized and tried to set things right. I wasn't about to budge. He was drunk, and I knew he had to get out, at least for tonight. As I pulled into the apartment parking lot, an instant metamorphosis took over Karl. With a flick of emotion he went from sorry to angry. Turning around, he leveled one more blow across my face, then jumped from the car and kicked a dent into the rear fender.

Gracie slept peacefully in the car seat behind me as I drove away. Tears rolled down my rapidly swelling cheeks, and blood from my nose and face poured down my shirt.

I needed to talk with Karl's sister, so I went to the dance club where she was hanging out and sat silently in the car to wait for her. Still trembling, I sniffled and waited . . . and waited. Finally the last call for drinks was done, and people began pouring out. I scanned the faces until I saw her, then I waved her over to my car.

"Karen," I warned her, "Karl is on another rampage. Keep him away from me tonight. We can't be in the same room until he sobers up," I added. "Don't let Karl out of your sight. I don't want him showing up until he's sober. Promise me."

She agreed.

Sleep did not come easy that night as I tossed and turned just trying to make sense out of this disaster. *My live-in relationship with Karl isn't working out. All we do is argue, and now we just slugged it out. We aren't good for each other, that's for sure. I admit defeat. My child and I can't stay here any longer.* I would wait until tomorrow to call my parents. After all, this was Saturday night, the night when pastors need their best rest of the week.

Yes, I would wait and call them after morning church was over.

Battered

The early morning light peeked through the curtains to bid me good morning. A knock sounded at my door. Fear gripped me by the stomach as I went to the door to peer through the peephole.

I was shocked . . . it was my mother!

When I opened the door, she looked at me with a pain that I will never forget. *How did she find out about our fight? Will I ever get my life straight? Am I so stupid that I didn't see this coming?* I did feel shame . . . how can my parents keep on loving me?

Karl's sister had woken to find him gone, and out of desperation Karen called to warn my parents: Early in the morning Karl was walking the eight miles straight for me! My mother gathered up the two of us and took us home—me, her "little girl," and her beloved innocent granddaughter.

A little later the church service ended and into the parsonage came my father, the associate pastor, a policeman who belonged to the church, and a few other stern-faced men. I slumped into the couch and began answering their questions. They were dead serious. Just the sight of my battered face and arms must have stirred many unspoken emotions in their hearts.

As the men talked, my mind drifted in and out of the murmur of conversation. The men organized a plan—we would meet up at a vacant parking lot at 1:30 that afternoon to travel together to the trailer and gather my belongings. These men hadn't needed to be asked. They wanted to help, had volunteered. Right on schedule, pickups with trailers came rolling in. The plan was set into motion. A friend, an Orange County Sheriff's Deputy, would supervise this potentially volatile operation. A female officer took an official-looking tablet and began taking notes as I gave my statement. She logged a description of my bruises. Then she asked, "Are you pregnant?"

I was six months along by then and my belly was starting to bulge. I answered a monosyllable, yes. I just wanted this over. I had to get my things out of that trailer, but I feared big trouble. My heart didn't want to go. I wasn't looking for trouble; I just wanted out.

"Battery on a pregnant woman is a felony offense," the officer informed me.

"What? What does that mean?" I asked. "I don't want to press charges."

Another officer replied, "It doesn't matter if you choose not to press charges. Karl is going to be arrested and charged regardless. It is out of your hands."

We caravanned down the road to the run-down trailer park and pulled around the front of our trailer. I sat in my father's car watching the men walk up to the door while Dad sat stern-faced in the car with me, doing his best to hold back his anger. The officer knocked, and a few seconds later the front door opened.

There he was! My heart raced, and my insides flipped. The moment was utterly terrifying. Fear . . . love . . . deception . . . pain . . . exhaustion were all roiling inside me. I trembled as I watched an officer read Karl his rights. He was handcuffed. I couldn't stop looking. *What have I done? I didn't mean for this to happen. I was only supposed to get my things and be gone.*

I sat in the front seat feeling horribly guilty as the officer took Karl to the squad car. As he was placed in the back he looked over his shoulder. Karl caught me with his eyes and mouthed, "I love you."

My father looked away as the tears fell from my eyes.

Then Karl looked back at me through the backseat window of the police car, taking note that I was the only one looking. I saw him mouth the words, "I'm going to kill you." In an instant my sadness turned to panic.

Not Listening

I spent the next few days mulling over my messed-up world: *Okay then, no job, third pregnancy, no money, pathetic excuse for a daughter, loser—yep, that just about covers it.* I was running low on options and up to my eyeballs in consequences. How many mistakes do you suppose one person could possibly make before wising up?

In my mind it was always somebody else's fault that put me in these predicaments. I was so far gone from listening to what God had to say that I couldn't even see my own blatant sinfulness. Each act of sinful behavior had placed another layer of cement on my ever-hardening heart.

My self-obsession to do what I wanted overshadowed my ability to love even my own parents.

Limbo

Karl's mother had gone to work immediately to get her son out of jail. She had contacted an attorney and a bail bondsman. The only kink in the plan was that neither of them owned anything of enough value to get him out on bail.

"Won't you please just talk to him?" his mother's voice purred across the phone line. "He feels awful and he misses you. He loves you."

"Well, I guess he can call me," I replied reluctantly.

The collect call came in shortly thereafter. Karl was all sweetness and apologies. "You know I love you, baby."

It didn't take long before I was heading to the bond office with the title to the house I had lived in with Jeff. The authorities accepted the house as collateral, and Karl was sprung from the county jail to await his court date.

Through a series of events, I learned that if a witness can't be found to subpoena, there's no case. It was as simple as that. I needed to disappear for a while. But where to go?

I didn't have many options to consider. In the end Karl and I decided that I would take off in my Ford Escort with Gracie and head for Wisconsin. I would be on the run until the case was dropped.

Why did I do this for someone who had beaten me? I guess it was because I had started the argument and felt guilty for the charges that were brought. I didn't want to be the one who put him in jail for a felony. I had wanted only safety, not vengeance.

Karl and his mother were quick to send me on my way. And I could hardly wait to be back with all my high school friends I missed so much. I had been away from Rhinelander now for almost six years. During my stay in Florida I never had made any lasting friendships, so when I wanted to talk with someone, I had still called my buddies in Wisconsin.

As far as I could see (and I certainly wasn't seeing very far), this was the best thing that could have come out of this whole mess.

Within the week I would be heading north!

Karilee:

Wendi had made arrangements to move back to her former haunt. "I want to try to make it on my own," was the reason she gave us. We later discovered the move was a mutual effort to have the charges dropped against Karl. It worked.

But this plan to move was just one more blow to my numbness—another hit that I accepted in my mind, but which I would not allow to filter down into my heart as reality. My mind was becoming adept at defense mechanisms, so as each traumatic event piled up, my mind automatically had begun to build walls.

I had to pull away emotionally from Wendi. It hurt way too much to love her intensely. So I stepped back emotionally and psychologically and found myself looking at her in a detached, disconnected way.

I helped her pack up her things, telling myself that she probably needed to experience the "pigpen" of the prodigal son before she was ready to admit her need for a Savior . . . her need for redemption.

Off she went with our cherished granddaughter to enjoy her "freedom."

Wendi:

The five-day journey filled me with excitement and anticipation. It was a wonderful bonding time with Gracie, now one year old. I had already missed so much of her life.

Four of my friends (who were now two couples) lived in a small three-bedroom house just outside of Rhinelander, and they were glad to take us in. The plus for them was the added rent money and the extra help with domestic duties.

It seemed a great fit for us all.

Drinking was minimal around there, since most of these friends were hard-core potheads. A houseful of stoned people is a pretty mellow place to be. My adorable little girl was the belle of the ball. Everyone absolutely loved her.

I felt an inner tranquility, and for a time, contentment. I even regained enough confidence in myself that I broke off all ties to Karl.

Had I finally found the peace I had been searching for?

Karilee:

Bittersweet

Relief, mingled with loneliness for our sweet granddaughter, settled in. Dan and I had given much of this innocent child's care, and we both missed her immensely.

But the circumstance was bittersweet to me because the raw pain of watching a loved one continue on a destructive path is excruciating. Now, though I knew Wendi was still running from the Lord, I didn't have to experience with her the downward spiral–step by agonizing step. I would not have to live each crisis, moment by agonizing moment. I would not have to know, firsthand, the sordid details of her sin-filled actions.

There was some relief in that.

CHAPTER TWELVE

Place of Refuge

Karilee:

TIRED . . . I ALWAYS SEEMED to feel oh, so tired.

For more than a decade, a great deal of our lives had revolved around the stress brought by Wendi's poor choices. I felt weary much of the time. God knew this. He lovingly provided some uplifting and refreshing times for Dan and me—one of which was Rob's marriage.

This Michigan wedding was sheer joy. Wendi drove from Wisconsin to witness the ceremony—a clear and moving testimony of the believer's relationship to Christ as the bride of Christ. Every aspect of Rob and Rhinda's union gave joyous praise and glory to God. Even Wendi noticed the difference. When the wedding was over, her comment was "Well, *that's* a marriage that will last."

Several months later, however, another wrench was thrown into our plans; what at first looked bad—even impossible—

became a time of blessing. Satan meant these things for evil, "but God meant it for good" (Genesis 50:20).

It began one day when Dan came home for lunch with exciting news. "Guess what happened today?" he said as he walked in the door. "Dr. Alan called from Baptist Bible College inquiring if I might be interested in joining the faculty as a professor."

One of Dan's great gifts is teaching. He speaks with strength and enthusiasm—and through that giftedness, he is a great motivator. I knew instantly this offer would be inviting to him.

"What did you tell him?" I asked.

"Well, I said I definitely would be interested in finding out more about it," Dan said, grinning. "Dr. Alan will be sending some information in the mail, but it's really amazing, Karilee. Everything seems to fit. One requirement was that I needed at least six credits toward my doctoral degree, and that's precisely what I have. Isn't that something?"

"Wow. That *is* something." My heart was smiling. Although Dan had dropped out of Dallas Seminary before obtaining any credits, he had accrued six credits through courses taken at a nearby Orlando seminary. Dan's mother knew he desired to work toward the degree and had generously paid for the courses—none of us realizing at the time how important those credits would become.

Dan pursued the job offer. After many hours on the phone and reviewing paperwork, the college confirmed the fit. Dan flew up to Pennsylvania for an interview and accepted the job on the spot. He would begin teaching that coming fall. We were elated.

Wendi:

As soon as I learned that my father had accepted a teaching position at a Pennsylvania college, I felt the need to head down from Wisconsin to Florida so that Jeff could spend one of the court-ordered visitation times with our daughter. This might be my last opportunity to have a free place to stay during visitation, so Gracie and I flew down for a weeklong visit.

It turned into six months.

Kurilee:

Wendi arrived as we were packing up and making preparations to move. Her arrival was a catalyst that sparked two unexpected turns of events.

Rattlesnake

The first event—and most far-reaching for the upcoming months—began by a knock on our front door. I climbed over the boxes, tape, and Bubble Wrap to answer the door. A stranger stood on the stoop asking for Wendi.

With a questioning eye she warily approached the entryway.

Quick as a striking rattlesnake the man shoved a subpoena into her hands. It was a divorce subpoena, requiring her to attend a hearing. Furthermore, she would not be permitted to leave Florida until the divorce was settled.

Well! Like an iron bar thrust into moving gears, our plans to move north ground to a sudden halt.

We had several problems. First of all, the deposition would be a couple months away at the earliest. Dan and I were to be out of our house within the week. Where would Wendi, who was in her second trimester, and Gracie stay? Wendi would need a doctor's care. What if Karl got wind of her being back? And there was the question of money for food and shelter, and, oh yes, the expense of hiring a lawyer. Our family had many decisions to make—and quickly!

This new dilemma took away my stomach. I was becoming sick and tired of this four-and-a-half-year roller coaster ride. Indeed, I did experience the Lord's comfort, grace, and peace in all of this. Truly I was able to turn over each new crisis to my Savior. My heart *did* find wonderful solace in the knowledge that God would take care of us, but even so, these things are physically and emotionally draining.

It's exhausting to be in the middle of a war. And it's excruciating to watch a loved one's life ravaged by sin's consequences.

Then there's the collateral damage. My heart ached for our granddaughter, who was being swept along in this rushing mudslide of destruction. And now there was to be another child involved—one born out of wedlock to a father who would be no father at all. Oh—what a horrid, horrid situation!

Rescued

In crises, the Lord uses His dear people—those He selects to bring aid in impossible situations—to provide encouragement and to supply specific needs (Philippians 4:18-19). He does this through different means—always with His tender love—thus enabling His children to bear the difficulty without being crushed and to come out on the other side giving praise and glory to God.

Our immediate rescue came through a wonderful couple

in our church who owned a retreat home on a lake. They had also overcome a severe life-problem and, as a result, wanted to help others in crises. They had dedicated their vacation spot to the Lord, naming it Faith Rest.

These dear friends took us aside the next Sunday morning. "We know you are looking for a place to stay while Wendi awaits the hearing," they said with soft, Southern drawls. "Years ago we dedicated our getaway home to the Lord, and He has put it on our hearts to offer it to you for as long as you need it. We'll open the downstairs right away. Just let us know when you need to move in."

This wonderful house was ours to use as long as we needed it—free of charge! The heavy burden of "what to do?" was lifted instantaneously. Dan and I decided it was best for me to stay back with Wendi and Gracie. Since we would be living quite a distance from any town, I would help run errands and drive Wendi to the hospital when she went into labor.

Faith Rest—oh, how the name fit! It was a secluded, restful two-story home on a lake. The name reminded me that my restoration could only come through day-by-day *faith* in the Lord and *resting* in His promises. Thank You, merciful Lord, for Faith Rest! And thank You for our beautiful, generous friends, Buck and Lib!

While Wendi and I settled in, Dan headed, alone, to his new job in Pennsylvania to prepare his classroom, structure his lesson plans, and locate a place to live.

This was *not* the way I had envisioned us starting together in his new job opportunity—but then most of what we were experiencing certainly wouldn't have been my choice either.

Wendi:

Ticked Off!

Being served with divorce papers and an order to remain in Florida really ticked me off. I was devastated to be corralled.

One would think that the constant pileup of bad events would finally bring me to my knees in repentance. But it didn't. I was still taking charge of my life, and I took charge again in completely the wrong way.

My parents are moving out of state and I don't have one single friend in Florida to turn to. What can I do?

What would be the dumbest thing to do?

That's what I did.

Desperate, and using no common sense, I gave Karl a call. We had an awkward conversation at a nearby park and decided we were capable of "handling things as adults." After all, he wanted to know his child-to-be.

Uh-huh.

Mother-Daughter Time

My mom had made a big sacrifice to stay with us out there in the snake and alligator jungle. She has a snake phobia, but her love overcame her fears. In fact, Mom and I were able to enjoy our time together in a way we hadn't for many years.

For the baby's sake I had quit smoking cigarettes and using marijuana, so my mind was clear and my attitude less combative. We sat in the sunshine, read books, rented movies, went out to restaurants, and discussed names for this child-to-be due in October.

I would not give my baby up for adoption this time even

though this would make me a single parent of two children. I couldn't bear another empty hole in my heart that comes with giving up a child, no matter how loving the motive. *I can do it! I am 24 years old.*

Karilee:

At Faith Rest Wendi and I fell into a bit of a routine. I basked in the solitude as we filled our days with walks, reading, and caring for "our" curious toddler. Talking on the phone with Dan, visiting with the lawyer, attending a deposition, and preparing for the birth of Wendi's baby filled many of the hours.

Therapy

An upright piano offered me soothing devotional "therapy." The old hymns of the faith became meditations of my heart toward the Lord. One song, especially, buoyed up my spirit. I played it almost daily, singing the words in my heart:

Be Still, My Soul

Be still, my soul: the Lord is on thy side;
Bear patiently the cross of grief or pain;
Leave to thy God to order and provide;
In every change He faithful will remain.
Be still, my soul: thy best, thy heavenly Friend
Thro' thorny way leads to a joyful end.[1]

Oh Lord, I'm waiting for that "joyful end . . ."

Weeks became months. Dan started teaching classes in September. Wendi was nearing her due date. Depositions behind us, we waited for a final divorce date.

How I wanted to be up north with Dan as the fall college activities began! Meanwhile, at Faith Rest, we had a labor and delivery ahead of us—and we still had the actual divorce proceedings looming before us with all the frightening battles of custody, state of residence, and claims for belongings.

"You Can Count on Me"

A second event began to occur as Karl, who had learned of Wendi's return to Florida, edged his way back into her life. Karl had a beautiful greeting card delivered to her with these words penned inside:

> Wendi, I have so much love for you. I know it's been some bad times. I probably wouldn't blame you if you never spoke to me again (NOT!). I just want you to know you can count on me. For once in my life you can count on me. I hope you feel better lately. I know we both probably feel a little less tense, for all we did was bicker all day. I'll really try to give you space you need. So if I don't talk to you by the time you get this card—please? Let's talk? I love you. I miss you. XO XO

After she read it, I could tell Wendi began to waver. What kind of spell did this unstable man cast on her that she would even waver at all? Did she forget he had slugged her full force in the face, breaking her nose? I had grave concerns over Karl's persistence in renewing a relationship and the fact that his child would soon be born.

Cool Water

Yet as we bided our time, the Word of God ministered to me as a cool refreshing drink of water quenching my thirsty soul: Verses in Isaiah captured my heart—

> Remember ye not the former things, neither consider the things of old.
>
> Behold, I will do a *new thing*; now it shall spring forth; shall ye not know it? *I will even make a way* in the wilderness, and rivers in the desert. (43:18-19, KJV, emphasis added)

Wow! My spirit lifted—God was giving me hope:

> For I will pour water upon him that is thirsty [right now that was *me*], and floods upon the dry ground: *I will pour my spirit upon thy seed, and my blessing upon thine offspring. . . . Fear ye not, neither be afraid*: have not I told thee from that time, and have declared it? (44:3, 8, KJV, emphasis added)

I clung to those verses and many more that the Lord used to quiet my fears and settle my churning thoughts.

Wendi:

My Little "Miracle"

Mom was by my side when I gave birth to my beloved little boy, who came a month early. "This baby is a miracle," remarked the doctor. "Look here, his umbilical cord is in a complete knot. If you had gone full term, this knot would have tightened, cutting off his life supplies."

He *was* my miracle. Twice God had kept him alive. First he had been rescued from abortion, and now he was born early by God's divine grace (although I didn't give thanks or praise to God at the time).

This little dynamo had been in constant motion in my belly. He kicked my ribs until I was sure they were broken. He arrived colicky, jaundiced, and in need of IVs and oxygen to get his lungs working right. The little scrapper had fought to be here, and he wasn't about to give up.

How I cherished him.

Karilee:

I was so pleased that Wendi asked me to be in the delivery room when her contractions began. We hurried over to the nearest hospital, and in a few hours she delivered a gorgeous baby boy. Two days later, there were now four of us at Faith Rest—Mommy, two children, and Grandma.

Self-Pity or Satisfying Praise?

The weeks dragged on.

Wendi, who was still required to remain in the state of Florida, focused on gaining back her strength and learning to care for two children. But the weeks started to become tedious because both of us wanted to move on with life. Still, even during those weeks, the Lord allowed me to learn something further—the importance of praise.

When things are going wrong, it is so easy to focus on the bad all around. It is second nature to grumble and complain about all the "poor me" circumstances invading our lives.

In these past few months I had been increasingly self-absorbed with *my* problems, *my* fears for *my* daughter and *my* grandchildren, *my* loneliness during the absence from *my* husband, and *my* inner anguish at all Dan and I had been facing throughout the years since Wendi's high school days.

I was viewing the world with an exaggerated "*my*-opia"—a self-centered nearsightedness that hindered any ability to see the world around me or to focus on others' needs.

When, through Scripture, the Lord convicted me about this shortcoming, I began a concerted effort to refocus my attention away from myself and toward God. I decided to start two-mile walks in which I would pray the entire time—with the self-imposed stipulation that I could utter only words of *thanksgiving* and *praise.*

I will not allow myself to pray about even one tiny complaint, one fear, or one worry during my daily trek, I promised myself. I would save my requests for other times. These walks were to be a dedication of praise to the Lord. I would thank Him, appreciate Him, and reach out to Him in nothing more than love and thanksgiving.

At first it was hard. After 10 minutes of praise, I had run out of things to thank Him for.

"Okay, Lord, I've made a promise not to dwell on negative things or personal requests. I want to simply praise You and thank You on my walk today," I'd begin. "First of all, I thank You that You love me in spite of my failures. *There are more than enough of those to list.* Thank You that I can come directly to You with my requests." My mind began listing some of those needs and fears. "*Oops . . . better not get started on requests. Sorry, God.* I mean, Lord, thank You that You hear my prayers . . . that You're never too busy . . . that You never slumber or sleep . . . that You love for your children to talk to You. . . .

"And Lord, I thank You so much for the safe arrival of our new grandson. . . . *Oh, how I wish Dan could see him. How I wish we both could watch him grow up in a normal, two-parent home. I really should pray for God to bring a Christian man into Wendi's life. . .*

"Sorry again, God." I seemed to always have requests pop into my mind . . .

After several such starts of finding my mind drifting back to "my poor situation" and apologizing again, I would thank Him that He understood my weaknesses—that He knew my frame—knew my very being better than I knew myself (Psalm 103:13-14).

I was back on track.

Soon verses flooded my mind—scriptures that highlighted reasons to praise Him or His myriad attributes. The two-mile walk was over before I knew it—and I was just getting started in praising Him! Each daily walk ended in my having a heart of true joy and gratitude.

Talk about healing for a sorrowful, self-centered heart!

What a wonderful, loving lesson the Lord taught me during those days. I found my heart daily filled with the joy of thanksgiving and the uplifting pleasure of "my two miles of praise." Paul's admonition became a reality for me right then—and it is an exhortation that applied directly to my everyday life: "*In everything* give thanks; for this is God's will for you in Christ Jesus" (1 Thessalonians 5:18, emphasis added).

Paul was not telling me to thank the Lord *for* everything that was going wrong. That would be dishonest, at best. No one can be thankful for the pain and heartaches of living in an evil and depraved world. No, Paul was exhorting me as a Christian to thank the Lord *in* everything, or *in the midst* of everything.

That is always possible—even in the worst circumstances.

I *could* do that because each day I thought about Him brought a newer and higher appreciation of who my Savior was and what He had done (and was doing) *for* me and *in* me.

There was another benefit, too. Being able to praise and thank the Lord in the middle of turmoil became a potent testimony to those watching. Without even trying, our family's problems became an opportunity—a platform—to talk with others. Dan's and my reactions to Wendi's situation touched not only family and friends, but also many strangers.

In the weeks and months ahead, the Lord would begin to use our circumstances to encourage other parents facing similar problems.

> "Blessed be . . . the Father of mercies and God of all comfort, who comforts us in all our affliction so *that we will be able to comfort those who are in any affliction with the comfort with which we ourselves are comforted by God.*" (2 Corinthians 1:3-4, emphasis added)

Ability to sympathize with others and comfort them through understanding *their* trials was one of the end results that praising God in adversity brought. Others saw the peace that praise brought to our hearts, and they wanted to know how we got that peaceful, joyful attitude.

Doing It Her Way

At last, Wendi signed papers for the marital settlement and a judge set the final trial date for November. I eagerly began making preparation to join Dan the first week of November.

Before we went our separate ways, I approached Wendi once more about her plans for the future. "Wendi honey, you know that Dad and I want the best for you. In a few weeks you'll be leaving Orlando to begin life on your own. You know that as a single mom, that won't be easy. In fact, it'll be hard because of your limited finances. With two children at home and a minimum-wage job, I don't see how you'll make it. Why don't you come up to Pennsylvania? I can help with the children as you work, and you can establish yourself again."

"Mom, I've told you. I want to try it on my own. I have friends in Wisconsin that I can use for baby-sitters, and there are a lot of people at the camp and church I can turn to if I need help. I think I can do it. I want to try."

Her mind was made up. Wendi and her children would move to an Orlando motel for the three weeks until the final hearing. Then she would return to Wisconsin. Wisconsin was "home," and that's where she would go.

Wendi:

Time Bomb

Everything began winding down and winding up at the same time.

Mom was anxious to join my father in their new home. Who could blame her? They had been separated for about five months. Karl was seeking to know his son . . . so I was easily talked into moving in with his sister; my motel rent money was mine to use for necessities. Of course, Karl moved in, too.

My infant son screamed incessantly. It seemed like this

child sensed the upheaval in the apartment. Money and food were scarce. Stress levels mounted all around.

Tick, tick, tick went the time bomb.

Karilee:

Together at Last

"Honey, I sure missed you!" Dan's hug was warm and strong as we kissed—five months' worth. It was wonderful to be back with Dan living a normal life again. With great satisfaction I dug into boxes for the pictures, curtains, knickknacks, and accessories that would make our condo feel like home.

We kept in close contact by phone with Wendi. Those three weeks in Florida were extremely difficult, I could tell. But she kept the details of any problems from us. A few days before the final court date Wendi and Jeff settled out of court to save money.

It was over.

In a divorce everyone loses. There are no winners. The husband and wife lose each other, and the family unit is destroyed. One partner loses custody of their child or children. Marriage—ordained by God—is dissolved by man. His holy decree and design is besmirched.

In Wendi's case, one child loses growing up with a dad. Another child is adrift without a dad. And Dan and I have lost the joy of seeing our daughter honoring God through obedience to His design for marriage.

There was no joy in this day of losing. Would joy come in the morning?

Wendi:

Hanging in There

So there I was, biding time with my children in a hellhole while awaiting the divorce. It was in huge contrast to the quiet kind of life I just left; I had forgotten the harsh shrillness of ever-constant arguments and drunken combat. *I just have to hang in for a little while. I'll be out of here as soon as this divorce is done.*

I did the best I could to console myself with hope for the future. Hang on . . . just a while longer . . . *just hang in there, Wendi.*

To help me hang on, I resumed my marijuana habit. Once a person uses marijuana to mellow out, his or her thinking becomes convoluted. I knew it was wrong—I knew my judgment would be impaired—I knew this habit was jeopardizing my children's lives—but I did it anyway.

Immediately, the marijuana made me not really care.

One sunny fall Florida afternoon Karl disappeared with my car. It wasn't hard to figure where he was. He had left with a guy who hung out at a strip bar just down the road. His sister kindly offered to go reclaim my vehicle for me. She returned in my car that now had both driver's side windows smashed out.

"I'm sorry to do this to you, but you guys are out of here." Her voice was shaking as she tried to hold back anger. She went inside, and the next thing I knew, all of our things were being thrown down the stairs from the upstairs bedroom.

"What in the world happened?" I asked.

"I was backing out of the parking place when Karl came running out of the bar in his usual drunken rage," she said still repressing her rising temper. "He's a maniac. He punched through your car windows with his bare fist, for #%$#'s sake, and tried to grab me. I had to floor the car to get away from him out of the parking lot. I don't want to put up with him any more. You'll both have to find another place."

I went outside to look at my little car, which was now filled with shattered glass from the front dash to the back hatch. *What in the world am I hanging around this guy for?*

But I knew why. I was desperate—and I needed his help to get up to Wisconsin. He wanted to help me move up there, and with two children I knew I couldn't do that alone. So I sucked it up for now.

A small loan from his mother, who, by the way, always defended Karl and not his sister, enabled us to set out looking for somewhere else to stay. We landed on the only place our barely existent money could get us—a dumpy motel 20 miles out of town in the heart of redneck territory.

The bugs, mainly cockroaches, were so thick on the walls that I had to decide which ones were big enough to get up and kill. I scrubbed the grime until my hands were blistered and bleeding. At night I would wrap my son's little handmade cradle with mesh netting to keep the bugs off him. We lived there until the divorce was finally over.

The day after the divorce we would ride off into the sunset to live happily ever after.

CHAPTER THIRTEEN

Shattered!

Karilee:

Now reunited with my husband at the college, I fell into the busy fall schedule with glee. School plays, sports activities, and choral concerts added an uplifting dimension to everyday life. The upbeat tempo of a college campus enlivened us as we immersed ourselves in getting to know Dan's students and searching for a church home. Another bonus was being near Rob, still in graduate school, and wife Rhinda, finishing her undergraduate work.

This was a year of sheer joy—my personal year of jubilee—for God would allow us an entire year of tranquility before facing another stormy onslaught of Wendi's problems. I felt as if I had recently survived monstrously stormy seas and an ensuing shipwreck, and was now cast upon a verdant and peaceful shore. I found myself basking in the sunlight—the sunlight of the Savior's love and the warmth of Christian fellowship. Ah-h-h, it felt wonderful.

Wendi:

"Where in the world did you find this guy?" my friends wanted to know. "He's an egomaniac, thinks he knows it all, and he treats you like dirt." Upon arrival in Wisconsin, Karl and I had moved in to stay with the same friends I had lived with prior to my six-month trip to Florida. It had only taken a few days for them to decide they did not like Karl at all. "Get rid of him, Wendi. He's nothing but trouble."

Instantly I found myself torn between my friends and my boyfriend as the situation intensified. Both of these couples were in the process of finding their own places to stay, but the arrangement of us all living together had damaged our friendship by the time they moved out.

Karilee:

Waiting for Morning

"Weeping may endure for a night, but joy cometh in the morning" (Psalm 30:5, KJV). Yes, joy *does* come in the morning. But Wendi's life was still in darkness—and the morning had not yet come. Her decision to follow this treacherous course would bring many more tears—to us both.

Wendi had found a nice little home to rent in Rhinelander—perfect for her needs, with room enough for the children. Karl had moved in with them apparently hoping to talk her into marriage. Wendi's creativity made the house attractive and homey, their make-believe "family" looking snug as could be as winter approached.

But the wood stove in the living room, providing cozy warmth in the frigid winter, was a complete antithesis of the true, cold harshness of their lives. Of course, Wendi kept silent to us as tension escalated.

Dan and I had not forgotten their violent past, however, and surmised that Wendi and the children were passengers aboard a sinking ship. She was getting what she thought she wanted—a relationship based on no obligations—her "freedom"!

Again, her life was imploding—and she could not blame circumstances on her father this time. She had chosen this life of living together—no strings attached. But she had not reckoned that "no strings" included no responsibilities, no commitment, and no self-sacrifice on either side. There was no God in their lives. Ultimately there could be no joy.

Wendi:

Eruption

A few months later Karl and I found ourselves alone in our own dwelling again. He had landed a job at a local factory but was drinking away every paycheck he earned right up until he lost his employment. Karl became surly and demanding. It was as if he were daring me to give up. He insulted me at every turn and took to criticizing my mothering.

One cold February evening he came through the door in an exceptionally evil mood. "What's the matter with you? You've been here all day and you couldn't even finish all the laundry. You're such a lazy *%#! And what's this? I told you I wanted sausage in my spaghetti, not this crap!"

I could have pled my case: "I've been taking care of the children and I did do all the laundry but that one load. And look, can't you see? . . . I've cleaned the whole house. You said you wanted sausage. This is sausage. How was I supposed to know you wanted kielbasa? Who's ever heard of spaghetti with that kind of sausage, anyway?"

I didn't plead my case—after all, I knew it was pointless. What I *did* do was explode. I was pretty good at erupting, too. I turned around with the frying pan full of bubbling sausage and let the pan fly across the kitchen, straight at his head. He saw the hatred in my eyes and took off down the hall out the door and was gone.

He stayed away long enough to let me gather myself before returning with his few burn marks from splattering grease. Somehow both of us had figured out the uneasy dance of avoiding each other's full wrath.

These types of situations became more and more frequent as our fury and frustration kept building. It came to a head one March evening shortly after Karl had come home from work and I ran to the nearby grocery store for a couple of items. When I got back, Karl immediately took off.

Gracie seemed unusually upset. Upon examination, I discovered a giant darkening red mark on her leg. She was only two and a half years old, and he had hit her—hit her hard. The mark was beginning to bruise and swell, and it was the exact shape and size of Karl's hand.

He can come after me saying and doing all the evil things in the world—but not her! He will not get away with abusing her! I was seething as I gathered up both children and loaded them in the car. I had no idea what I was going to do, but I *did* know that he had to pay. Either I was going to exact retribution from him, or the law was. This time it wouldn't bother me one bit to see him suffer.

I knew I had to stay away from the house. I wound up driving to the Social Service building and filing an abuse report. They took pictures of Gracie's leg, which was still darkening.

Our next stop was the police station, where I filed another report and asked for assistance to go retrieve a few of my things. With plenty of various bruises on my arms and legs, too, the officer eyed us all. I still remember the officer telling me to take my children and go somewhere safe. "After all, your things can be replaced. You can't."

The children and I spent that night with some friends who lived way out of town on a little dirt country road. No way could he find us there.

Havoc

The following morning I had an uneasy feeling. I knew Karl's temper well enough to figure our departure would have set off another rage, so I drove past our house to scope things out. The windows were all covered with sheets. *What . . . ? Something was up.* I thought it best to check in by phone, so I went to a friend's house to call.

"Hello," Karl answered.

"Why are the windows all covered with sheets?" I asked.

"They're broken."

"You broke the windows? Is anything else broken?"

"Everything is broken."

"What do you mean *everything*?" I probed. This statement jolted me. I had seen him shatter mirrors before—but everything? My mind fastened on my personal treasures. "What about my ceramic eagle?" (This was a beautiful spread-winged eagle landing on a branch, hand painted by my mom. It was magnificent—two feet tall—and I cherished it.)

"I said, everything is broken. Even your eagle." He

sounded ashamed and even contrite; he was an expert at apologies after a rampage.

My heart sank. "I want to go in and look but you can't be there," I demanded. "You start walking, and I'm going to wait a half hour before heading over. I expect to see you at least a few miles down the road."

He obliged.

With my best friends by my side, I pulled into the drive. I could see some of my things lying out near the trees across the drive; other things were scattered over the snowy yard. I took a deep breath and opened the back door.

Glass crunched under my feet as I slowly walked into the bedrooms. Mirrors, dressers, toys, knickknacks, everything I saw lay shattered. My legs weakened. I dreaded what I would find with each step as I approached the living room.

Rounding the corner, I felt my energy drain right out my feet. Everything was destroyed! The walls were smashed in, marred by huge, gaping holes where the TV or fish tank or perhaps a chair had been hurled. The microwave, dishes, and my precious Josef porcelain angel collection, all my children's toys—absolutely every breakable that I owned was destroyed.

My eyes landed on three goldfish lying lifelessly on the carpet (Huey, Dewey, and Louie, who had resided in a Little Mermaid fish tank). The house was in shambles—a shell full of broken glass shards.

We entered the bathroom. This horror was too much. The medicine cabinet had been ripped from the wall and smashed into the tub. Most unbelievable was the huge amount of blood splattered over the walls, bathtub, and sink. *What in the world?*

I had lost everything except our clothes, many of which

were stained with blood and saturated with shards of glass. I was sobbing by now, as fear gripped me.

With their arms around me, my friends helped me stumble back to the car.

My body shut down for two weeks. I couldn't think, eat, or sleep. I went to the doctor and received some sedatives to help get through the trauma.

Looking back, I realize that God was merciful to me, even then. A touch from His hand lent a tiny flicker of insight to my steely resolve of independence.

Knee deep in yet another despicable mess, a Christian woman (the mother of a childhood friend from Fort Wilderness camp) reached out to me. She had seen through me as a teen, and knew I was "trouble." But this day, in spite of my past, she offered to take me to a doctor's appointment, knowing I was in no shape to drive.

This loving lady picked me up from my friends' house where the kids and I were staying; during the ride into town she actually apologized from her heart for the bad feelings she had harbored against me as a teen. She asked my forgiveness! And because of her humble spirit, her impact on me was profound.

Mrs. Guthrie's kindness and transparency registered deeply with me, staying with me as a totally new revelation. A glimpse of God's love had shone through the barriers I had built. My stony heart had been touched.

Friends donated their evenings to help clean up the mess. They shoveled *750 pounds* of my things into the back of Karl's pickup truck, and one load at a time my possessions were hauled off to the dump. My feelings yo-yoed from angry to forlorn to lonely, as I camped with my children at friends' houses, trapped by my circumstances.

My friends informed me of the progress being made to the house. Karl was still residing there and had replaced the windows, removed all the glass from the carpets, and shampooed them thoroughly. He wanted to talk to me. I had no other future, so again out of desperation for love, I let him call.

He sounded so sincere with each plea for forgiveness and each promise for love. "Baby, I'm so sorry. I don't know what came over me—I guess I thought you might have skipped out on me. You know I need you."

He would stop drinking because he loved me so much. I desperately wanted his promises to be true. I desired that more than anything in the world. He seemed truly repentant and sincere. I talked myself into believing that this time things would be different.

We went back to him.

One Last Attempt

It was such an eerie feeling to walk into the empty house that had once harbored my belongings. Somehow Karl had come up with a few hundred dollars and used it to take me shopping for some new things.

For the first few weeks back together Karl was wonderful. He didn't raise his voice once or criticize me or complain about my cooking—until I discovered him sneaking off time and again for a few drinks. "I'm running to the store for a pack of smokes. Be right back," he'd say. Each trip started getting longer and longer as he lingered at various taverns or just drove the country roads chugging a six-pack of beer.

As soon as the daily drinking resumed, angry, filthy garbage began to spew from his mouth. Arguments reappeared and we found ourselves right back where we had started. Ugliness and viciousness flew from both our mouths without regard for little frightened ears and eyes. We were two growling pit bulls circling one another, ready to fight to the death. And if we fought physically, it actually *could* mean death for one of us. To smooth out my days, I lived on marijuana, complementing it with drinks now and then. My thoughts seemed constantly jumbled.

"Sometimes I watch you sleep and I imagine the different ways I could kill you," I threatened him spitefully one evening. His look of surprise was quite enjoyable to me. I, myself, was perpetually incensed and increasingly unstable. *Is this what insanity feels like?*

I wasn't sure I could trust myself anymore. I felt he wouldn't hesitate to harm me, for every argument had escalated physically, with more slapping, strong-arming, and punching each time. Verbal threats were commonplace.

But could I harm him?

I convinced Karl that some time apart would be best for us. The plan I presented to him was that we needed to fix ourselves separately so that we could come back together and function as a family.

Karl agreed to head to Florida for a while so that we could pursue individual counseling. It was my elaborate secret plan to get him as far away as possible before telling him that we were through. Fear for my life had led me to this decision. *He can't kill me over the phone, and hopefully once he's back in Florida he'll lose interest.*

It was that night I penned these words:

> **JOURNAL ENTRY:** April 22, 1993—Today is the first day, once again. Two years have slipped by now. Another chapter concludes.

> Once again love has hurt me deeply. Yet I continue. . . . I love, I cry, I hate!! I am with my friends now. They are dearer to my heart than I can describe. I have a son, a precious boy. His smile can warm the coldest hour. My darling little girl—to see her is to love her. She feels the sorrow in my heart. I hold her close, I love her intensely. Oh, that she can have all the love she deserves. Why do I feel the need for companionship? Perhaps I am afraid of confronting myself!! This time it will be a long, hard road to mend my broken heart. I have had my dignity taken from me. I have lost many precious things. I have concluded that love is not only wonderful, it is also evil. You see there are two equally intense sides. It can be compared to flipping a coin. Tails—I win!! Heads—I lose!! When I look at beginnings and follow through to the end, I see everything has a purpose and a way of working for the best in the long run. Thus, I choose tails to win. Inside my mind I am easily swayed. Desperate for love. Dying to love. Eternally optimistic. My heart has been broken by my manipulated mind. Heads—I lose.

Karilee:

This volatile relationship had come to an end. *Thank You, Lord!*

When we received the news that Karl had left, a glimmer

of hope replaced the huge burden our concerned hearts had carried. But our hearts still ached for Wendi, who always seemed to need to learn the hard way. She had borne so much pain. But we especially hurt for our poor grandchildren—both had experienced such great traumas already in their young lives. Knowing that there was much Wendi had not shared with us we could only imagine the frightened hearts of our grandbabies! Yes, we were greatly relieved that Karl was now out of their lives.

Little did we know we would soon face a new and harrowing challenge.

CHAPTER FOURTEEN

Terrorized

Wendi:

KARL NEVER SAW IT coming. It wasn't until he arrived back in Orlando that I told him of my decision to break up. "That's why you were crying so hard when I left. You knew it was over. You're going to pay for this, you #!%!" His threat came across the phone line loud and clear. That is how a new phase began.

Karl spent the next full year terrorizing me.

My phone rang constantly for the first two weeks after he left. I heard Karl cursing, "You #^!%! I should have known what the %#$!* you were up to. You're trying to keep me from my son, you no good #&%! I'm going to come up there to kill you—but first I'll teach you a lesson. You won't know when I'm coming. But I'll be there—you'd better not sleep at night because I'll walk right in while you're sleeping."

Sometimes the phone would ring, and when I picked up

I heard only breathing. But I knew it was Karl. Other times, when he began cursing, I'd hang up. Seconds later the phone would ring again. This was repeated and repeated.

I started keeping the ringer off. Many times when I wanted to get a line out, I had to pick up the phone, hang up to disconnect it, and immediately pick it up again. It seemed he was always there—menacing—on the other end.

At times Karl would start out sweetly, saying he missed me; quickly that would turn into telling me he was coming after me.

Where is he? Florida still? On the road? Around the corner?

Never before or since have I felt the panic those calls inflicted. Cold fear pulsated through my body. Each and every waking minute, as I went about my business, I was ready to fight for my life at any given moment. I contemplated getting a gun.

After several weeks the calls became fewer, but they were still constant. I could always tell when Karl was on a drinking binge, for that was when the phone rang incessantly.

One night after an evening with friends, I drove my sitter home while another friend watched the kids. When I returned she showed me a log of the phone calls that had come in while I was gone. I still have that log: 6-24-93—11:10, 11:10, 11:10, 11:11, 11:11, 11:11, 11:11, 11:12, 11:12, 11:12, 11:13, 11:13, 11:14, 11:14, 11:14, 11:15, 11:15, 11:15, 11:15, 11:16, 11:16, 11:16, 11:17, 11:17, 11:18, 11:19, 11:19, 11:20, 11:20, 11:20.

He had called 30 times in the 10 minutes I was gone. And this was two months after he had left.

I was terrified. Might he come back and carry out his threats?

Karilee:

Tender Farewell

As Wendi dealt with Karl's phone stalking in Wisconsin, back East, the Lord was tenderly preparing Dan and me for his mother's home-going. God so lovingly intertwined details and events that still today we stand in awe, thanking Him for His graciousness and mercy.

Every spring the college held a formal banquet, a time for students to follow their hearts and to invite a date for an enjoyable, romantic evening. Dan and I were especially blessed on this occasion because we had a family table for eight with both sets of parents and Rob and Rhinda joining us.

The evening was magnificent. Joyous and uplifting. Our featured guests, the Back to the Bible Quartet, drew our spirits heavenward, immersing our souls in dynamic songs of praise and glory to the Lord.

Amongst the musical program of the evening, two songs especially reached into my longing heart for Wendi, so I purchased two CDs even though we did not yet own a CD player.

That evening during the banquet intermission we asked a friend to snap a group picture of all eight of us for our memory book, knowing it would be a long time before all of us were together again. Rob and Rhinda would soon graduate and leave the area, and both sets of parents rarely came to visit at the same time.

Throughout the event Mom Hayden commented how pleasant the evening was. "Isn't that music wonderful," she exclaimed, "but I wish I could be lying down while listening. I'm so weak, I feel like I might be getting the flu or something." At intervals she would lay her head forward on her crossed arms, which rested on the table.

As soon as the program concluded, we whisked Mom into Dad Hayden's awaiting car. She was so weak she literally fell into the front seat to begin the two-hour journey home.

An early phone call awakened us the next morning. Dad Hayden's broken voice told Dan, "Mom's gone." Mom and Dad had no sooner gotten home when she collapsed in the hallway from a massive stroke. She had died instantly.

How privileged we had been to have shared her last evening on earth! It had been a night of inspiration and gladness. Our memories were precious—and we even had a photo of that treasured time. Thank You, dear Jesus.

Mom Hayden was a sweet, gentle woman—a pastor's wife for over 50 years—and I had become very close to her. I fondly remembered how she had instantly taken me into her heart when Dan and I became engaged. Many times we had laughed together, giggled together. In her loving spirit I had found the very qualities I so admired in my husband: compassion, gentleness, love for others, love for Christ. I cherished her memory—and, oh, how I missed her!

One afternoon I was in the bathroom washing the tears from my face when I sensed her saying to me (not audibly, of course), "Karilee, stop crying! I'm so happy now—so satisfied. I don't hurt anymore—rejoice with me, please, Karilee . . . laugh with me!" It felt like she was speaking to me face-to-face. I sat at my desk scribbling those thoughts and words:

Rejoice With Me

LAUGH WITH ME—do not mourn.
While on this earth my heart was torn
With heartache, sorrow, pain, and grief;

Today I walk in sweet relief,
For all my tears are wiped away.
COME LAUGH WITH ME—be glad today!

SMILE WITH ME—please do not cry.
My dearest ones, I did not die;
I live! I breathe! I walk . . . I run!
I'm in the presence of the Son,
Enrapt in His sweet loving gaze.
COME SMILE WITH ME—behold His face!

SING OUT WITH ME—but no lament.
Let songs of praise be upward sent,
For I with angels now do sing . . .
A myriad voices echoing
A glorious song of jubilee.
COME SING WITH ME—joy's melody!

GIVE THANKS WITH ME—no heavy heart.
My gracious Lord bid me depart.
Remember, if for me you yearn,
Ev'n if I could, I'd not return.
I'm now complete—so satisfied!
GIVE THANKS WITH ME—I'm glorified!

REJOICE WITH ME—do not ask "Why?"
Tho' I have gone, it's not "Good-bye,"
For when your time on earth is through,
With open arms I'll welcome you
To morning's light—Eternity.
REJOICE IN HOPE. REJOICE WITH ME!

My sorrow had been for myself because I missed her so. But when I began to sense a measure of the exquisite joy she was experiencing in the presence of the Savior, I realized anew that she was, for the first time in decades, free from pain. My heart was comforted and encouraged.

Token of Love

A few weeks after Mom's death, Dad Hayden called. "Dan and Karilee, I want you to know that Mom was thinking of her children in the last few months and had put away money for each child. She was going to give a money gift to each of you personally, but I'll be sending the gift in the mail on her behalf. Please receive it as it was meant—a token of her deep love for you."

Dan and I knew immediately what we would do with that money—it was the exact amount needed to purchase a great sound system, complete with CD capabilities. We did just that. From that day on, and because of Mom Hayden, our lives became immersed in jubilant Christian music—a constant poignant remembrance of her forethought and love.

And there was still *one more* intertwining blessing to be had.

One of the CDs I had purchased at the banquet became a touchstone of hope for me in regard to Wendi. As soon as our sound system arrived, I played the CDs from the Back to the Bible Quartet. Quickly the two songs that had touched me at the banquet became my heart-songs for Wendi. I sang them over and over almost every day in the years to come.

I want to share one of them now, and the other one at the end of this story. The beautiful song below expressed my deep longing and prayer, and each time I played it I sang with Wendi in mind—especially during the chorus:

Turn Your Heart Toward Home

Late in the evening when everyone was sleeping,
The father of a wayward son slipped out in the night.
He looked toward the city and wiped away the tears,
And prayed his son could hear his father's cry:

Turn your heart toward home,
Turn your heart toward home!
You've been gone so long,
Turn your heart toward home . . .

You've been gone so long,
Please don't wait too long . . .
Turn your heart toward home![1]

Oh, my wayward, beloved Wendi—*please* turn your heart toward home!

Wendi:

Running on Nerves

When my father's sweet mother passed away, I was in no shape physically, emotionally, or financially to go to her funeral in New York.

She was the first of my grandparents to die, but I was incapable of dealing with the loss, so I buried the sadness in my heart and went on. Each frustration I felt—sadness, disappointment, loss, injustice—was stuffed away and left in the attic of my soul. I really had developed a talent (honed with the help of pot) for not feeling.

The kids and I took up residence at the local shelter for battered women. But I didn't feel safe in Rhinelander anymore because Karl was still phoning threats to my friends. *He could come back whenever he chooses!* I decided to relocate 60 miles south in Wausau for a while.

The children and I moved to a trailer park with low rent and unpacked our meager belongings in a run-down, dark-paneled, two-bedroom trailer with walls as thin as tissue paper. *Well, here I am. Now what am I going to do?*

Without a specialized degree I couldn't find a job that would cover day-care expenses, much less pay my bills. So, what does a single mother going absolutely nowhere do?

I sought out the drinkers in the trailer park and hooked up with some "fun" gals who knew all the baby-sitters around. I blew my welfare checks and let my rent fall behind. I drank to oblivion, using alcohol to drown my fears and hide from my own thoughts.

I really can't remember much of those weeks of hopelessness. My mom's cousins who lived in a nearby town lovingly helped with money and food, but I was so far gone I hardly said thank you to Dyann and Rick. I was incapable of managing anything—my life or money.

One night I went out to shoot some pool. When a greasy-looking older man started coming on to me, I felt nothing but disdain. "Hello, beautiful," he said sidling up close to me as I steadied my cue for a shot. Ignoring him, I continued my turn until I missed the pocket, allowing my opponent to take over.

The grease-ball stood nearby watching the game, throwing out comments of encouragement and praise to me. "Ya know," he said, "you are really quite pretty, and your long hair is really nice. I think you'd be fabulous with a permanent in your hair." He rambled on, tossing more compliments my way.

What a loser. I can't believe he thinks I'm buying this.

"So how about it?" My eyes widened as he handed me a hundred dollar bill. A total stranger was handing me one hundred dollars. For a perm!

What do you think I did? I tried the con right back on him, talking him into another $50. Soon after, I ducked out when he went to the bathroom. I had taken money from that poor lonely man without a qualm. I never saw him again.

Feelings of shame and hopelessness grew inside me each time I woke up from a drunken party to find my kids on the kitchen floor digging through the packages of food they had scavenged from the refrigerator.

It was a sheer miracle that some authority didn't step in to take my children from me.

And I was constantly on edge and becoming paranoid about Karl returning. On windy nights the trees outside would scrape along the tin siding. I would awaken trembling as I lay silently in my bed listening . . . listening . . . *Did he find me? It's just the wind, calm down.*

Soon it didn't matter where I was. If I heard a telephone ring, I panicked. In fact, any sudden noise made me jump. On edge and jittery, I lived each day constantly looking over my shoulder, fearing for my life.

I had disintegrated—was incapable of making rational decisions (the alcohol and marijuana sure didn't help either). Each day in Wausau I had lain around, exhausted from running on nerves, trying in vain to figure out my next step—that is, until my father made an offer to come get us and move us out to Pennsylvania with them. It was like asking a drowning person if she'd like a ride on your boat. Of course I'd go. My stay in Wausau totaled only a month and a half.

Both of my parents drove (a pickup truck and their car) across the country to my hovel. Everything I owned, including the kids' beds and dressers, fit into the back of that truck. What a despicable excuse for a person I was. The entire stay in Wisconsin had lasted 11 months.

Karilee:

A Known Shelter

Well, one of my longings was now fulfilled.

Wendi and her children had come back to our home physically. As a grandma, I wanted to nurture my sweet grandbabies. But as usual, Wendi kept herself emotionally and spiritually estranged from us and the Lord. With nowhere to turn, she had come in desperation to a known shelter.

Wendi arrived scared and totally depleted. The harassing calls filled with vulgarity and verbal threats had not followed her to Wausau, but they had accomplished their purpose because her fear had continued to mount.

We soon discovered Karl hadn't given up. Even though he couldn't call Wendi in Wausau, he somehow managed to find our Pennsylvania phone number and began calling our home.

An outstanding warrant for his arrest most likely had prevented him from returning to Wisconsin, but what would prevent him from showing up at our home now? He knew Dan's place of employment, and should he desire, it would be easy for him to discover our home address.

Now Dan and I, too, became victims of his stalking. Many times I picked up our phone to hear someone breathing on the other end. He would threaten Wendi if she answered but never said a word to me or to Dan. It didn't matter—I could feel the threat tangibly.

Usually I hung up instantly, but once or twice I thought I'd wait him out. After the first "hello" with no response but breathing on the other end, I waited. But he never hung up first—that in and of itself was frightening!

This was the first time I had felt true, tangible fear. Karl *was* unstable. I knew him, had seen his stubbornness and cold, calculating anger. He was certainly capable of violence. . . . It was easy to let my mind run with those kinds of thoughts.

So we put in place several home security measures, alerted the college office concerning his description, talked with the local police, and called Focus on the Family counseling services.

Fearing for your life or bodily endangerment can become an all-consuming emotion—if you let it. On weekends when Dan traveled on speaking engagements, I slept uneasily . . . one ear tuned for unusual noises. Would Karl show up? Little creaks in the nighttime hours triggered an instant wide-awake response. Sometimes I'd slip out of bed to check the doors and windows before finally settling again into a restless sleep.

Whenever Wendi or I ventured out into the public, each of us kept a watchful eye, expecting to see Karl's face in a crowd. Always aware of my surroundings and looking over my shoulder I, too, had become jumpy.

The calls kept coming—for weeks. We stayed vigilant. And we kept praying.

Then, with a change to an unlisted number, the calls ceased. When several more months went by without any more disturbances, we began to relax.

Wendi:

Laid Back and Lovin' It

I spent the first few weeks in Pennsylvania recuperating. I quit smoking and drinking for almost a month. After several weeks I went out and found myself a job at a gas station just down the hill from our townhouse.

Within a few months I had paid off all the debts I had accumulated in Wisconsin. Now all the money I made was mine to spend however I chose, a bad state of affairs for someone as selfish and undisciplined as I.

Knowing full well the troubles that followed my habits of smoking and drinking, I jumped back into that lifestyle anyway. I now found myself at my parents' house, confined in a cage with nothing to do but think. I craved the drugs and alcohol—needed a fix to numb my mind. So I searched for new friends at work.

The first friends I found enjoyed good, clean fun and spent weekends watching movies and shooting pool at the local fire station. My boss, too, seemed to be a fun-loving person. So one winter night when she asked if I'd like to go with her to a little hole-in-the-wall tavern in downtown Clarks Summit, I was game.

We walked through the bar door, and immediately I knew this was where I wanted to hang out. The music was loud (the Grateful Dead played on the jukebox) as people in tie-dyed shirts and tattered jeans goofed around with each other. Everyone knew everyone else there. I can spot a pothead a mile away, and this place was crawling with them. I was home!

It's hard to explain just why I continued to purposefully

seek the wrong kind of friends. I had no interest at all in attending church with my parents, although sometimes I attended just to keep the peace. And even though my brother, Rob, and his wife lived nearby and attended the Christian college where Dad worked, I held everyone at arm's length. Christianity seemed dull and smothering compared to living a fast-paced life. I can only say that my eyes were totally blinded to spiritual things and my heart was not only closed but double locked with sin.

Getting to know this new crowd was a breeze. I discovered that the majority of these flower-child rebels were from money and had simply chosen not to grow up. Most of them had gone to high school together and still lived at home with their parents. Just like me, their paychecks were theirs to spend. No bills—no worries! Mixed into the brew were a few hard-core party animals who lived in small houses with their boyfriends or girlfriends.

My life became one big party. I would work till 11 and then head to the bar till closing time. Sometimes I'd go home around midnight, and other times the party kept going and so did I. It would have been easy to live there forever.

Karilee:

Moving On

Spring arrived. College graduation this year—Dan's second year of teaching—was a joyous celebration because both Rob and Rhinda were graduating; he from seminary, and she from college. We hosted a small party for them in our townhouse, inviting Rhinda's parents and friends from Michigan, along with my parents from Wisconsin and Dan's dad from New York. With high spirits we discussed Rob and Rhinda's future plans, and simply enjoyed the fellowship with one another.

Amid the festivities Dan's father casually mentioned that he was being treated for prostate cancer. Being a nurse, I questioned him and found that his disease was progressive. He had undergone surgery, and although very upbeat, I think he, too, realized the gravity of the situation.

That very same week we received notice that we must be out of our rental condo because the units were being sold. We were given 90 days to be gone. We began house hunting in earnest but found nothing in our price range after several weeks of diligent searching.

Then word came that Dad's cancer was invading his body with a vengeance. Dad, who lived alone in upstate New York, was knee-deep in a nonprofit retirement housing project. With his illness he could not handle the bookwork, let alone the management. Would it be possible for Dan and me to come up to help? New homes were being built in this project, and if we could help, our housing would be provided at cost.

It would be a two-hour commute to the college. The drive seemed long, but we discovered that many people who worked in New York City commuted that distance. It was doable.

Well, we reasoned, *we soon must vacate our present residence, and we weren't able to find a home these past few weeks . . . the housing offer must be God's provision.* After prayer and discussion we decided we would make the move to help Dad in his project as he received cancer treatment. Once again we packed up our belongings, this time heading for Ithaca, New York, site of Dad's ambitious project, Sunrise Acres.

Wendi and children were coming with us, and this time we had an additional shred of hope that she might be turning her life around–she planned on attending college.

Wendi:

"I really hate to see you move away," my friend said when I gave him the news. In that short year, I had found a boyfriend. We had spent endless hours telling dumb stories (some real, some not). We were friends—with no pressures from either side. Both of us knew that one day each of us would move on with our lives. But for now, why not enjoy life?

This friendship had given me a shred of hope for the future. I had found a person who listened and interacted without a hidden agenda. When it was time to go, I left with some small repairs to my heart.

CHAPTER FIFTEEN

Forward and Backward

Karilee:

A WHIRLWIND.

That pretty much describes the next two years in Ithaca. So many eddies of activities, commitments, and responsibilities swirled about our lives that I felt like Dorothy in Kansas being sucked into a tornado.

The three of us were busy, busy, busy—each individual's activities blending into one whirling concoction of chaos called life.

Wendi jumped into the community college with a full course load. . . . Dan commuted two hours each way to teach his college classes, many times staying several days in a row to save time, gas, and energy. . . . Both Dan and I delved into Dad Hayden's nonprofit project to aid its development. . . . I became Mommy-Grandma during Wendi's school days, babysitting full-day stretches. . . . Speaking engagements filled

Dan's weekends and many of the next summer's weeks. . . . I was diagnosed with an extremely hyperactive thyroid, and began a regimen of medications—antithyroid, heart-rhythm stabilizer, and a high-blood-pressure beta blocker. Fatigue ruled. . . . Dan's dad remarried our second summer in Ithaca as his health continued to decline. He began an aggressive cancer regimen.

A Happy Surprise

In her college world, Wendi astounded us by coming home with straight A's in all her accounting classes. The teachers, recognizing her abilities, asked Wendi to tutor others in math. She made the dean's list. She was nominated for and inducted into Phi Theta Kappa.

She was blowing us away!

Wendi's diligence in school and academic self-motivation encouraged us tremendously. Since her efforts in high school had only been halfhearted, we really hadn't known how she would fare at college.

Like starving refugees at a banquet, we savored every achievement she received. Ever since her teen years there had been precious few things to brag about in her life. We felt satisfied in supporting her every way we could, hoping that through this degree, she would discover fulfillment in an enjoyable career.

We prayed always for a spiritual awakening in her heart.

Wendi:

I entered a community college to earn a degree in something I could use in real life—accounting.

The school year started off smoothly, and as the first of

my tests and papers came back I was pleasantly surprised. I was nailing straight A's! *I'm not dumb? I'm not stupid? I'm not an idiot? Who would have guessed?!*

At school I joined the writer's guild and submitted my first poem. Someone liked it so much they printed it and made a poster for me.

The poem was an expression of my inner feelings, but because I still refused to seek God, these feelings were directed upward to a beckoning moon. This was a lyrical love poem. I am that wolf and my intense longings are shown as unobtainable desire.

Wolf Rune

I wait for you, friend full moon,
Foretasting your mastery, we'll be together soon!
For your genius, my wild soul—
Your power so captivating as I watch you grow.
The forest dances tonight;
I almost glimpse the wind by the strength of your light.
Lustrous rays drop like rain,
Penetrating me once again.
Intertwined, bonded, strong—
Spirits soar, we belong!
Head thrown back, eyes shut tight,
Crying the song of love tonight.
Dancing with you I am free:
The gift of insanity given to me.
Good night love and dearest friend—
Come, take me once again!

Karilee:

The Bond of Abuse

Dan and I were overjoyed at Wendi's academic achievements, but it wasn't long before we realized that the friends she was making at school were, again, the troubled ones—students with hard-life stories. Many of her new girlfriends were, like her, overcoming adversity.

One gal, who became her best friend, had also been abused and was currently supporting a preteen daughter and teenage son who lived with her. This friend also battled a significant drinking and smoking habit and was caught up in an unhealthy abusive relationship. Unfortunately, the bond of being victims of abuse drew these two together, and their friendship grew.

A whirlwind of evil soon swept into Wendi's life.

Wendi:

Two of a Kind

I met Jodi during tennis class. I was with several other girls volleying off the wall when I heard one girl talking about what a *!%# her boyfriend was. I kept slamming the ball while she slammed him. What a refreshing thing it was to hear *someone else* talk about her miserable relationship. Of course I could identify completely.

"Men! &#%* men! Who needs them?" She whammed the ball with vengeance. "You can't live with them, and you can't shoot them . . ." Slam! More rude comments flew from her mouth, and before I realized I had spoken, I had conjectured a like-minded remark.

She was intrigued. The conversation began flowing, and by the end of class we decided to get together after school. She became my best friend for the next two years.

The first school year whizzed by and I completed my first year of studies with a 4.0 GPA. The incredible thing was that I had once more taken up a serious drinking habit and had hooked in with the pot-smoking, party-going crowd. I would study in taverns until I had drunk too much to study anymore. Somehow I was mixing oil and water and, to me, they were blending marvelously.

Jodi and I were two of a kind in many ways, one of which was that we both sought adventure. Something inside of me always seemed to cry out to try things on the edge.

The edge for us varied: drunken downhill skiing, cross-continent road trips, camping out for days at country music festivals, biker rally weekends in Pennsylvania—it didn't matter. We wanted to be where the action was, and we lived each moment as though it were the last.

We laughed at life and at the strangeness of every living being (including ourselves). Of course everything is much funnier through drunken eyes.

We shared some bad times too. She received her second DWI (Driving While Intoxicated) by smashing into the back of a black Jeep "invisible" to her drunken eyes at night. I broke my tailbone falling down the stairs while leaving a Cornell frat party. She broke her front tooth and had gravel wounds on her face when she stumbled while running across a parking lot. I broke my thumb downhill skiing while drunk. She got beaten by her boyfriend. He smashed three windows out of my car with a two-by-four.

I think that paints a clear enough picture.

Blind, Mute, and Deaf

I was having fun! For the first time since high school I didn't feel trapped or worried. My parents were basically raising my kids and doing a wonderful job, much better than I could do at the time. Jodi's daughter was an excellent baby-sitter for my needs. It came together so well.

If someone had tried to tell me I was doing wrong, they'd have been barking in the wind. In fact, my dad did sit me down again—for a fatherly talk, sharing the gospel once more. To me, he was just being a dad—and what he shared didn't seem relevant to my fast-paced life. Religion was for old fogies.

I honestly couldn't see my need for the Savior. I think it would have taken a sledgehammer to break through the layers of hardness. To say I was blind, mute, and deaf to the true spiritual battles going on in my life would be correctly stating my condition.

Not until I had gone through the fires of my own hell-on-earth would I hear Jesus standing at my heart's door and knocking. I had to bottom out—to come to the total end of myself—before I listened.

It would be God who moved in me. He alone would bring me to Him. It would be *His* timing, not mine. I know He has loved me from the very beginning. But He would not force His love on me. He would let me learn my need for Him the hard way—my way.

Karilee:

In our two years in Ithaca, we could not draw Wendi's interest in church or any other spiritual activity. We reached out to many of her friends in Christlike love, but they all kept their distance. Wendi's nights were often late—especially the summer between the two years she attended school.

Our heart's deepest desire continued to be that she would discover the grace of Jesus Christ and the peace and joy of life in Him. Wendi treasured the world and what it had to offer: "For where your treasure is, there your heart will be also" (Matthew 6:21). Her treasure was "partying" and having "fun," and her heart was into nightlife and all that comes with that lifestyle—so far away from the spiritual realm of life.

We watched her. We counseled her. We prayed earnestly that her heart would not become irreversibly hardened, that she would not stay away from Christ too long: "*You've been gone so long, please don't wait too long turn your heart toward home . . . ,*" my heart kept pleading.

Wendi:

A Turning Point

It is difficult to reflect on disturbing past events—horrific happenings. I have many terrible memories, but one incident became a pivotal life experience.

Anyone who has ever been gripped by a bad habit—alcohol, overeating, pornography, smoking, and so forth—and finally found the strength to conquer it, will no doubt remember the turning point. The exact moment or the period of time in which you finally saw through to the truth will be etched in your mind indefinitely. That sure is true for me.

I shudder to think about the events surrounding this turning point. I would still spend four more years in unrepentant sin, but during my second year in New York,

I saw firsthand the frightening and disturbing side of hardcore drug addiction.

In my mind's eye, I still vividly see the series of events that changed my view on these illegal narcotics permanently. It was as if someone took a highly charged electric cable and thrust it directly into my soul. I was jolted by a friend's rapid demise, and it caused me to instantly stop dabbling in drugs (all drugs other than marijuana, that is).

Crack

Charice was enrolled at the same school as me. Married, she had two children—a daughter (with a severe neurological disease) from a previous relationship, and a son from her current marriage. I found Charice to be a sweetheart and a lot of fun. Jodi, who had met her first, introduced us and we hit it off immediately.

It only took a few months from when we first met until Charice fell to crack. Crack cocaine was a hot item in Ithaca at that time. My last year in New York I was given many, many opportunities to smoke crack. And I did try it a few times—but for some reason it only made me sleepy. Crack dealers accepted cash, jewelry, food stamps, stereos, and basically anything that had value. A 20-dollar rock would give a few hours' high.

Crack is a highly addictive drug and tends to wreak havoc on anyone using it. Within a short period after trying this drug, Charice was gripped.

Charice would disappear for days on end only to show up at home unbathed and strung out. It didn't take long before her husband made her leave. She lost 45 pounds in less than a month. She was a very pretty redhead with a stunning smile when I met her, but in just four short weeks, she had become a jittery sallow-complexioned scarecrow. Her once beautiful skin now looked dirty and leathery. Her matted hair had lost its shine as she picked at her scalp. It tore me apart to watch her disintegrate so rapidly.

Once I tried to get her out of town to sober up by taking her out to my parents' house for a week while they were gone on vacation. We also brought her daughter along with us—a very sick little girl who took her food through a stomach tube and breathed through a tracheotomy.

At my place Charice did sober up for a few days, but then she became antsy. She approached me about borrowing my car. "Wendi, I just can't stay cooped up in a house for this many days. I need to get out. There are some things in town I have to pick up—I need to run home. Could I just borrow the car for a few hours? I'll be careful with it."

"I'm not worried about something happening to the car," I answered warily. "But you're clean now, and I'm worried that you'll get pulled back into your crack habit." I couldn't go along with her because her daughter could not be left alone. "Why don't we line up a baby-sitter, and I'll go with you later on—maybe tonight or tomorrow morning."

"I'll be okay just for a few hours," Charice promised. "Honest. I really need to blow off some energy right now. Please." She checked her watch. "Look. It's one o'clock. Let me take your car and I'll be back by four. I promise I won't get into trouble."

So I let her borrow my car for a couple of hours. She didn't return.

There I sat, alone in a house with a child who needed specialized care. I was completely untrained to care for this little girl, and try as I might I wasn't doing the job right. It scared me silly, especially at night. The tracheotomy kept clogging and had to be suctioned. I couldn't get her to breathe right! For two days and nights I labored over her, hoping Charice would show up. She didn't.

Desperate, I called my friend Jodi, but she was stuck at her house without a car. I began to panic. *If I didn't suction her right, might she suffocate? Might I kill her by neglect?* I made the decision—I couldn't do this anymore. I called the 911 operator and reported that I had an abandoned child.

After the medics took Charice's daughter away, I got a ride to town and enlisted Jodi to help me search for my car. We walked the streets of downtown Ithaca knocking on every door in the drug section of the city. We told anyone we saw, "Tell Charice we are going to report the car stolen if she's not out here within a half hour." That worked. I got my car back and she remained in a crack house—childless.

You may be wondering, *How can a person sink that low?* How about even lower?

Charice's sister came to Jodi and me in tears one day. She had gone with Charice the night before to party. She had gone in search of fun, knowing it wasn't going to be "cookies and milk." But what she got was far worse than she had imagined.

Charice had taken her sister to a run-down house inhabited by a couple of stocky drug dealers. She talked to them for a few minutes and then told her sister she'd be right back. Little did this trusting sister know—her own full-blooded sister had just "sold" her to one guy who remained in the room.

Charice had made a deal for crack. She walked out of that room to smoke the crack, leaving her sister to be raped.

Sickened as I heard her sister's story, my whole being was jolted into the realization that drug addiction is not an optional activity. All around me I had seen it. But now because of my good friend, it was personal: Addicts in need of a fix will do whatever it takes to get that next high.

For my friends and for me, it was so easy, so inviting, to try drugs—and nearly impossible to quit. Every one of us thought we were the exception. Each of us thought we could quit when we wanted to. Now I knew differently. Charice couldn't quit—even when it was killing her.

Why did I play around with crack myself and not like it? Why did my body react completely differently than most to this drug? Why hadn't I succumbed to crack's deathly pull? I cannot explain it. It must have been God's grace in answer to my parents' pleas for mercy on my behalf.

I still feel sick inside when I think back upon this incident. My opinion of hard drug use was changed forever that last year I lived in Ithaca. I still had other lessons to learn, but I would never forget this one.

I was done with hard drugs.

PART THREE

The Long Journey Home

Just so, I tell you, there will be more joy in heaven over one sinner who repents than over ninety-nine righteous persons who need no repentance.

—LUKE 15:7 (ESV)

CHAPTER SIXTEEN

Back to the Pigpen

Karilee:

FALL 1995 WAS SPECTACULAR. Flaming leaves—vivid and bright—danced below a brilliant azure sky as I snapped a picture of Dad's red apartment-building barn standing serenely by a pond's edge. The stately two-story building, snuggled in front of this colorful backdrop, reflected so clearly it could have been sitting by a mirror. As always, autumn had captured my heart.

But mingled with my appreciation of this splendor of God's creation was the sad realization that Dad Hayden was quickly succumbing to his cancer. By October he had become bedridden. By Thanksgiving Dad was on an IV morphine drip. Our beloved energetic and vibrant father whom we loved so much died on December 21.

Now, in addition to dealing with the challenges of Wendi's behavior and the grief of losing Dad, we were immersed in the gigantic task of sorting through Dad's personal estate along with Sunrise Acres—a multifaceted and complicated project. Dan continued his 95-mile commute to the Bible College while I spent hours sorting through boxes, files, documents, account books, and receipts. The barn-apartment-complex and three erected homes must be sold. Heavy equipment, tractors, and other vehicles needed to be liquidated. We contacted lawyers to oversee the dissolution of Dad's complex nonprofit organization. It would take at least a year to bring Dad's affairs to an orderly conclusion.

Dan resigned from the college in the spring to take charge of Dad's affairs. Perhaps he would be able to return in a year—but for now it was impossible.

The Agony of Watching and Waiting

Watching loved ones continue to turn their backs on righteousness is an excruciatingly painful experience—especially when they're living in your home.

Somehow it was easier for me to bear Wendi's rebellion when she lived away from our home. During those times, my heart grieved, but the pain was somehow not so raw.

The mother in me loved having Wendi and her children in our home with us. But the daily pain was agonizing.

We watched her come home in the early morning hours, we met some of her drug-addicted friends, and we witnessed her actions deeply entrenched in ungodliness. We grieved profoundly. Seeing her self-destructive way of life brought intense, searing pain like that of vinegar poured into an already festering wound. At times it seemed more than I could bear. *How long, O Lord, how long*? (Psalm 6:3).

Yes, we could have kicked her out of the house. But foremost, we wanted the influence upon our grandchildren—and secondly, our hearts were drawn in love to Wendi's friends, all of whom so desperately needed Christ, too. Several allowed us to share Christ with them. So we hung in there, praying, and awaited God's intervention.

This wait for God to answer a specific prayer was agonizingly difficult. We had been waiting, literally, for years. God seemed silent. Should we give up?

Never!

Paul's exhortation brings resolve:

> We are afflicted in every way, but not crushed; perplexed, but not despairing; persecuted, but not forsaken; struck down, but not destroyed; . . . *Therefore, we do not lose heart,* but though our outer man is decaying, *yet our inner man is being renewed day by day.* (2 Corinthians 4:8-10, 16, emphasis added)

In the midst of these difficulties, emotional fatigue and ensuing discouragement were an ever-present danger. For me during these excruciatingly painful days in Ithaca, I made a conscious decision to take my eyes off of my problems and fix them on the Lord.

I clung to an analogy that Dan had taught while we worked at Fort Wilderness in Wisconsin. Several times Dan had the opportunity to teach Bible lessons on a weeklong sailing junket, and I was privileged to go along.

One day when the wind was very strong, Dan asked the captain just how his vessel (a three-mast schooner) could sail headlong into the winds blowing against us. The captain explained that when a sailboat is sailing against a strong wind, the vessel can't make progress, and, in fact, endangers itself. What the ship has to do is to tack back and forth—*sail at an angle*, creating a vacuum on the back side of the sail that actually pulls the ship forward.

Dan has used this analogy many times in his teaching, applying it to hardships in life. Gleaned from our 20-year journey of the harsh winds of Wendi's rebellion, we can speak with assurance—this works.

Dan expresses it this way: Don't face directly into the problem, but rather, when adverse winds arise, just turn your mind toward the Lord. Then, "as the troubles come toward you, let them just whip on by. As they do, it will create that pull toward God. In that way the trials of life will pull you toward the Lord. Learn how to tack as you sail spiritually against the wind."[1]

It was a great focus tool for me. Adverse winds had been blowing against us for over a decade. Instead of facing these problems head-on, which would knock me off my feet, I needed to get myself at an angle *setting my face toward the Lord.*

Turning my eyes toward the Lord took my eyes off the problem and helped me actually make progress in my spiritual life-journey instead of being "blown away."

> Turn your eyes upon Jesus,
> Look full in His wonderful face;
> And the things of earth will grow strangely dim
> In the light of His glory and grace.[2]

A Dog Returning to Its Vomit

Wendi was only one course away from graduation when she decided she wanted to move back to Wisconsin. One course!

We pled with her to complete the graduation requirement while she could. "It will be extremely difficult to find time to complete that last course when you're out in the working world and raising two children," we cautioned. "Just one more course—one more semester—and you'll have your diploma. . . . You'll have earned a college degree in applied science. Hang in there. You can do it!"

But whatever force was drawing her back to Wisconsin—it pulled her like metal to a magnet. She *had* to go. Her mind was made up. She *would* leave—she would finish her last course in a nearby Wisconsin college.

For me, this was such a discouraging decision. It seemed so foolish—so dangerous. I couldn't help but think of Proverbs 26:11: "Like a dog that returns to its vomit is a fool who repeats his folly." She was returning to her vomit—returning to a place that always pulled her down.

It seemed more than I could bear.

This point in Wendi's life became my lowest moment—ever. I began to slip into the slough of despair.[3] Wendi's waywardness had continued for so many years that I was near giving up hope. Everything looked so dark, and there seemed to be no light at all shining through. It would have been easy to let the pain of the circumstance take over. To quietly slip into a state of depression. To stop caring . . . about anything at all.

At times like that—when it seems that God is silent and you see no hope ahead—faith can ebb and discouragement or bitterness can settle in. The fatigue of the battle—this spiritual battle of daily entrusting Wendi to the Lord, and praying earnestly on her behalf—began to overwhelm me. I was being swallowed up by the monster of hopelessness.

But my God is a faithful God. My "God of hope" would

again bring me back to a place of joy and peace (Romans 15:13).

Wendi:

Old Stomping Grounds

Severe restlessness had overcome me again. I began making plans to move back to Wisconsin as I signed up for the last two required classes offered in the first summer school session in the Ithaca area.

One of those required classes just so happened to be a subject I had deliberately been putting off. Science is not my forte and this was stab number two for me since I had dropped biology the previous summer. It only took a couple days in this class for me to realize I was going to drop it again. I did finish one further course requirement, but my science requirement was not completed. Still, I was determined to make my move back to my old stomping grounds.

Yes, I can hear you, "What is the point of going to school for two years only to leave without a degree because of *one class*?"

I was stubborn. My plans did not call for staying around Ithaca any longer. I wanted to go to Wisconsin and nothing was going to stop me. Why the urgency? Did you notice the words "my plans" and "I was"? *Self*ish, *self*-centered, and *self*-absorbed, I wanted to do what I wanted to do.

Disenchanted with the hard-drug scene, I had become homesick for my old cronies—my friends in Wisconsin. When a person turns her back on God, a vacuum of restlessness is ever present. I had to find more excitement. I had to move on.

I wanted to be back in Wisconsin in time to go to the

summer Country Fest. My imagination already was captured by the excitement of sixty thousand people camping out for 10 days on the fairgrounds while partying and being entertained by the hottest stars in country music. This was my party—one I hadn't missed in years, and I wasn't going to miss it now.

And so the 22-foot Ryder cab-truck was loaded, with my car hooked up to the back. Yes, I said 22-foot Ryder truck. Everything the kids and I had owned fit in the back of a pickup truck when we moved East; now I possessed a truckload of beautiful furniture, thanks to Grandpa Hayden.

After being allowed to dig through the storage at the barn to find furniture and household fixings, I had everything I needed and more; everything, that is, besides a job, a house, or any money. But those little details didn't bother me a bit.

I took a friend from school with me who had a substantial crack habit. She was along for the trip and the 10-day party, after which she would ride the Greyhound back to New York.

I drove the entire way, wheeling this large truck through the center of Chicago and on up to northern Wisconsin. I had made this trip four times during my stint out East and knew the way by heart. Anticipation to see my friends built as the states passed behind us. I was almost "home"!

Karilee:

Trusting God's Heart

Wendi's choice to return to Wisconsin devastated me, but again, God met my need. For it was at this point—this lowest point—that I found new encouragement in pondering the character of God.

How can one *not* be encouraged in meditating on the fact that God is *loving* and *good* and *full of mercy*! How can one's confidence *not* be restored while pondering the Savior's *omniscience* and *omnipresence.* He is *all wise* and sees the picture from beginning to end, and He is with me each step of the way. How strengthening it was to realize afresh that my very own Father in heaven is *immutable . . . faithful . . . holy . . . just . . . supreme . . . all powerful . . .* and *sovereign*![4]

Oswald Chambers' book *My Utmost for His Highest* helped me to understand this. He asked, "Have you been asking God what He is going to *do*? He will never tell you. God does not tell you what He is going to do; He reveals to you *Who He is*" (emphasis added).[5]

My heart was nearly breaking in two. In near despair, I clung to my anchor, my fortress, my rock—Jesus Christ. I pored through the Bible, writing down verses about God's character. I began committing many of these verses to memory. And as I played our CDs over and over, another song lifted my soul, a song titled "Trust His Heart."

This poignant song shifted my focus from trying to figure out the *hows* and *whys* of our ordeal to *whatever, Lord.* Even though I couldn't understand how Wendi's struggles could ever be of value, I *could* trust that God is in control.

He is God. He never makes mistakes. And all that He does for His children is intertwined in love, mercy, and goodness. Bottom line: If I never discovered God's purpose in what was happening in our crisis—I *could* trust His heart!

Though I could see nothing changing in Wendi's heart, even though she continued to go her own way, I clung tenaciously to the assurance that my God—my loving, wise, and all-knowing God—was in control of all things pertaining to my life and to our prayers.

I determined that I would remain firm—*I would trust His heart.*

CHAPTER SEVENTEEN

In Alcohol's Grip

Wendi:

I WAS BACK! AND it was all I had hoped for.

I went directly to the bar where my friends used to hang out. A high-school buddy now owned it—a rock 'n' roll party saloon that was an "anything goes" kind of place: be free, be yourself; enjoy the window-shaking, music-blasting ambience of tattoos, long hair, Harleys, whiskey and beer, drinking games, poker playing, and beer pong—a Ping-Pong drinking game. You name it, the wilder the better.

Landing a place to live only took a day, and my friends helped me unload the truck. I'd unpack later. It was time to have fun and enjoy myself, and I did! The saloon owner offered me a job bartending until I could get on my feet. House—check! Job—check! Money—check! It was a breeze. Everything was coming together just like I planned.

There was just one detail—actually, two living details—that

I hadn't quite thought through. My parents weren't going to be around to raise my children.

One thing that drugs and alcohol do is keep a person from thinking clearly and growing up. When a person doesn't have to look at life through realistic eyes, how can she possibly mature? Play, play, play, and sleep off the hangovers. I certainly was unprepared to be the grown-up of the house. None of my friends had to, so why should I?

Two weeks after I had left New York, my parents drove my kids out to join me in Wisconsin.

There we were—the three of us—in our little upstairs apartment. What fun! Or should I say, "What fun?" I scrambled for baby-sitters and landed on four different kids, children of my friends ranging in age from 12 to 14, who loved the freedom of hanging out at my place.

But it only took a week to completely annoy my landlord, who lived below us. "Keep it down," he'd angrily shout to the sitter who answered his pounding on the door. The "baby-sitters" would nonchalantly agree and turn the rock music down. Wrestling matches or scrambling to catch a Nerf ball or the blaring TV would draw the landlord up the stairs again. "It sounds like you're tearing the place apart. I want it quiet up there—and I mean it! Tell Wendi I want to see her when she gets home."

Within the first month we were served with eviction papers. Because I had no place to go and I drank away each paycheck, the "ends" were nowhere close to meeting.

Karilee:

Desperate Living

"Dear Lord—merciful and loving Savior, again I bring my heart's greatest longing to You. Wendi continues to run from

You. She continues to make poor choices. She is getting entangled so deeply in her sinful ways . . . I don't even know if she's gone beyond hope. But I ask for Your mercy upon her and our grandkids. Father, I pray that Your Holy Spirit will break through her heart of stone. Almighty God, I ask that You draw her unto Yourself. I commit her into Your keeping—again—for *this* day, even though she is so far from You. Please deliver her from the evil one, I pray. Amen."

Each and every day we lifted up Wendi and the children in prayer before God's throne. Every week, every month, every year that she refused to turn her heart toward the Savior in her relentless pursuit of sin, I had to face the question I feared most: Would her refusal to seek Christ take her to a point of no return? Would she become so entrenched in her profligate lifestyle that she could not hear the voice of God? We hoped not. We prayed not!

We beseeched God to continue His pursuit of her. We prayed that His Spirit would somehow break through the barriers she had built around her heart and soul.

Wendi:

"We've closed up the cabins for the winter," the resort owner explained. "They're not insulated and can't be used after the frost arrives. I do have one trailer back in the woods that I could rent you, but that's it."

I stored the majority of our furniture and moved into the little "tuna-can" trailer. It was flimsy, dark, and a bit creepy. But that was all I could afford for now. We settled in. The kids and I lived in shambles. The yard of pine needles was constantly strewn with the kids' messes, and since my schedule brought me home from work at three o'clock in the morning, nothing inside was getting cleaned either.

My son started going through great emotional outbursts. He needed his grandpa-dad, not the insane lifestyle I offered him. Out of sheer desperation I called my parents to find a solution. My dad drove to Wisconsin and took Nolan back to New York for a six-week stay. This time Gracie and I made it just over a month before getting evicted.

Karilee:

Traumatized

It was difficult to know what to do about our sweet grandchildren. The move seemed especially traumatic for our grandson, who began one- to two-hour nonstop screaming sessions. After a couple of weeks without improvement, Dan drove from New York to Wisconsin and brought Nolan back. The tantrums immediately stopped, and he began to settle down. For six weeks we tenderly showed him love, and finally he was able to return to his Mommy and sister.

Our hearts were being torn apart like a carcass being pulled by a savage beast. We despised the lives our grandbabies were forced to endure: gloomy, barren rooms; morsels of leftover food and fast-food meals; the general bedlam of Wendi's undisciplined lifestyle.

Yet as we prayed and prayed some more, we felt it best for the children to remain with Wendi. She was their mother, and she needed to assume responsibility for them. Additionally, the children felt great love for her. We knew she loved them, too—it was just that she loved herself more.

Wendi:

My bartending job started losing its appeal after a few months. On the nights I had a sitter I would drink excessively during work; I was polishing off an entire bottle of whiskey in an evening on a regular basis now. I commonly woke up not knowing how I'd gotten home. More often than not, I had driven myself the four miles along the winding wooded roads completely drunk.

While Nolan was in New York with his grandma and grandpa, poor Gracie had to come to work with me to save on child-care expenses. Her evenings were spent roaming around the dingy tavern or coloring in the kitchen area behind the bar. At bedtime she curled up to sleep on the carpeted stairs, which led to two empty bedrooms upstairs.

What in the world am I doing to this already traumatized little girl? Over and over I tried to shove such thoughts out of my mind.

But I knew that change was due, so I set out looking for a better job. It only took a couple of weeks until I was hired to organize the medical supplies at a large in-house care facility. My official title was Medical Supply Technician.

At the same time the kids and I landed in a little two-story house on the main drag of town. Gracie would be able to remain at the school where she had started her kindergarten year, and it seemed that a small semblance of order was slowly appearing. The people at this new job were great, and my job responsibilities allowed me to use my much-neglected organizational skills. Things were changing for the better. We were surviving.

As an extra source of income I kept bartending on the weekends, which I thought worked out quite well. The additional income was usually enough to pay off my bar tab.

Help, I've Fallen and I Can't Get Up

"Happy New Year!" My first New Year's Eve back in Wisconsin opened my eyes to the excessiveness of my drinking. I started out the evening at the bar where I worked, drinking my usual whiskey and root beer, but as the New Year arrived everyone was handed their own gratis bottle of champagne. I promptly chugged down the entire bottle and decided to head off with some friends to a nightclub.

The nightclub was one of those "pop dance" kinds of places where the college kids and yuppies hung out. By the time I threw back a couple more mixed drinks, I was schnockered. Noticing that a couple of my friends played in the featured band, I decided to go over and say hi to them. I stood on the flashing disco floor and leaned in to talk—and fell right over into the lights, wedging myself in so awkwardly that I had to be pried out. All the people dancing got a good laugh on me.

With enough humiliation for one night, I decided to go home. In the parking lot I hitched a ride with the first people heading to town. My ride took me as far as downtown, and from there I had to get myself the rest of the way home.

And so I started the walk home. I had eight blocks to go. Sound easy enough? Well, heavy snow had fallen for a few weeks, which meant that the sidewalks were buried and huge snow banks stood at the end of each block. The first snow bank took me three or four tries to get over.

So I decided to walk in the road. The only problem was that for every step forward, I took two or three backwards and sideways. This was no good since I would have been completely incapable of getting out of the way of any approaching traffic.

Back to the sidewalk I went. It took me over an hour to go eight blocks. I must have fallen down a hundred times. Do you sense my humiliation? The memory of that evening still makes me cringe.

But each stupid mistake I made removed a little more self-esteem, leaving only the desire to forget about it all. That New Year's fiasco initiated a growing realization that I had a severe alcohol problem.

My solution? I decided to put my drinking in the backseat behind pot smoking . . . another way to forget problems. I still drank, but I cut back to avoid those nasty hangovers.

Irrational Thoughts and Decisions

Through my bar life I got to know a lot of people in town. One particular couple came in to drink fairly often. They seemed to get along fine and I had no idea about their relationship—until one day this guy caught my attention. Doug was standing alone at the bar.

I busily worked that day as I watched him drink his beer with huge tears in his eyes. *I wonder what's going on.*

I was about to find out.

You see, the girl he had been living with had been married, and, in fact, still was. Evidently, she and her husband had agreed to take a year off from their marriage and date other people. The year was up, so Doug was out. That morning she had notified him to move his things out of her house because her husband was coming home.

Does that break your heart?

It broke mine.

Doug and I started talking and connected so well that we decided to go out snowmobiling together. He even offered to supply me with a pair of thermal boots that had belonged to his deceased mother (I later discovered they were stolen from his previous girlfriend).

We hit it off. We were two lonely hearts searching for love.

Within a few weeks, we became an item. Doug lived with his father just one block from my house, and he came and went as he pleased, and so did I. I was falling for him, but there was something I couldn't put my finger on. Something was wrong.

I now know what that something was—lack of common sense and maturity. I was a mental basket case and so was he. My brain was frying from too much alcohol and pot, and his brain was pickled from alcoholism.

These disjointed thoughts (unstable at best) were penned by candlelight on a cold winter night:

> **JOURNAL ENTRY:** March 7, 1997—I'm home! What a journey it's been. The kids are sleeping and I'm bored out of my mind.
>
> I'M LOST!
I'VE GONE TO LOOK FOR MYSELF!
IF I RETURN BEFORE
I GET BACK,
PLEASE ASK ME TO WAIT!
>
> So, what have I accomplished? Good question. Love has come and gone—see ya!! I am a wild animal in a cage—we'll see if I can be tamed. I am having feelings that are strange. Love pangs? How depressing. Can I open my heart? Can he? I want it all and I won't stop. But I just may get lost on the way. Friends slowly drift apart. . . . My independent streak is

gone. I must be aging. I should be telepathic—I see no reason for me not to be. My brain is in overdrive. I don't want to be sitting here right now. Compulsive—I am, I have been, I will always be. Why? I am going completely insane. Will I fall in TRUE LOVE—will he? I want it bad. Shut up! I do believe I've started talking to myself. Imagine that. How could I have gone over that edge? Come home to me. I want your breath. Sleep departs and thoughts run wild. Yes or no? Right or wrong? And how long? I have no answers—only questions. Today? . . . Tomorrow? . . . Forever? . . . Grow old with me. Be my friend. Let me offer my mind, heart, and soul. I have an empty pedestal to decorate. Patience is a virtue they say. In reality, patience calms over the insane and makes the mind wander. Forgive and forget, love and be loved. Too much too fast? I am ready for my once-in-a-lifetime. It's almost Saturday . . .

Karilee:

Although there was not a day or week that went by that Dan and I did not uphold Wendi in prayer, the Lord enabled me to distance myself emotionally. As her relationship with Doug evolved, I watched from afar—curiously detached. My heart could not bear that raw pain again, yet all the while I interceded strongly for our dear, innocent grandchildren.

Why did Wendi latch on to these hard-drinking guys?

This was alcoholic number three. I could not begin to fathom why Wendi had chosen again to put herself and her children in such jeopardy. Only God understood her heart and mind—I couldn't figure it out.

Wendi:

Ignoring the Warning Signs

My heart dived into my new relationship with Doug despite all the flashing warning signs. We were a complete disaster from the first hello. Our snowmobiling excursions took us from tavern to tavern. It was a sick kind of Bonnie-and-Clyde relationship, but he made me feel important. He needed me.

He also had an acute bleeding ulcer that required careful attention, so I doted over him, trying to fix all his problems. It became an obsession. I'd wait to eat dinner until the late hours of the night, just to sit with him. He'd call to say he was on his way—"Be there in 15 minutes"—only to show up four hours later, drunk, and mad at me for feeling let down.

Desperate to figure this mess out, I tried to fix, fix, fix. Psychologists call this problem codependency. Whatever the technical name, it doesn't matter because it is a destructive path of action.

Our bickering grew daily. We drove each other nuts when we were sober and argued incessantly when we were drunk. The only times we enjoyed each other were when we could go out together drinking.

A Way to "Save Money"

Doug discovered a three-bedroom, single-wide trailer out of town on wooded property. "Hey, Wendi," he said one night as we headed for another bar, "I found this trailer for rent and if we moved in together we could save a lot of money on rent. We're with each other so much we might as well move in together. How about it?"

I began figuring. We'd save $200 a month on rent, and I'd have help paying my bills. I wanted this relationship to work out so badly. I moved in with him.

He just so happened to have five days' worth of jail time to serve (for a drunk-driving accident). His appointed time to be in jail landed on the same weekend we were scheduled to move; so while he did his time, I moved my family's things by myself to the little mobile home.

Everything started out smoothly as we settled in. I was even able to throw a 10-girl slumber party for my daughter's birthday. I signed up to take a botany course through the University of Wisconsin, which would complete my accounting degree. My medical job was proceeding well, and I was still able to get Gracie to the same school.

Then the company Doug worked for laid him off for the winter. Alcoholism and boredom don't mix well. As tensions built, I decided to drop my botany course. Doug had all the time in the world to barhop, and I began to resent his laziness and drinking.

Karilee:

A Bit of Heaven

The dissolution of Dad Hayden's estate and Sunrise Acres was nearing an end, and we began to look ahead to the upcoming year, wondering what direction Dan should take as he hunted for a job. It was fall—almost a year after Dad Hayden's death—when Dan traveled from New York to Michigan to speak at a weeklong Bible conference. The church holding the conference was without a pastor and the leadership approached Dan to consider that position. Several weeks later, Dan accepted the call to Grace Church.

In God's exquisite timing, we made the move west to this thriving church in Grand Haven, Michigan. What a God-ordained joy it was to serve in this body of Christ—a young, vibrant church of people who appreciated Dan's teaching gifts.

Unhampered by Wendi's problems, we thoroughly enjoyed our first year of ministry—another year of refreshment, immense satisfaction, and blessing. In fact, it felt like a bit of heaven on earth.

CHAPTER EIGHTEEN

Hitting Rock Bottom

Wendi:

THERE HE WAS, PASSED out cold in the bar parking lot as he sat in the driver's seat with the truck still running. Doug's winter layoff had left him with all the time in the world and nothing much to do. His entire life—and now mine—centered on one thing: feeding the craving to drink.

"Doug, wake up!" I yelled as I shook him. But he was in a deep, drunken stupor, and I couldn't move him. So I climbed on his lap and drove home. Then I had to walk back to the bar to retrieve my own car.

Alcoholism in its late stages is all consuming. While I would pass out and sleep off my drinking binges, Doug woke up a few hours later needing another drink. We kept a bottle of vodka in the freezer, which would last only a few days. Many mornings Doug woke up at six o'clock to head off immediately to the bar.

I couldn't find Doug most of the time—he was good at disappearing; so was my money. Most nights I slept with dollar bills stuffed in my pillowcase, and I was getting sick and tired of the whole mess. My resentment toward him intensified.

Late November when my birthday rolled around, I was broke. All my life I had enjoyed our family's custom of choosing a favorite meal for birthdays. No one else had planned a celebration for me, so I borrowed 20 bucks from a friend to make some curried chicken the next day for myself.

Happy birthday to me . . .

I woke up on my birthday morning to find Doug gone along with my borrowed 20 dollars. *That's it!* I was furious. *He's done taking advantage of me!* I jumped in my car, leaving my kids with a baby-sitter, and drove the half mile down the road to the local country bar.

His truck was there just like I knew it would be. I jumped out, stormed inside, grabbed the six dollars that was left off the counter, and told him I was leaving. I went back in a rage, poured all the alcohol we had down the drain, grabbed my kids and some clothes, and left.

My children and I spent the next week in a cheap motel just out of town. Daily I went hunting for still another place to live. We found a tiny little cabin way out in the woods that would do just fine.

When Sunday arrived, I wheeled into the driveway of the dumpy little place Doug and I had shared. I was accompanied by a dozen friends with two trailers and three pickup trucks. It took less than an hour to haul all of my things out.

The next few weeks were spent avoiding him like the plague . . . and wondering what he was doing.

Yes, I missed him.

Big Proposal

We started talking again. No surprise there, I'm sure. He had realized his drinking problem and "decided to change." Blah, blah, blah . . . of course, I bought the lie. I wanted to believe . . . needed to believe.

Doug offered a "master plan," and it involved our relocating to Antigo, a little farming town just 45 miles south. He planned to take up cross-country truck driving again and had already landed a job with a company down there. All we had to do was find a nice little house to live in, and oh yeah—*would I marry him?*

We rented a pleasant little ranch farmhouse in the middle of a bunch of potato fields. The house, surrounded with pines, even had a garden out back. It seemed perfect with its three bedrooms, two baths, and a finished family room in the basement.

Doug's truck driving usually took him away for five or six days and brought him home on weekends. I began planning our wedding and reception with a degree of excitement, and his homecomings were great.

Our big day drew nearer and our loving little family flourished in our charming little home. My beautiful garden produced a divine crop of carrots, beans, cucumbers, lettuce, corn, and raspberries. We were practically Ward and June Cleaver . . . for a few months.

Two addicts living in seclusion from reality is a spring-loaded situation. It wasn't long until we began rationalizing: *We can handle a few drinks as long as it doesn't get out of hand.* After all, I still had my pot (so I didn't need much alcohol), and everyone knows a truck driver is subject to random drug testing and can't use drugs, so he deserved a little alcohol.

The few days a week Doug was home we started frequenting a tavern just across the highway. Everything seemed to be under control . . . so why not keep a bit of beer at the house? I was clueless—or wanted to be clueless—to the intensity of an alcoholic's cravings. I believed him when he assured me that he drank only occasionally—only when we went out together. Uh-huh.

Then one morning I opened a drawer in the bathroom and discovered a hidden can of beer with condensation still dripping down the sides. Doug vehemently denied it was his, even though it was still cold.

His problem was back, and we were back to square one.

On with the Show!

Our wedding was now just a few weeks away. I was pensive; should I actually marry this guy? Yet he was so convincing with promises to treat me "like a princess." I chose to go on with the show.

Our day arrived with great anticipation. We'd been able to rent a small cottage on a lake for the weekend, planning to honeymoon a month later. We had a quaint little ceremony (to which he showed up slightly intoxicated). The reception, at which we partied into the early morning with all of our friends, took place at a tavern donated by a friend.

We had done it—I was now Mrs. Drunk Guy and he was married to Mrs. Stoned Gal.

We settled back into our domestic lives and planned our honeymoon. We had two options: One, take a load out east in his truck and visit Ithaca along the way. I still kept close communication with Jodi and wanted to visit her. Two, go up to Rhinelander for my favorite party—the Country Fest. We chose to travel. The trip started out especially fantastic. We enjoyed each other's company, and I took pleasure in seeing some of the country I hadn't traveled before. Doug's load was delivered right on schedule in lower New Jersey; now it was time to go have fun! . . . until the company sent him in the complete opposite direction from where I had planned to go next.

His bosses didn't care that they were ruining our honeymoon. Imagine that!

I had missed Country Fest, and now I wasn't going to see Jodi in New York, either. I was bummed. *What in the world had I come all this way for anyway?* The ride back to Wisconsin gave me plenty of time to fume, and plenty of time for him to wish he'd never brought me.

Karilee:

After Doug and Wendi's wedding, Dan and I agreed to watch the grandchildren during their "honeymoon." There was no way we wanted our grandchildren cared for by the troubled friends that Wendi had accrued (they all seemed to have their own deep problems and addictions). Additionally, we wanted to influence our much-loved offspring with God's love and truth as much as possible. Never would we say no to babysitting, if we could help it.

So we gathered Gracie and Nolan into our home in Michigan and nurtured them with a grandma and grandpa's abounding love.

The Final Downward Spiral

For Wendi, the last year living in Wisconsin with Doug was nothing short of a hell on earth. Her final downward spiral was beginning. My heart aches even now as I recall those last dark, evil, and angry years.

Our precious grandchildren were again innocent victims of alcoholism, and it wasn't pretty. There is never, *never* enough money when it is spent on compulsive drinking, and so the family was always short on cash for food or clothing.

Wendi told us that Doug's lying and stealing was a common game and she had to hide her money whenever she got paid. She said that being a truck driver gave Doug many opportunities to "blow" their money because in addition to his drinking habit, a growing penchant for gambling added to the destruction.

This is what we knew; we were unaware of Wendi's heavy drinking and addiction to pot, however. As a result, the situation for our grandchildren was even more precarious than we imagined. During this last year I could only continue crying out to God with pleas for His mercy, grace, and divine intervention. Wendi's life was so out of control and her family situation so desperate that it would truly take a miracle from God to bring any kind solution to the mess she was in.

Would He do a miracle in Wendi's life?

Please, Lord, don't turn your back on her.

Gentle Breeze of Encouragement

God again tended to my discouraged soul precisely when I needed it. An unexpected encouragement, like a gentle breeze, blew into my heavy heart by way of a book. It arrived unannounced in the mail one day—a gift from my cousins Rick and Dyann. I held the book, titled *Fresh Wind, Fresh Fire*, in my hands and flipped to the inside flap on the front cover. It read, "The times are urgent, God is on the move, now is the moment to . . . *ask God to ignite his fire in your soul*!"[1] At that particular time the flame in my soul was barely flickering . . . I needed God's voice to fan the flame.

Once I began to read this book, I was mesmerized—it was as if God Himself were sitting face-to-face with me speaking loving, encouraging words of hope. When I came to chapter 4, I burst into tears. Tucked quietly into this powerful book Jim and Carol Cymbala shared a poignant story of their prodigal daughter, Chrissy, who at the age of 16 began a two-and-a-half-year rebellion. This inspirational anecdote grabbed my eager heart. In seven short pages, Jim Cymbala had painted a word picture of exquisite hope and stunning victory through Christ and the power of prayer. God had miraculously intervened in Chrissy's heart, leading her to unexpectedly return home, repentant. Soon after walking in the door of her parents' home, Chrissy told them what had happened.

> "In the middle of the night, God woke me and showed me I was heading toward this abyss. . . . I was so frightened. I realized how hard I've been, how wrong, how rebellious.
>
> "But at the same time, it was like God wrapped his arms around me . . . as he said, 'I still love you.' "[2]

It was just the spark needed to reignite my depleting faith. My heart soared with hope. Truly my God—again—had shown Himself to be a "very present help in trouble" (Psalm 46:1). With goose bumps, I humbly thanked God for His personal and timely message of encouragement.

We serve a gracious God. God not only answered the specific prayers of the Cymbalas, but true to His sovereign and loving ability, He turned a bad circumstance into good by using Carol Cymbala's anguish at the time of her deepest need to minister to others. Out of her personal struggle during her daughter's waywardness rose this inspiring song, "He's Been Faithful," written during her struggle. The lyrics express God's faithfulness in times of trial:

> In my moments of fear,
> Through every pain, every tear,
> There's a God who's been faithful to me . . .
> He's been faithful, faithful to me,
> Looking back, His love and mercy I see.
> Though in my heart I have questioned,
> Even failed to believe,
> Yet He's been faithful, faithful to me.[3]

My heart indeed remained deeply saddened when I considered Wendi's life circumstances. But as a piece of tough meat can be pounded by a mallet into tenderness, God was using Wendi's despicable life events to "tenderize" my inner being. Using this book as a catalyst, His Spirit directed my prayers in a restful dependence upon His almighty power in a way that drew my heart into a deep and indescribable peace.

Wendi and her family were at a place where only God could work. And that's the best place to be. Ever.

Wendi:

Following our "honeymoon," Doug and I returned to Antigo and still had time before our children would join us, so with "great insight" we went out to see what the bar life was like in that town.

After some deliberation, we went to a place where one of Doug's coworkers frequented. It was actually a lot of fun. The gal bartending seemed like the kind of person I could hang out with. As I started to get drunk and relax, I got to telling jokes. Pretty soon a dozen or so of us were all whooping it up and having a ball.

Not Doug though. He was drunk, ornery, and wanted to go home.

I ordered a double order of fried cheese curds and begrudgingly joined him as he headed to the car. Who would drive? I was the most sober, so I offered. Knowing it would be safer to cruise the back streets, I exited the parking lot at the far end and started toward home.

"Where are you going?" he grunted.

"I thought I'd see if I could get lost and still find the way home," I joked.

Doug didn't find my humor in the least bit funny and immediately copped an attitude toward me. For the next two or three miles he insulted me on every little thing he could dredge up.

Never to be outdone, I took action. When we pulled up to a stoplight, I rolled down my window, grabbed the cheese curds off his lap, and promptly dropped them out the window onto the road.

The argument heated up from there.

By the time we pulled into the driveway, the words were boiling over in vicious spurts. "You can just get out of my house," he snarled. "Everything in here is mine. You're not taking anything out of this house."

Now then, remember the 22-foot moving truck I had

driven from Ithaca? Just about everything in that house was mine, given to me by my parents and inherited from my grandfather. *Mine!* I'd go down with the ship for this argument.

I plowed through the bathroom door so I could set him straight once and for all. "How dare you . . ." I started.

He turned and charged at me with a lunge. We wrestled and tumbled, but the scuffle lasted only a few intense moments before he was kneeling on my arms, my back to the floor, his balled fist heading toward my face.

With all the might left in me, I stretched my head forward and bit into his leg, causing him to leap off me in pain. As he jumped, he turned to land a few kicks before hobbling off.

What a lovely honeymoon this was turning out to be.

Bruised but Not Broken

The next morning I struggled out of bed in disbelief. I stood looking at myself in the mirror, inspecting my battered body. I was a giant bruise from my shoulders to my toes. And it hurt to move.

Doug was long gone by then, but he finally called from southern Wisconsin to let me know that he wouldn't be back for a week and a half—and he was sorry.

I had marijuana to deaden the pain.

A few weeks later, Doug was fired from his job. He had racked up a large debt by gambling at truck stops over the past few months, so once again we faced bills that would not be paid. It was time to move on.

One load at a time, we put my things into storage in Rhinelander for the winter. Doug had friends on the other side of Rhinelander who owned a resort. They offered their unwinterized cabin to us up through October. It was now

August, just two months into our marriage.

The new lodging was a nice fit for Doug since there was a bar just two buildings over. He landed a job driving a truck for a local company. I found new work caring for elderly women. One would think that with steady employment that maybe we had a fighting chance to work things out.

Not so.

Doug worked long hours and went straight to the bar next door every night, leaving me alone in the run down little shanty they called a cabin, where the water was not fit for consumption and the ceiling was caving in. The septic backed up under the raised floor, creating a mold that shut my asthmatic lungs down quite painfully. I took up bartending a few nights a week to bring in a bit of additional cash with the hopes of getting out of there ASAP.

Back to Square One

Doug's drinking was completely out of control by then, and we were surrounded by drunks in every cottage. His drinking continued daily from early morning until bedtime.

It was when he took up drinking until all hours in the night with the girl next door that I gave up.

I packed up the kids and myself and off we went (again). By the way, for those not keeping count, this was move number eight for the children and me in a three-year period.

We went back to square one—winding up in the same resort that we originally stayed in at our second move, only now it was under new ownership. We moved into a small three-room cabin next door to our previous "tuna-trailer." The front door opened into what would be my bedroom; the other tiny rooms were a small kitchen area, a bedroom that the kids would share, and a bathroom with a stand-up shower stall—only the basic requirements for housing, but who could be picky?

Making a decent income with my elder-care work, I had moved from bartending to cleaning the bar on Saturday mornings. For once I sensed a feeling of reward with my jobs. The elderly ladies I worked for were wonderful—dear, sweet women with very special needs. They truly appreciated my help. What a change that was for me. Caring for these needy ladies brought some degree of fulfillment and satisfaction.

With the first frost Doug left his unheated cabin and once again came crawling back. Myself pathetic, I took my pathetic excuse for a husband back into my abode.

Same Ol' Same Ol'

The results were the same once more. Doug went from bar to bar; the difference now was that winter had set in and the woods swarmed with snowmobiles. Doug and I had acquired two snowmobiles, and we found a bit of compatibility on the trails—a never-ending nexus to infinite taverns throughout the north woods of Wisconsin and Upper Michigan.

The problem was that Doug was constantly out running the trails, calling in sick to work, and of course, spending all our money.

Midwinter when Doug crashed my snowmobile and returned home at four in the morning, another middle-of-the-night argument escalated into the need for me to file a restraining order. The next afternoon he called to apologize, but I wasn't going to play the game. I told him when he could come and retrieve his things.

Karilee:

Alcoholism breeds a vicious, vicious cycle that takes those involved around and around in circles—but the circles converge into a funnel—and it goes nowhere but down. Promises were made, followed by more promises. Lies and more lies, arguments and more arguments—all of this before wide-eyed growing children—*our grandchildren*!

These two little ones had been forced to live so much of their lives in filthy cauldrons of boiling, seething emotion—rank with vile drunkenness and instability. I couldn't even imagine what their little eyes and ears had been forced to hear—what their little hearts had to factor into their thoughts as the hostilities and vulgarities played out through the years.

Protect them from permanent damage, dear Jesus. . . . Guard their precious hearts, I pray . . .

Wendi:

Reckless and Lonely

I finished the rest of that winter living alone with my children in the tiny cabin. As an escape, I spent many hours on my snowmobile trying to flee the ever-growing madness in my head. Once again I took to playing the daredevil, looking in the eyes of danger and laughing.

My cabin, located at a resort on the Wisconsin River, sat just two miles upstream from the bar where most of my friends hung out. To get there by snowmobile, there was the long way around (the safe way) or the quick path (a more treacherous route)—the way I often chose.

The challenge was to get across the 15 or so feet of open water that never froze due to the strong current, followed by a 90-degree turn immediately after the water. The way to get across was to get a good start, sit way back on the seat, fly under the bridge between the cement walls at full tilt, and then kick out the tail end to make the corner.

Looking back, I believe my reckless behavior resulted from losing all hope—daring God to "take me out." (But most likely if I *had* fallen into the icy water, I would have changed my mind quickly.) Clouded minds aren't sure just what they think. Still, even in that state of mind, I didn't look to the Lord for help. At that point maybe I was a little afraid of God—knowing how badly I had lived my life. . . .

Big "Turnaround"

Spring had sprung, taking the sledding season away. I found myself facing my loneliness again. Rumors floated around about Doug's big turnaround and my interest was piqued. He sent me a letter explaining his decision for sobriety, leaving the door open for me to come to him in a trailer he had just purchased.

In keeping with my hopeless lifestyle I went back yet again!

Summer Country Fest was rapidly approaching and Doug convinced me that he could drink for one week only—then quit cold turkey. I didn't drink much anymore due to the fact I was having such a hard time recuperating those days.

So we went to the Fest—"my party." Of course Doug's drinking sparked his alcoholism into full swing again.

Meanwhile, I had struck a deal with myself to stop smoking. I would be turning 30 in a few months and could feel a definite deterioration in my health. I had been smoking for nearly 19 years, and it was slowly killing me. Right on schedule, the Monday after Country Fest, I quit smoking cigarettes.

After the Country Fest, Doug and I would make one last attempt to make a go of our marriage. Unfortunately, it was just that: an attempt.

How can you build on something that has no foundation?

CHAPTER NINETEEN

Glimmer of Hope

Karilee:

I REACHED UP TO the shelf, carefully taking down the Precious Moments figurine that had been given to me in Orlando. Many times I held this favorite figurine—my touchstone of hope—a bonneted girl holding an open-winged butterfly in her outstretched arms. The title of the piece was "We Are God's Workmanship," but the moment I'd laid eyes on it, I had given it another name. I called it "Something Beautiful," from the Gaither song—and also from the chorus "In His Time," based on Ecclesiastes 3:11—"He hath made every thing beautiful in his time" (KJV).

This little figurine embodied my deepest desire for Wendi. The butterfly represented new life—metamorphosis from an ugly, slow-moving caterpillar to a colorful, graceful, newly created thing of beauty. *Someday, Wendi . . . someday you, too, will be made beautiful when you escape the cocoon of sin shrouding your life and are released into the freedom of God's grace.* Each time I handled this Precious Moments piece, I breathed a prayer for her.

Someday . . . Someday.

Wendi:

Doug and I had discovered a tranquil chunk of wooded property for sale. Fifteen acres located perfectly—across the street from my best friend, my maid of honor. Somehow we finagled enough money to purchase the land and started the laborious task of clearing it for a pad site, with the hopes of putting up a double-wide modular home.

Doug worked weekdays, and while the kids were in school I hauled wood. I hauled wood by the truckload out to the clearing to stack or burn. It had always been my dream to own property like this—a dream that seemed to be coming true.

I spent evenings and rainy days relaxing out in our small trailer at the trailer park. Doug was trying to quit drinking (again) but hadn't been able to quit cold turkey, so the kids and I had plenty of time to ourselves while he was off drinking.

My Body Cries Out

Kicking my smoking habit with nicotine patches, I began reading books to occupy my mind. But my body had been so strongly addicted to nicotine, that when I quit smoking some debilitating side effects took over. As I tried to wean myself from the patches, a headache the size of Texas landed in my eyes and forehead for the next two years, along with tremors throughout my nervous system. Besides enduring constant, excruciating headaches, I was a jittery, shaky mess. (I have since learned that research has linked anxiety disorders to teen smoking; I was the perfect lab rat.)

With great interest I discovered the self-help section of the public library and began soaking up all the secular knowledge I could lay my hands on. I moved into self-discovery literature and eventually landed on the subject of alcoholism, which led me straight into codependency information. For the first time I realized how truly sick I had become, both mentally and physically.

As I pushed forward with our building project, I decided to seek psychological help. I soon discovered an organization that offered assistance to alcoholics and their families. They assigned me to a wonderful woman counselor who brought new insight to my life.

I now truly saw that I had severely neglected myself (and consequently, the children). My counselor discovered that along with several other ailments, I was also dealing with stress-related hives. My ability to handle tension was depleted—my body was screaming out at me. As part of my treatment, I was asked to write a letter to myself from my hives.

> **JOURNAL ENTRY:** March 30, 1999—I am your hives. I live inside your nerves. I am here to tell you when you need to handle life differently. I have been living inside you for all of your life. We first met sixteen years ago when you were in high school. I would visit you when you daydreamed in class. I was climbing through your skin and blistering. I love to make you itch. You never listened to

> me—so when you were seventeen I decided to get your attention at night. You never pay any attention to your own needs—it makes me so mad at you. So, I come visit you during the only time you slow down enough to think—at night. I want you to care for yourself—so when you lay in bed worrying about everyone else, I come out. I crawl in between your toes and fingers and light fires. I make you itch so badly—I make you listen. I make you pay attention to yourself. You don't like me, but I love you. I want you to take care of yourself. Stop worrying about what you cannot change. Recently you made me so angry that I decided to raise hell in your body. I went wild. I set so many fires, I'm tired. If you would have let me out, I would have set fires to all the anger you keep inside. I want to break things—scream out all the injustices you endure. I am your unresolved traumas, lost loves, fears, resentments, and your despondency. I do not enjoy hurting you. Please stop hurting yourself. Take care of yourself so I can get some sleep. You know what you need. I shouldn't have to remind you!
>
> Sincerely, Your Hives

For the first time in years, I began seeing my life from outside my personal tornado. As my thoughts began to clear (off marijuana), I began to evaluate my past and future. I quickly realized that I had been going absolutely nowhere but down. *How had I missed the fact that I was destroying myself and my children?*

A Dream Realized

Now, I immersed myself into the "house project." I did all the subcontracting, including a four-car garage, plumbing, well, electric, phone, cable, cement slab, excavation, and landfill.

My headaches grew intensely. Still I labored on.

I was beside myself with anticipation on the day that our modular home was due to arrive. My best friend and I sat in lawn chairs at the end of her driveway and watched as the beautiful four-bedroom, three-bath house with fireplace and two-by-six construction came rolling in. My heart jumped with exhilaration and I took pictures each step of the way. This was a most exciting day, one that I was eager to share with Doug.

But evening came, and then night fell, and there was no Doug. He had gone out drinking after work and didn't come home until eleven that night. My enthusiasm was replaced with sadness and frustration again. I couldn't fathom that he hadn't even come to see our new house.

Mid-September we moved into our beautiful home and everything quickly fell apart. Doug was drinking so intensely that I ended up having to move all of our possessions by myself, including furniture (after all, I had worn out my welcome with all my friends—they were sick and tired of helping me move). During this transfer, I injured my neck and ruined my knee permanently.

Additionally, Doug was trashing our new home in drunken blackouts, falling asleep with lit cigarettes, urinating in the living room behind the couch, and now he was vomiting blood from his bleeding ulcer.

> **JOURNAL ENTRY:** October 13, 1999—It's not supposed to be like this. What happened to all the promises? Why is there alcoholism, God? I am so broken. I let him back and I gave him all of my heart. It's so broken. I'll never love again—I can't. I'll love him forever. It's like mourning a death.

It's interesting, looking back, to see that in my crises, though ignoring God all my life, I tended to blame Him for my troubles. Like God invented alcoholism? Right.

Sick and Tired!

It took another month and a half for me to completely fall apart. I was so sick—completely exhausted. My constant headaches were incredible. I'd get my kids off to school and go back to bed until they came home. Somehow I'd manage supper for them, and then get them to bed by eight so I could fall into bed, too.

Finally, I applied for state insurance and got myself in to see a doctor who prescribed a narcotic for headaches and sent me on my way.

One night at four in the morning I heard Doug throwing up in the bathroom. He had finished off all of the alcohol in the house, and in dire need of a fix he begged me, with absolute desperation, to go find him a drink. He wasn't going to make it without one.

This was the night I gave up.

I walked across the road and up the driveway of my closest friend, knowing that I was going to have to wake her and the family so that he could drink. I felt so ashamed to be there.

The next day Doug came back from the tavern sometime midafternoon with a new scheme to earn money. He had decided to deal drugs from our house. Yes, I had smoked pot, but never would I jeopardize losing my kids by dealing drugs. When I set my foot down about this scheme, he exploded in anger.

His outrage scared me to death. I had seen this kind of rage before—and I knew I had to get out pronto.

This time I turned to my father for advice, something I hadn't done in years. He told me of my need to seek the Lord and suggested that I bring the kids to Michigan to live. There in my lowest hour, I agreed. I had no idea what would take place from here on out, but at the moment nothing really mattered. My journal sums it up.

> **JOURNAL ENTRY:** December 2, 1999—I tried again. I can't do it again. My heart has done enough.

Saying Good-bye to the Dream

The plans took some doing, but things came together. I was forced to obtain another restraining order against Doug so I could have the time to get away.

My brother made a trip from Michigan, loaded some essentials into his van, and hauled them back to Michigan. We rented a storage unit in Wisconsin for furniture and miscellaneous things we could live without. On December 14 we left Wisconsin—and my shattered dreams behind.

The numbness inside me left my mind bogged down,

and despondency engulfed my soul. I couldn't cry or smile. I simply existed.

Doug remained in the "dream home" I had left behind, while I continued to pay the mortgage from Michigan. His calls started coming in each night as he cried the drunken tears of "love" and loneliness. He wanted to get better. He admitted he was sick. He needed me. He truly needed me.

Every night I lay in my parents' guest room with a gaping vacancy that ate at my soul. Each day took humongous effort to simply endure the loneliness that was my life.

Doug's and my hearts still clung together like cancer clings to its victim.

I wasn't going back—I simply couldn't; so he decided to come to me. It took a few weeks for him to sell off some assets and put the house up for sale, and then he was on his way. His arrival to Michigan was quiet as he found an inexpensive motel in which to hole up temporarily.

I'll never forget Gracie's reaction when she learned that Doug was moving nearby. Now 10 years old, she understood the pain that we all had endured because of this man, and she adamantly voiced her displeasure.

Shortly after Doug arrived, my parents offered to take us all out to Red Lobster for dinner. Mom and Dad, Doug, my two children and I awaited our table in an uneasy truce. Gracie refused to look at Doug or speak to him—she burned with anger toward this person who had caused so much pain and so many tears.

Dad had a purpose in mind in setting up this dinner. He told Doug firmly (but nicely) what he expected of us. We were to attend a marriage seminar (put on by Campus Crusade), and our family was to attend church regularly.

I was ready to learn, and hoped that somehow God

would step into this mess I called my life.

Karilee:

Baby Steps Toward God

Somehow Doug had talked Wendi into allowing him one more chance. His move across the Lake (from Wisconsin to Michigan) was a last-ditch effort, I believe, to hang on to this marriage and to simply survive—but I also firmly believe that God was at work in a special way in Wendi's soul.

Dan and I had arranged for Doug and Wendi to attend a weekend Christian marriage seminar in a large, beautiful Grand Rapids hotel. Both were desperate enough to try anything. Wendi came back from the seminar with some enthusiasm and hope. The gospel message and straightforward talk of the importance of a Christ-centered marriage had been forcefully presented. Doug said all the right words, but we could tell his heart wasn't in this "Christianity" stuff. Both of them (and the children) attended church together, not missing a Sunday, and people of our church reached out to them in warmth and love.

Wendi:

Truly Over

Within a month Doug and I had rented a little apartment and set up house. We had begun attending the church that my father currently pastored, fulfilling our promise to Dad. God began to soften my heart through His Word. In addition, Doug and I began Christian counseling, but I could see Doug was simply jumping hoops for me. There was no interest on his part to complete the assignments our counselor gave us, and no improvements in our relationship resulted.

On Sunday mornings before church, Doug would fill up with a dose of rock 'n' roll and cigarettes so he could endure the service.

I watched him consume outrageous amounts of Mountain Dew, which meant he hadn't truly sobered up. In my quest to understand alcoholism I had read that sugar has the same effect as ethyl alcohol in an alcoholic. Doug had replaced drinking alcohol with extremely large doses of sugar. I saw him manifest what is termed as a "dry drunk." That is when an alcoholic experiences the mood swings of drinking without having consumed any alcohol. He was constantly surly and rude.

Doug had been in Michigan less than three months when I confronted him about his intentions. "If you don't plan to work on getting better, I'd like you to leave," I declared.

That's all it took. He'd had enough. We loaded all his things from the apartment into the back of his truck, emptied the bank account for cash, and he was gone. This time I was sober when the truth of the finality of it all hit me like a tidal wave. My feet were swept right out from under me as I succumbed to this tsunami. It was over.

Truly over.

Karilee:

For Doug, it had all been empty. Working on the marriage, attending church, and cutting back on his drinking were all self-efforts. It wasn't working because the Lord was not in it. He wanted out. On the Sunday Doug walked out of Wendi's life, she told us he lit up his cigarette and departed with an expletive.

Two additional blows came a few weeks later. When Wendi received her credit card bill, she discovered that Doug had used it to gamble en route to Wisconsin. Wendi showed us the bill: Doug had racked up hundreds and hundreds of dollars. That evening Wendi shared another incident with us: In phoning Doug about this debt, Wendi was shocked to discover that already he had moved in with another woman.

Believe it or not, although living with another woman, Doug had actually tried to sweet-talk Wendi into giving him another chance.

"No way," was her answer.

In the midst of this turmoil Wendi determined to finish the science requirement to secure her graduation diploma and signed up for a correspondence course of environmental science. Battling excruciating headaches and with tremendous effort, she put in arduous hours of study and completed numerous papers. Though physically ill and emotionally drained, her tenacity and determination won out and she graduated in absentia with highest honor.

Incredible!

And in the meantime God was beginning to soften her calloused and hardened heart . . .

Wendi:

I called a new friend in Michigan (one my parents had prayed into my life) and Jackie came straight over to help console me. I shared some of my burdens and fears with Jackie—one of my concerns being Doug's drunk driving. He was currently driving a pickup registered in my name, and I feared he would cause harm in his drunkenness, putting me into further financial liability.

Within a week, I filed for divorce and Jackie and I drove round-trip to Wisconsin and back to retrieve my things from storage.

By then my health was shot. I felt sick constantly, catching every virus that came within a mile. A mixture of strong prescribed medications did not relieve the relentless, pounding head pain. But worse yet, the heart pain was unbearable. Valiantly trying to do things right, it was hard to find my way by groping in the dark.

> **JOURNAL ENTRY:** July 1, 2000—Never have I felt this alone. With sobriety comes the awful pain of reality. However fine the folks are here, I don't feel a connection. I am bottled up and it is so sad. I want affection, yet all I feel is the pain of my broken heart and my neglected body. Sometimes I want to recede into the wild, away from all humanity. It all is so alien to me and I do not fit in. I try to do what I should but I remain hollow with pain. Each day melts into the next—I cannot even distinguish them any more. I send my prayers and I go on. I don't do "lonely" well. The pain is too much. I did it again—for the last time . . .

Death Wish

Overcome with the realization of my total failure after Doug left Michigan for good, I cried myself empty and prayed for only one thing—I wanted to die. I wouldn't take my own life, but "God, would You please do it? Take my life . . . please, God!" I had tried and failed. I had no desire to try anymore . . . to live anymore.

For two weeks I was all alone. I had driven Gracie to Florida to visit her daddy, Jeff. Nolan, who always enjoyed being with Grandma and Grandpa Hayden, was staying in their guest room and also enjoying spending time with great-grandma and great-grandpa Cronk, who were currently living with Mom and Dad.

Then my dear Grandpa Cronk, lying on a hospital bed in my parents' home, passed away. Mom and Dad called my apartment with the news. After hearing about his death, I hung up the phone, my body crumpling to the floor. The waves of sorrow and loneliness crashed over me . . . pounding me down. I had finally hit rock bottom.

There I was in a heap on the kitchen floor, numb with pain and too weak to fight any longer. Everything had fallen apart. Cursing the day I was born, I continued to cry out to God, "Lord, if there is truly any mercy—please take my life!"

Grandpa was gone and I had been witness to his last months. I still don't know what hurt more: to see a man who was truly loved and truly had given love, now gone from this world—or the thought that it should have been me who died.

I felt my grandmother's grief with every fiber of my being. Grandma and Grandpa were best friends, and now she was alone. I understood the pain of "alone." But I didn't understand what it had felt like to have been truly loved by your mate. I could only imagine that.

Two days later I drove once more to Wisconsin for the final divorce hearing. I stood in the courthouse foyer, trembling as I waited for our case to be called. There stood Doug—the man to whom I'd given my last shred of dignity. I felt so cold inside—then suddenly so angry!

The stench of stale alcohol lingered in the air as he approached me, audaciously asking if we could be friends. Could he come visit me—take me to dinner? My quavering voice spat a hardened "no!"

Our case was called—and my marriage was over as quickly as it took the judge to drop his gavel and pronounce it so. Just as easy as that. Every inch of my body ached with the pain this divorce brought. In my own twisted way, I had truly loved this guy. Lord knows I had tried.

The next morning I awoke with eyes swollen and puffy, then began the nine-hour drive back to Michigan in an all-consuming exhaustion.

Physically sick and consumed with despair as I drove, my questions shot heavenward. *Why, God? I gave this marriage all I had. And why, God, why my grandfather now? Why, God, am I living in Michigan away from all my friends?* Automatically I had turned to God with the questions racing through my mind. Tears blurred my vision as the world outside went on without a care.

Finally I arrived home and collapsed onto the couch. I slept from Tuesday afternoon until Friday as Mom and Dad watched Nolan and Gracie, who had returned from Florida. God would soon begin to mend me.

> **JOURNAL ENTRY:** August 6, 2000—A month passes with long labor and deep sorrow. I have traveled to North Carolina and to Tennessee. I do things with others—yet always alone. My grandfather has departed into the heavens. I try to imagine my grandmother's sorrow. I cannot conceive—

> not for a moment. With his departure my marriage has ended only two days after. The hole is so vast in my heart. I see lonely days ahead with no prospect for future joy. My smile is only ornamental. A flicker of light is all that is left.

I cried often, praying the same prayer over and over—pleading that God would take me away. I'd tried and failed. My will to live—my sin-filled will—lay buried in the rubble of the wreckage I called my life.

Emotional and physical strength depleted, I lay exhausted in bed, no longer able to care for myself or my children. But the Lord had quieted my spirit and allowed me a deep rest while surrounding me with caring angels of mercy—family and church members who reached out to me in my deepest time of need with homemade meals and child care.

Unbeknownst to me, the spiritual wheels of my life were loosening and beginning to turn. During these days, my leaden soul began to awaken and my spirit, newly stirred, began wrestling with God's Spirit.

Karilee:

Wendi and the children were rebounding yet again from another broken relationship—Wendi's second failed marriage. This time the façade of her rough exterior cracked open, and her heart allowed others to reach out to her in love. This time she didn't run back to her past friends. The blinders on her spiritual eyes fell off, and she witnessed true Christianity at its best—and it reached her soul. *This time* the soil of her heart was fallow and prepared to receive God's personal message to her heart.

A burgeoning new life would begin to blossom.

God had used the death of my father as the catalyst to bring Wendi to total brokenness. Mom and Dad had moved into our home as Dad fought bone cancer. He had needed physical care that Mom was unable to give. Caring for Dad at home with the help of hospice was both rewarding and tenderly painful. Day-to-day care brought with it unsurpassed joys and excruciating sorrows. I was holding Dad's hand that morning when God ushered him into eternity . . . a thrilling time for him, and a poignant struggle for me.

Oh, how I would miss him!

Good-bye's Heart-cry
A Prayer

My heart is pained, Lord!
A living, writhing, searing pain
    that rips and tears in rushing waves.
So tight pain's grip I cannot breathe!
I did not wish for him to leave . . .
    But he is gone.

Oh, how it hurts, Lord!
Remembrance marred by suffering's glare:
    Each raspy breath, each muted groan—
Those wasted limbs on feeble frame—
Once twinkling eyes so filled with pain . . .
    I miss him so!

With so much love, Lord,

We tended this once vibrant man
turned feather-frail with whisp'ring voice.
A parch-lipped smile for all who came;
He never murmured or complained!
Put others first.

He taught me much, Lord.
Needs met by strangers as he lay
entwined in tubes and sterile garb.
No secrets now! No privacy!
He bore all this with dignity
and grace.

To You I run, Lord.
I need Your tender, strength'ning touch—
Your strong arms wrapped around my pain—
To feel the ointment of Your love
Wash through my soul so I can breathe.
Be still my soul . . .

In You I hope, Lord!
Bring back the meter to my song—
Restore a melody once more.
Dad's time on earth was o'er, I know,
For numbered days and Your wise ways
decreed it so.

Amen. With hope, Amen!

Wendi—tenderhearted being that she was—had spent a lot of time with her Grandpa, enjoying his wry sense of humor and simply soaking in his presence. The Lord called

Dad home in the middle of July 2000—and He was calling Wendi back "home" into the fold of His children at the same time.

CHAPTER TWENTY

Morning Has Broken

Karilee:

"HOPE DEFERRED MAKETH THE heart sick; but when the desire cometh, it is a tree of life" (Proverbs 13:12, KJV). Our hope—the 20 years of longing, praying, waiting . . . hoping—was now soon to be realized.

Morning had come!!

Oh, what inexplicable joy the realization of our hopes and desires for Wendi would bring to our hearts! Ah, the sweetness of the scent of God's presence in her life we were now to behold!

As I write this, a daily fountain of thanksgiving and praise to our merciful and gracious God is ever springing in our hearts. Like watching Lazarus rising from the stench of the tomb, we see a new and resurrected life in our daughter, and we weep with joy!

Intertwined with the beauty and sweet aroma of Wendi's

new life, however, are the jagged fragments of the debris of 20-plus years of sinful living: Physically her body bears scars and chronic illnesses resulting from her abusive habits; the ever-present guilt and sorrow for the hurt she brought to people's lives must continually be turned over to the Lord; and the damaged hearts of her children require special care and gentle restoration.

Years lost are never truly regained—but God's mercy, strength, and wisdom are hers in abundance just for the asking (Philippians 4:6, 13; James 1:5).

Wendi:

Welcomed by My Heavenly Father

My Father in heaven looked down upon me with His loving eyes knowing that I would come to Him soon.

The pain of reaching rock bottom was harsh and cold, yet I was surrounded by the shining warmth radiating from Christian coworkers. A new job placed me in a loving, Christ-centered environment. Each day I listened to Christian radio programs and Christ-honoring music while I worked. And as I wrestled with God inwardly, I soaked up this healing environment where I was warmly received and unconditionally loved. But oddly, this unconditional love hurt. *How can I be loved when I don't possess love myself?*

I had missed many, many days of work and yet hadn't been fired. I asked so many questions, yet I never felt that I was an inconvenience. These believers were living God's words:

> Love is patient, love is kind and is not jealous; love does not brag and is not arrogant, does not

> act unbecomingly; it does not seek its own, is not provoked, does not take into account a wrong suffered, does not rejoice in unrighteousness, but rejoices with the truth; bears all things, believes all things, hopes all things, endures all things. (I Corinthians 13:4-7)

Not Pharisees, not in-my-face preachers, not overbearing or demanding—they lived each day in God's love and illuminated His grace. They didn't *tell* me to be like them. They *created a desire* within me to be like them. They ministered with Christ's compassionate kindness.

A million questions, like fiery darts, flew from my troubled mind into my heart, burning . . . burning . . . burning. I had walked away from "American cultural Christianity" at age 12. In spite of that, I was a Christian, right? I had asked Jesus into my heart when I was a little girl. I was baptized, too! What did these people have that I didn't?

And . . . what were these new sensations?—I began to feel! Remorse. Embarrassment. Despair. Deep yearning. Hope? . . . Yes, a fresh desire to seek answers emerged. I wanted truth.

Each week that passed mingling with my new coworkers helped tear down the self-protective walls I had kept up.

One Friday night I found myself alone at home with unwanted time to face my vacant heart. All my life I had run from my problems. I had learned to escape from difficulties through alcohol and drugs, but I wasn't drinking or using drugs now, and there was no hiding from the pain and emptiness.

Alone—at that moment—the incredible agony of reality finally broke through the stone of my heart and soul. I saw myself—the unvarnished, wretched, sinful Wendi—and I fully understood my need for Christ.

Passion broke through to my heart's core. Collapsing to my knees, I cried out to the Lord with tears of repentance that fell like rain. *God, I am so unworthy of any good thing. I am desperately messed up! I'm so sorry for all the horrible things I've done. Please forgive me. I want to do what's right, Lord. I don't want to run my own life anymore. I give myself to You.*

In the seclusion of my little apartment the Holy Spirit ministered to me, making me a new creation. Me, a broken addict. Me, a single mother twice divorced. Me, a rebellious preacher's kid. Twenty years after I had rejected God, and thousands of poor decisions later, I let go of the steering wheel of my life and trusted Jesus, who had died for *my* sins to take total control.

I returned to my Father broken and empty. I had absolutely nothing to offer, but He took me in anyway. I had done so many awful things to disgrace Him, but He showed me my debt had already been paid for by His Son. Jesus had borne my shame (and it was enormous) when He died on the cross—for *me*.

For many years, Jesus had been knocking at the door of my heart; but I had to open the door myself. I had to see my sinful, broken state and fall to my knees in repentance. Jesus led me—Wendi, the sinner—in a personal and unique way to the cross where I was made clean.

I have never felt alone since that night.

Karilee:

Our Family Fabric Restored

So there you have it—the unraveling of our family's fabric.

In chapter 1 of this story, I mentioned the fact that little snags and loose threads can unravel quickly. Indeed, in the early years of child rearing, our family-life fabric had a number of snags and dangling threads. But the hard yank on a thread—the day Wendi became pregnant—started an unraveling we could not control. Seams burst and edges frayed while the world looked on in disapproval.

But, we praise the Lord for the many people—God's people—who saw beyond the disintegrating fabric of our lives . . . to tomorrow's possibilities. They stood by us, prayed with us—and waited . . . and waited . . . until one day, 16 years after the unraveling had begun, they witnessed our family's garment restored.

This new garment—exquisitely crafted by God, the Master Designer—reflects His beauty in such a way that others can't help but notice.

It Is Never Too Late

Before Wendi writes a final word to you, our readers, I want to share the other song (previously mentioned) that ministered so strongly to my heart during our years of praying and waiting for God's intervention in Wendi's life and heart.

This song voices a *hope for parents* currently carrying the burden of a beloved, wayward child. And the words carry a strong message of *hope to the prodigal son or daughter.*

This, then, is the message—both to the teen filled with hopelessness and anger, and to parents who are waiting . . . waiting . . . and waiting: It is never—*never*— too late to come to the Savior asking for forgiveness—to receive eternal salvation, and gain purpose and fulfillment in life. Whenever a person comes to God with a repentant heart, He is willing and ready to forgive, for no one has ever gone so far into sin that God's love cannot reach. *It is never too late. . . .*

There Is a Way to Come Back Home Again

There is a way to come back home again—
A way to be clean and be made whole again.
Regardless of your past or how far away you roam,
There is a crimson path leading to the Father's throne.
Yes! There is a way to come back home again.

The deepest stain of sin—
The hopeless wandering—
The longing to begin the process to be clean . . .
Trust in Him today,
He'll wash the stain away—
The guilt, the debt, the loss
Overshadowed by a cross.

Don't let your heart grow cold,
Don't give in to the pain!
Don't let fear take its hold,
Don't let the hate remain!
His arms are open wide—
You'll never have to hide!
Come stand before His throne
And know that you are home . . .
You are home!

There is a way to come back home again—
A way to be clean and be made whole again.
Regardless of your past or how far away you roam,
There is a crimson path leading to the Father's throne.
Yes! There is a way to come back home again.
Yes . . . There is a way to come back home again![1]

Wendi:

Beginning to Grow

It has been several years now since I placed my life in God's hands. I am learning many, many lessons.

One incredible early lesson came to me in a song.

A few months into my walk with God, I purchased a three-album CD of Phil Keaggy's works. By this point I was devouring God's love through four different Bible studies, reading five or six books at a time, and memorizing most every song I heard on Christian radio.

I was also planning a move, incredibly, to Orlando—and I felt like Daniel going into the lion's den. My job with the ministry was transferring me down to the city in which Karl and Jeff still lived, and I was scared. But I also knew that many missionaries face danger in their work, and so I was willing to follow Christ wherever He led me.

This particular day I was alone in my garage preparing for a yard sale and singing along with Phil. I had known this song "Our Lives" for many years, but on that day I *felt* the words. One line in the simple chorus impacted me profoundly: "When love's a gift, how then can it be earned?"

Right then and there I bowed my head and with tears running down my face I thanked God for this incredible revelation.

God's love is a gift that cannot be earned!

God had recently shown me that, and it overwhelmed me to think that I could actually be loved unconditionally, especially since the One who loved me knew my every weakness and failure. What an incredible realization that was to me—someone who had depleted her health by trying to earn someone else's love!

On this day, though, He showed me something more: that true love—the kind we are commanded to give—is also a gift I could learn to give to others. "This is My commandment, that you love one another, just as I have loved you" (John 15:12).

It dawned on me that not only had God intended even me to be loved like this, but *I, too, could learn to love others in this way*. My whole life had been centered on Wendi: watching out for Wendi, taking care of Wendi, loving Wendi first and foremost.

Now my heart was being stirred with the thought that perhaps God wanted to use me—the rebellious kid and foolish young adult—the one who made mistakes galore—the headstrong prodigal—He wanted to use *me* to reach out in love to others.

Amazing!

Since that moment I have been learning—a lot! I have daily struggles due to the life-long consequences of my sinful behavior. Some ramifications of bad choices can never be undone. But along with the struggles, I've enjoyed unbelievable blessings, too. I'm beginning to learn how to put aside my strong will and self-centeredness, and to lean on Jesus.

Perhaps someone is reading this, feeling alone and unloved, and wondering how to go about receiving this kind of love. Let me share how God worked in my heart. First, I had to realize that God already loved me completely, sinner that I was. But more incredible than that, He really wanted—He yearned—to have a close and personal relationship with me.

Me! All I needed to do was ask.

Yes, He loved me unconditionally. But I had to acknowledge my sin and ask for forgiveness. First John 1:9 says "If we confess our sins, He is faithful and righteous to forgive us our sins." It was that simple. Once I admitted that I had a sin nature, and confessed my sins to the Father in Heaven, all I had to do was to invite Him to come into my life. That's it.

Jesus was always ready and waiting for me to come to Him—to have my sin washed away, and to love me with His perfect love. The same holds true for you. What will you do?

To those of you who love the Lord your God, let my story bring this challenge: To what degree do you show God's love to the unlovable? Do you continue to show love toward your prodigal even when he or she is so very difficult to love? Unconditional love can be overwhelmingly frustrating at times. It may be heart-wrenching as was my parents' love toward me.

But *your love is a gift to be given* to your rebellious loved one. Your love for the child for whom you weep, mirrors Christ's love to him or her. Your child cannot earn your love. Give it freely in spite of constant antagonism toward you.

This kind of love creates a longing in even the coldest of hearts.

Many, if not all, hurting souls cry out for nothing more than to be truly accepted and loved. My parents' consistent love (20 years' worth of love to a closed heart) finally broke through my hardened heart, and helped me see the Savior's love for me.

And so, as one story ends, another begins.

I'm still in Michigan, and didn't end up moving to Florida. God simply gave me an option to obey Him, and when I chose to do so, He lovingly set me back down in Michigan.

Additionally, the Lord, in His great love, led me to a patient, serving, Christian man, to whom I'm married. God put us together to grow in Him and mend both of our broken lives. We are learning how to lead and love our blended family of five children, and to reach out to our community and church.

Personally, I have fallen flat many times. But at last, I now seek God's will and not mine as I strive to grow up.

Giving up my very strong will is not an easy task!

Another big change—I do not run from my problems any more. Letting go of my sin nature is by far the hardest thing I have ever done. But I am not alone—Jesus walks with me each step that I take. With God's grace I now seek to love and nurture my family—to teach them by example.

Day after day, I sing to my heavenly Father with praises lifted to His throne. My cup really *does* overflow. My body is broken; yet my soul is mended. The best way to describe it has already been done in the famous hymn "Amazing Grace":

Amazing grace! how sweet the sound,
That saved a wretch like me!
I once was lost, but now am found,
Was blind, but now I see.

'Twas grace that taught my heart to fear,
And grace my fears relieved;
How precious did that grace appear
The hour I first believed![2]

In spite of myself, in spite of my past, God is using me.

I will praise the Lord no matter what happens. I will constantly speak of his glories and grace. I will boast of all his kindness to me. Let all who are discouraged take heart. (Psalm 34:1-2, TLB)

Asking the Hard Questions

Karilee:

As we have shared our story with hurting families throughout the country, we've often talked with aching parents needing encouragement. Over and over, certain basic questions resurface as moms and dads struggle with their personal feelings of disappointment and dashed hopes. Dan and I don't pretend to have all the answers, but we *have* grappled with many questions and God has given us helpful answers through this experience, and from His Word. It is our hope that what we have learned in the crucible of pain and prayer will be helpful to parents enduring crisis circumstances in their own lives.

The following questions are those we have been asked repeatedly—some are addressed to us as parents, and some are addressed to Wendi. Above all, we wish to strengthen hurting Christian parents in the Lord, bring comfort to those anguishing over their current situation, and point to our eternal hope—the Lord Jesus Christ, who always delights in hearing our prayers and comforting our hearts.

QUESTIONS

To Us, the Parents:

Q. Early in Wendi's life, you prayed consistently that the Lord would protect your daughter. Yet she had two children out of wedlock, got heavily involved in drugs and alcohol, had live-in relationships, and experienced two failed marriages. Do you feel that God failed you?

A. As a mother, of course I would have preferred that God had miraculously intervened in Wendi's life the moment she began to stray. From the day she was born I dreamed of only the best—wishing for her a wonderful, carefree, God-centered life. Dan and I guided her the best way we knew how, praying that she would make wise choices. She didn't.

Our Creator-God has made each one of us, and He places within each individual a free will to choose or not to choose things that are righteous. For many years, our daughter chose to rebel and live contrary to God's will.

Did God fail us? Never.

Every step along our treacherous journey with Wendi, the Lord met every single one of our needs. *Every single one.* He brought comfort, peace, direction, and a deep sense of His presence.

Personally, I learned about prayer. I learned about patience and leaning on Him. I learned of His person and presence in a real and tangible way that could not have been discovered had my life happily bounced along free of difficulty. I learned about myself—that my ways and thoughts are very often totally opposite to the Savior's.

No, God did not fail us. He used our family tribulations to perfect us and draw us to Himself in a special way (James 1).

But most importantly, when I look at the big picture today—now that our prodigal has come home—I see so much more. God *did* protect her. He *did* answer that particular prayer. But He did it His way and not mine:

1. He *didn't* protect her from pregnancy. But He *did* protect her two times from taking the life of two children by abortion. *Thank You, Lord.*

2. He *didn't* protect her from drugs and alcohol. But He *did* prevent her from hard-drug addiction and from overdoses. Wendi tried a lot of drugs in high school and her early 20s; she used acid and crack cocaine in her later years. I don't know why, but she didn't become addicted to these things. She should have. *Thank You, Lord.* God mercifully spared her from HIV and AIDS. *Thank You, Lord.*

3. He *didn't* protect Wendi from herself and the wild and dangerous lifestyle she lived. But He *did* protect her from societal predators when she twice tried to run away or jumped into a car with complete strangers or was picked up by strangers in bars. *Thank You, Lord.* He protected her from bodily harm when she skied drunkenly or rode snowmobiles carelessly over open ice. *How I thank you, Lord!*

Yes, my Shepherd—Wendi's Shepherd—heard each and every prayer, and He mercifully brought her safely through the dark places and into the light (James 5:16).

Q. It seems that so many times you were taken by surprise by your child's actions. How could you have been so blindsided by her rebellion?

A. This question brings a twofold answer. First of all, because Dan and I had an open and loving relationship with both of our children, our hearts *wanted* to believe what they told us. From early childhood we had instructed them in God's ways, stressing the importance of truth—no matter what. Since Wendi's nature was not argumentative, not displaying an in-your-face defiance, it was very easy—too easy—to accept her lies and excuses.

Often she listened to our admonitions silently and then went her own way. We wanted to believe her, even though we never truly trusted her.

As Dan and I questioned Wendi and followed her habits as closely as we could, we suspected but could not prove things. It took us three years to uncover Wendi's smoking habit because we never caught her smoking—never discovered cigarettes in her room or in her purse or glove compartment of the car. Never did we know of her marijuana habit—or her drug habits, although we had eventually learned that she drank alcohol. I guess that makes us very naïve. We certainly tried our hardest to discover a way to reach her.

Secondly, Wendi was extremely clever in lying and cover-ups. She thought things through and had her stories prepared. And she enlisted many friends to help in her deceptions.

To be honest, the times I tried to expose lies, I felt like the KGB interrogating an innocent citizen. For example, one day I searched her room for drugs and discovered a tiny blue-green pill on the floor. Aha! Now I had her. When she returned from school that afternoon I confronted her with my evidence.

I felt pretty foolish when I found out that the pill was from the veterinarian's office—a prescription for one of our ailing cats.

Recently I watched a secular TV special about children who conceal their wild lifestyles from their parents. One young man shared his many ways of "covering" his evening activities. When this teen came home later than curfew he had as many excuses as he needed: "I got held up in traffic because a car accident blocked the highway; I had to take a couple friends home who lived across town; I had a flat tire; I ran out of gas; we were watching videos at so-and-so's house and lost track of time; I was riding with Scott, and was the last one of a bunch of kids to be dropped off . . ."

This young man often climbed out of his upstairs room in the middle of the night to party with friends; for years he had successfully concealed his drug habit from his loving and careful parents. Only when he finally landed in jail because of a wild party at a friend's house, did his shocked parents discover his deceptive ways. They had no idea of their son's problems because he was an expert at cover-up.

I can only say that the problem (having the wool pulled over parents' eyes) seems to be widespread. Some children are blatant in rebellion (e.g., arguing and disobeying rules openly, or immersing themselves in punk dress, hairdos, or tattoos in spite of parental wishes). Others, like Wendi, rebel quietly and secretly.

We *were* certainly caught unaware and did not learn of Wendi's troubling addictions until she was an adult. It is embarrassing and a bit humiliating to realize how much we missed. "The sins of some . . . [people] are conspicuous, going before them to judgment, but the sins of others appear later" (1 Timothy 5:24, ESV).

Q. Who were the people who helped you in your prodigal experience? Which people hurt you? Why?

A. I've summarized this in two parts.

Part One—Those Who Helped

In the circle of family and close friends, we found great encouragement through those who showed their love by simple words like, "We're praying for you," or "We want you to know we love you all," or "I'll pray each week especially for Wendi." Asking, "Is there anything specific for which we can pray?" gave us the opportunity to share our current heartfelt need.

Nosiness or asking questions that probed for the sordid details, though, were an instant turnoff. Parents of wayward children will share things they wish to share and nothing more. I shared details with those closest to me—but even then I wasn't comfortable laying everything out on the table.

The best friends to us during our pain were those who simply supported us by their presence. Who helped the most? Those who put an arm around us. Those who prayerfully stepped back to let *God* show us His own direction and purpose—who let *God* bring to us His comfort and peace—whose steadfast prayers beseeched *God* to work in His merciful, loving way. They stood by us, and *let Him do the work.*

Concerned strangers ministered to us in various ways. Some had already been through similar circumstances and could encourage us through their instant empathy or stories of God's provision and answers to their prayers. We loved hearing success stories of other prodigal children!

Also, as Dan traveled and spoke at conferences, he sometimes related in a broad way our hearts' burden for Wendi. Oftentimes encouragements would come our way later by means of letters or personal comments from strangers and casual friends asking, "How's Wendi doing? We have been praying for her" (sometimes for years). For example, just recently a woman pulled me aside at a conference. "How is your daughter doing? My husband and I have been praying for her for six years."

What a thrill it is to realize that God's people upheld our family (and Wendi specifically) in their requests to the Savior. What a joy it has been to tell them, "Wendi has come back to the Lord! She is a changed person. She is studying the Bible and growing by leaps and bounds. Thank you—*thank you so very much for your prayers.*"

The prayers of others were an integral part of God's work in our family's crisis. I'm sure we'll meet still more people in heaven who shared our burden with us in beseeching the Savior on Wendi's behalf.

Part Two—Those Who Hurt

Sometimes, however, even well-intentioned people can be hurtful. Several times onlookers approached Dan or me with platitudes such as, “Perhaps God is going to let Wendi wallow in the pigpen for a while,” or well-intentioned comments as to how some children “just have to learn the hard way,” and so on. These comments, though perhaps true, were of no comfort to me personally. I wanted love. I wanted understanding. I wanted hope—and I wanted nothing more than to have others join with me in prayer for my beloved daughter.

The few well-meaning people who tried to comfort us with unsolicited advice or “a word from God” came across to me like Job’s “friends” (who weren’t real friends at all) as they tried to ascertain the root cause of our difficulty.

When these people came out of the woodwork to tell us what we should do, or how to discover the “good” in our bad situation, we found their words to be more hurtful than helpful. Regarding the discovery of the “good” that God is working in a painful circumstance, Sandy Lynam Clough says, “It can be months, years, or even a generation before the good, like the last piece of a puzzle, helps things make sense. We simply cannot pull the ‘big picture’ into focus by guessing how God will work.”[1]

Finally, great hurt was inflicted upon us by those who condemned—the few who let us know that we were doing things wrong, or who offered unsolicited advice as to how we could “do things right.”

We knew we were not perfect. We knew we had made mistakes. No one had to tell us that. But do you know what? We were doing the best we could. We were seeking

God's direction—and here's what happened:

Amidst our inadequacies our daughter struggled in life—she rebelled, but our sovereign Savior persistently sought her and patiently brought her back. *We praise God for this.*

But additionally, *in spite of our inadequacies*, our son walked with the Lord, was a bold witness in high school and college, and today he and his family are missionaries. *We praise God for this.*

Two different children with the same parents and the same upbringing—with two different responses. God met both of our children according to their individual needs.

Unfortunately, in the body of Christ, one can always find judgmental people. These folks may truly love the Lord, but they seem to have a temperament in which all matters of life are black-and-white—right or wrong. Tim LaHaye names the "Choleric" individual as a prime example—a person who "tends to be decisive and opinionated, finding it easy to make decisions for himself as well as for others."[2]

For example, one man who ruled his daughter with an iron fist exhorted us to do the same. What this well-intentioned man did not seem to understand, however, is that what works for one child may not work for another. Through the years we have watched prodigal stories play out for countless families. Some fathers were strict—others were lax. Some parents responded in anger and even banishment—others prayed in love through many tears. Guess what. The results were varied in spite of the approach taken. There are no pat answers. There are no formulas to guarantee the prodigal's quick return.

The point is this: When another family is confronted

with an unrepentant, rebellious child, tread softly. There is nothing more powerful than your prayers on their behalf. Covenant to pray for them. Offer your love and support. They need your concern, not your criticism.

If, *and only if*, they ask for advice, give it gently and lovingly. Point them to the Word of God. Encourage them to seek their pastor's help or the help of a qualified Christian counselor. Above all, be a good listener and offer to pray with them.

Condemnation and harsh words only add to the pain and guilt. Even if the parents *are* doing everything wrong, ask the Lord to intervene in His own way. Someone has said, "The Christian army is the only army that shoots its wounded." Let's not be one of those merciless shooters.

Q. What are the important things to tell families who currently have rebellious children? What things should always be done? What things should never be done?

A. I've given some guidelines below.

1. Seek to do these things:

- *Never give up on your child.* With God all things are possible (Matthew 19:26).
- *Remain steady before Christ.* It's vitally important to continue living a Christ-honoring life—thoughtful toward others and obedient to God's Word. Your example of true godliness may be one of the significant enticements to bring your rebellious child back to Christ. Rebels are not impressed by hypocrisy.
- *Love your child—especially when they're unlovable.* Ask the Lord for His enablement to show Christ's

unconditional love. You may have to exercise tough love, but let your child see that you love him or her in spite of his or her actions.

- *Be prepared to hang in there for the long run.* Many children return to the Lord in a short period of time. Others have rebelled for many years. There are no formulas—no precise timetables to follow.
- *Enlist friends to stand with you in prayer.* Carefully choose one or two close friends or a family with whom to confide and share your heart. You do not need to bare all—but a close friend sharing the load is a tremendous encouragement, especially in the darkest hours.
- *Seek professional help when necessary.*
- *Christian counseling can bring invaluable help.* Medical evaluation may be necessary for bipolar disorders; ADD, ADHD, and other physical or neurological conditions, and drug and alcohol addictions. If the problems seem severe, a complete physical exam is warranted.
- *Accept responsibility for any blame that may be yours.* Seek help if change is needed in your own life for
  —personal alcohol or drug problems
  —unresolved anger due to divorce or other issues
  —abusive behavior
  —bitterness toward God
- *Turn to Christ.* If you, as a parent, do not know Christ personally, seek Him now. Read the following verses, and then meet with your pastor or Christian advisor: Romans 3:23, Romans 6:23, John 3:16, Ephesians 2:8-9, Acts 16:31, 1 John 1:9, John 1:12.
- *Entrust your child's welfare to God.* Relinquish the

well-being of your child to His care.

- *Pray daily for your child.* His or her turnaround is something only God can bring about.
- *Pray for yourself, your spouse, and your family.* Ask God for wisdom and direction each and every day. Ask for physical, emotional, and spiritual strength.
- *Immerse yourself in God's Word.* It's in the Word of God that you will find comfort, encouragement, and help. It is through the Word that God will speak personally to your heart—give you personal direction and personal advice.
- *Learn about the character of God Himself.* Kathy Troccoli puts it this way: "God . . . may not reveal His plan. But He has revealed Himself."[3] It is through God's Word that we learn of His character and faithful ways.

2. Avoid these things:

- *Don't close the doors of communication to your prodigal.*
- *Guard yourself against anger/hostility.*
  - "[Parents], do not provoke your children to anger" (Ephesians 6:4)
  - "Let the words of my mouth . . . be acceptable in Your sight, O Lord" (Psalm 19:14)
  - "Cease from anger and forsake wrath" (Psalm 37:8)
- *Guard your tongue.*
  - "A gentle answer turns away wrath, but a harsh word stirs up anger" (Proverbs 15:1)
- *Don't give in to despondency or bitterness.* It is frighteningly easy to withdraw or become reclusive out of

embarrassment. Despair and despondency are slippery paths that can lead to bitterness. Don't give in to these emotions! A response of humility, love, and sincerity may be the means of touching others.

Q. I have friends whose teen is doing things the parents don't know about. I feel I should warn the parents but am hesitant about risking our friendship. Should I confront the teen?

A. This question is difficult to answer because several factors enter into the equation.

Confrontation in general is not a profitable way to go about restoring a wayward teen. Confrontation connotes hostility and opposition. Few people (let alone struggling, mixed-up teenagers) respond well to confrontation. So, don't approach them with condemnation like, "I know what you're up to, young lady, and you'd better stop or God is going to punish you" or "You look hideous with your tattoos and body piercing . . . the devil must have hold of you." I know I'm overdoing it a bit—but you get the picture.

There's a fine line here because acceptance of unwanted behavior (thinking they'll grow out of it) can also be dangerous. Furthermore, some children get caught up in the dark side of spiritual things—the occult and the macabre—or they get sucked into addictions that are hard to overcome. Intervention may be imperative in these situations because certain behaviors (including those arising from demonic influence) can lead to suicide, crime, and even murder, as we've already seen in high schools across the country.

Consider these two questions when approaching a rebelling teen:

1. *Are you burdened for this teen or simply angry and condemning?* Bathe your concern in prayer and ask God to put His love and understanding in your heart for this teenager. Make sure your approach is caring and sensitive.

If your heart remains angry or bitter toward the teen, it's probably better that you don't try to confront him or her. Wisdom may lead you to simply continue praying. Ask God to change your heart of condemnation to one of love. I've seen the hearts of angry people make a turnabout as they uplift their "antagonists" in prayer. The same can happen regarding *your* attitude toward a troublesome teenager.

If you embrace a genuine, loving concern for wayward teens—and they sense this—then, after praying for God's guidance and timing, an approach in love may be warranted. Put your arm around them and ask how they're doing. Tell them you care and offer to take them out for a hamburger or pizza. If there's a specific problem that's out in the open, tell them of your love and that you are praying for them. Offer to be available at any time to talk. Then leave it at that.

2. *Have you established a relationship of trust or are you merely interfering?* I believe that genuine helpful advice should be given only by those who have already established a genuine relationship with the prodigal teen. If you are perceived as a friend, he or she is more likely to listen.

Q. Should I warn unsuspecting parents?

A. Again, tread carefully. This is an especially difficult issue because lifelong friendships can be damaged. What is your motive in approaching the parents? Be sure that the Lord is leading you to do this (by first seeking His direction in prayer). God can care for things without your intervention, you know. But there are times, especially when the children are endangering themselves, that you might feel an urgency to warn the parents. If this is the case, consider these issues:

1. *How well do you know the parents, and how do they respond to their children's actions in general?* We all know parents who, when informed by the school of their child's bad behavior, are defensive of their child who "can do no wrong." They may even threaten to sue the school, or make things hard for the administration if things don't go the child's way. If the school threatens to expel the student for bad behavior, this type of parent becomes angry and hostile. They are the ones to make excuses for their son who landed in jail, or blame the companions and friends of their teen when a group is busted for drugs or alcohol at a party.

If the parents of the child for whom you are concerned are like this—it will accomplish very little to confront them with their prodigal's activities.

Even if the parents are loving and dedicated, exposing the waywardness of their child can still be precarious. For instance, when Wendi was struggling in her high-school days, a dear Christian friend approached me with something horrible she had heard about Wendi. I didn't want to believe it. Then later when I asked Wendi about it and she denied it (of course). I chose to believe Wendi. Go figure. I *wanted* to believe Wendi because it hurt to think otherwise.

The unfortunate downside in this situation was that

from then on, I felt embarrassed when I was around my friend. Our friendship was strained because she believed something shameful about my daughter. (Even though later on I learned it had been true.) We did remain friends, but things were different, and in the end her confiding in me hadn't changed a thing as far as Wendi's behavior was concerned.

If you are a relative (aunt, uncle, grandmother, cousin), the same holds true. If after much prayer, you still feel constrained to talk with the parent(s), then, proceed with humility and much love, showing genuine empathy and sensitive support.

2. *If your concern was triggered by a specific event—say, your daughter told you about something that happened while she was with the wayward teen—bear in mind that her friendship with that teen will be in jeopardy if you confront the parents.* Teens are adamant about being true to their friends. They don't want to be known as informants. Furthermore, if you break a son's or daughter's confidence with regard to their friends, you may damage your relationship of trust with your own child.

3. *Covenant to pray every day for the prodigal.* God's intervention in his or her heart is what is needed. Only God can figure out the details—entrust the matter to His sovereignty and loving-kindness. He might use you in the situation. But then again, He might not. The one thing you can do—and *should* do—is pray.

Q. What is your biggest regret in child raising?

A. All of us as parents have regrets when looking back on our child-rearing days. Even if our children sailed through life without difficulty or incident, most likely we can recollect a time when we lost our tempers, came down too hard on our children, took something too lightly, or even punished the wrong child for a family mishap.

Regrets are usually nonproductive feelings. Hopefully we learn from our mistakes, and move on. However, if we *have* responded incorrectly or impaired our child's emotional development (through neglect, alcoholism, or abuse), we might need to seek professional help to work through the difficulties in a healthy manner. With the guidance of a counselor or pastor it will be important to ask our child for forgiveness (after we've confessed our failure to the Lord).

So with that in mind—let me share two of my regrets.

1. *Busyness.* In the ministry (as can also be true in families with secular jobs), schedules can be horrendous. In our case, there were months and years in which Dan left the house before the children were up, and returned after they were in bed.

That was a primary reason our family moved from Madison, Wisconsin, to Rhinelander. One day after the Sunday morning message, one of our children had approached Dan as he stood in the back foyer greeting people. "Dad," this little one said, "how are you doing? I haven't seen you for so long." That question sliced deeply into our hearts, and we determined to make a change so that we could have more time with the children.

But busyness continued to be a struggle to overcome, and I dare say it's a prevalent obstacle to parent-child communication in many homes today.

2. *We have recently come to believe that our daughter,*

Wendi, most likely suffered from Attention Deficit/Hyperactivity Disorder (ADHD). I regret that we had no inkling and therefore were not able to provide her with all the help she needed. ADHD was scarcely mentioned in those days—but now that we've studied this ailment (two of our grandchildren suffer from it and are being treated), I am confident that many of Wendi's problems might have been averted (at least tempered) had we had access to a physician's help and medications if warranted.

These days it is recommended that parents whose child seems overly compulsive, restless, agitated, or unable to focus his or her attention for any length of time seek an evaluation as to whether or not that child suffers from a physiological disorder. A bipolar condition can also be manifest by abnormal behavior. Medicine has come a long way in assisting children with such difficulties—and an increasing number of schools are aware of these diagnoses and can help our children through their adolescent years in a safe, productive manner.

In Wendi's case, I believe that a part of her waywardness stemmed from an ADHD physiological need to live life "on the edge." Dr. James Dobson describes this desire for high-risk activity:

> Even as children, they can be accident-prone. But, as they get older, rock climbing, bungee jumping, car racing, motorcycle riding . . . and other high-risk activities are among their favorite activities . . ."
>
> "Adults with ADHD are sometimes called 'adrenaline junkies,' because they are hooked on the 'high' produced by the adrenaline rush associ-

> ated with dangerous behavior. Others are more susceptible to drug use, alcoholism, and other addictive behaviors."[4]

Many resources are available today by way of books, magazine articles, and Internet medical sites which can aid parents of children with ADD, ADHD, bipolar disorder, etc. So parents—be prayerfully alert to your son's or daughter's behavior patterns. Should your child suffer from one of these ailments, seek a physician's help and immerse yourself in self-education. You can increase the probability of your child's success in life and live with a sense of hope.

To Wendi, the Returned Prodigal:

Q. Is there one thing or are there certain persons you blame for the course you took in life?

A. Before the Lord reached into my heart I could have written an entire book naming every person who had ever wronged me!

Chapter one would no doubt have been an exclusive on Mr. Farris, my seventh-grade teacher. But I wouldn't have stopped there—I could have happily told of the countless "Christians" who betrayed my confidence, criticized my life, and gave their expert advice derived from their "perfection."

Blaming others for my personal difficulties was certainly a trap that ate me alive. During my rebellious years I blamed *circumstances* (our family moved too many times), *my parents* (too strict), *friends* (can't trust them), *disabilities* (my grades are poor because I have dyslexia), *luck* (how did I get that horrid teacher?), or *God* (He could make things go better for me if He wanted to).

Now, as I look back, I'm embarrassed at how expert I was at judging and blaming others.

Jesus says, "Do not judge so that you will not be judged. For in the way you judge, you will be judged; and by your standard of measure, it will be measured to you" (Matthew 7:1-2). When my eyes were opened to the spiritual dimension, I found it extremely hard to admit that I, Wendi—not anyone else—had messed up my own life. The good news is that God was there waiting to forgive each and every mistake and to help restore peace to my life.

So my answer is yes, I have one specific person to blame for the course I took in life . . . and that person is me.

Quite frankly, I now find it easier to fess up and ask for forgiveness. There's a wonderful freedom in owning up to my mistakes by confessing them to God, and starting over again, clean and forgiven.

Q. If your parents would have "put you under lock and key," do you think that would have helped?

A. This particular question (put to my parents during my rebellion) triggers myriad responses, such as: Literally? Maximum-security school for wayward girls (all of whom are just like me)? My bedroom (with bars on the window perhaps)? Handcuffed to my obedient brother? Grounded for life?

Obviously some cynicism emerges with this thought.

Yet, I don't believe you can cage a wild animal and call it domesticated. "For man looks at the outward appearance, but the LORD looks at the heart" (1 Samuel 16:7).

I'm reminded of the story of a little girl who was punished for bad behavior by being required to sit in a corner with her face to the wall, hands folded in her lap and head bowed. Time after time she was placed in the corner for naughty behavior and told to sit with head bowed, praying, until she felt repentant.

One day, after a particularly belligerent episode toward her parents, she was sitting silently in her corner chair with head bowed. Her older brother approached her as she sat facing the wall. "You sure look different than when you threw your tantrum at the dinner table today," he commented. "You must be pretty sorry for screaming at Mom and Dad. I guess it really helps to have you sit there in the corner, huh?"

"I may be sitting down on the outside," she angrily replied, "but I'm standing up on the inside."

So, you see, we can lock up, punish, withhold from, yell at, or scourge our children, but changes only come from the heart. It's possible to require a conformed behavior, but if the heart screams of injustice and hatred, nothing good has been accomplished.

Of course children do need guidance, rules, consequences, and structure. And in some instances an increased structure and greater degree of monitoring behavior is justified for the child's welfare. But even when children act in their most rebellious and defiant manner, unconditional love is essential. That doesn't mean accepting wrong behavior. It means facing the extreme frustration toward our disobedient kids and teenagers and communicating that we still love them in spite of their sins.

I am now a parent of teens myself, and I see my past self in the actions of my children. I'm learning as I go, and God is teaching me many valuable lessons. But this I know: We, as parents, have an incredible opportunity to shine Christ's love through our own lives. When we do this, our kids will be touched by His love as well.

Q. What advice would you give to parents that might prevent children from making the mistakes you made?

A. There are no guarantees, but good communication, unconditional love, and forgiveness are paramount.

Sure, it's easy to kiss the little toes of our precious newborn. And we have no problem doting over our cute-as-a-button little tykes. We can even enjoy our goofy preadolescents.

But what about an angry teen?

Do we look at these awkward, prickly offspring and feel the madly-in-love feelings that were alive when they came home from the hospital? Are we intrigued with their dreams? Are we getting to know and befriend their frustrated friends? Do we lift them up in love and prayer even when they fail? Do we step back and let them fail sometimes?

Or is our response to them a long and tyrannical list of dos and don'ts? Or constant nagging and criticism? Or indifference because we're sick and tired of dealing with them? Or such deep worry and fear that we're ineffective in making any kind of decision . . . so we do nothing?

Kids know if we're genuinely interested in them or if frustration rules the relationship. I would encourage parents to consciously seek out their struggling teen and learn everything possible about them. Talk to them and listen carefully when they speak. Get help, if you need to . . . but do something positive (instead of always being negative).

I will never know what creative technique could have saved me from myself, if any. What I do know is that I based my life on the moment—each new experience was all that I lived for.

And because I grew up in a sheltered little part of this world, I was shocked . . . and delighted . . . when I discovered the pleasures of worldly living. The lure of the world was tantalizing and attractive to me. I was unprepared for and unconcerned about the repercussions of my actions, so I didn't think beyond the moment. Then, when I put up barriers and became withdrawn and surly, I was nearly impossible to communicate with. Once communication was lost, the battle for my parents was uphill.

Still, even with an uphill battle, it's important to make every effort at communication couched in Christ's love. When we as parents blow it (and we will), we need to come to our kids and ask their forgiveness.

Condemnation, banishment, constant yelling, and criticism burn the bridges of communication and make future restoration nearly impossible.

Q. What advice would you give to young children who are exhibiting rebellious behavior? To teens who struggle in their relationship with their parents and authority in general?

A. **To children—elementary age or younger:**

So many times as children we have to do things that don't make a lot of sense to us. Sometimes that makes us really mad. It's easy to get so angry that we do things we know are wrong just to show how angry we really are. Doing wrong things because we are upset is called rebellion. God tells us that rebellion is a sin. Did you know that even moms and dads can rebel?

But there are rules for everyone who lives on earth—even Mom and Dad have rules they have to obey. Adults have to obey rules when driving a car, or traveling to work by airplane, or running a business. Police have the job of making sure we all obey the rules (or laws), and so do judges in the courtroom.

Actually, rules are what help us all get along together, and they help make sure that everyone is being treated right. That's why God says it's so important to obey rules.

God gave us the Bible, which is a written-down copy of His words to us. Some of what God says in the Bible includes rules that will help us have a good life. One important message in the Bible is written directly to you—to kids: "Children, obey your parents in the Lord, for this is right. Honor your father and mother (which is the first commandment with a promise), so that it may be well with you, and that you may live long on the earth" (Ephesians 6:1-3).

We may not understand why our parents have the rules that they do, but God does, and He thinks it's important for us to obey. As a matter of fact, it's so important to God that He says a person who is obedient may live longer than someone who won't obey. Wow!

So the next time you think about being naughty and want to break the rules because you are mad, remember that God sees you. When you do what is right, you make Jesus happy!

And if you've already done wrong, it's okay to say you're sorry. In fact, that would show that you are growing up.

To Teens:

You are in a unique place of your own in terms of your age. By law your parents are still accountable for you, yet physically and mentally you are the decision maker for much of your life. Your thoughts are independent. If you don't feel that you can trust the adults in your life, you keep your thoughts to yourself.

Much of the time it might seem that adults have lost the ability to understand. One would think they could remember what it's like to be a kid and give a break or two every now and then. Most teens aren't out to hurt anyone—they're just trying to have a little fun, right? So, what's up with all the nagging and controlling?

First, let me say that parents often forget they're talking to young adults when they talk to teens, and that can be frustrating to you. But the way you respond to them will affect the rest of the conversation. Act like an adult. Respond with dignity, and you'll be surprised at the outcome.

Second, parents have survived being kids themselves. Believe it or not, the reason they say no to you is that they sense danger or possibly a bad outcome from your desired activities. I realize some parents have more rules than others—but their boundaries will benefit your life.

How? you ask.

Well, when you're 18 and move out of your parents' house, all that freedom you could hardly wait for . . . will not exist.

Huh? I'll be able to stay out all night long. I'll be able to say anything and do anything I want. My money will be my money. Whatever . . . whenever . . . whoever . . . it'll all be my decision.

But it doesn't work out that way. I've been there, and I know. Let's follow the scenario.

Okay, so when you stay out all night, it'll be hard to stay awake in class (if you attend college), or you'll mess up on the job (you *will* need a job, by the way). And with every job comes a boss. A boss is a lot like a parent. A boss has rules, and wants tasks done right. You'll be expected to be on time, work hard, and show courtesy.

You'll have a landlord, too. You'll be expected to take care of your residence. Trust me, I know. I've been evicted because I lived like a pig. In addition, if you spend all your paycheck on having fun, your landlord will not have the mercy of Mom and Dad, and you'll get kicked out.

Besides jobs and landlords, there will still be lots of rules to follow. Life will always carry with it people who are in authority over you.

I am a person with ODD (not an odd person)—the letters stand for Oppositional Defiant Disorder. When I was rebelling I broke every rule—twice! But in doing so, I made life for myself very, very difficult. I fought the law—and the law won.

So here I am in my 30s, and I'm just now learning to accept authority in my life. You know the "you can't teach an old dog new tricks" thing? Well, you can—but this dog is learning some hard lessons.

God puts it plainly: "Everyone must submit himself to the governing authorities. . . . The authorities that exist have been established by God" (Romans 13:1, NIV).

Why fight it? God always wins. And we win too, when we obey Him.

Q. Who in the Christian community was a hindrance to your attitude toward the church and Christians? Who influenced you in a positive way, and why?

A. For me, one particular mind-set damaged my thinking and turned me (and many of my friends) off more than any other negative influence: people who piously condemned others and who displayed a constant negative attitude of "don't . . . don't . . . don't." It has taken me a long time to get beyond those who condemned me.

I had to discover for myself that Christianity is not about every small mistake we've made. It's about hope. It's about a Person—Jesus—whom we love. And because of Him, Christianity is exciting—not exacting, for Christ came to save us, not to revile us. Scriptures says, "Therefore there is now no condemnation for those who are in Christ Jesus" (Romans 8:1).

I like to contrast the modern-day Pharisee with the modern-day fruit bearer—that sweet person who bears the fruit of the Spirit instead of negativism. God used this type of person several times to reach into my rebellious heart. Think about it. Who wouldn't be attracted to a person who displays love . . . joy . . . peace . . . patience . . . kindness . . . goodness . . . faithfulness . . . gentleness . . . self-control? (Galatians 5:22-23).

People who exhibit those qualities are often the ones who draw the hardened hearts to Christ—for they can be trusted.

Kids are incredibly perceptive. They sense motives a mile away. Their radars detect phonies. Does an adult say things that project an image of self-righteousness? They see it immediately. Is there condemnation . . . at all? If so, forget trying to get through to troubled teens, for they've closed off those people before a word is said.

But genuine concern is felt. Unconditional love is always understood, and even if outwardly rejected, the person who shows love will be remembered and listened to, and their words and actions will have an impact.

Q. How would you respond to a kid who says, "I'm a teen, just having a bit of fun—dabbling in alcohol, and every now and then popping a pill or two. I feel like I have control of my life, so what's the big deal? I'll buckle down when I have to—after all, you're only young once"?

A. I believe strongly that a person cannot simply "dabble" with drugs or alcohol. I don't know of anyone who has ever decided, "Hey, I think I'll become an alcoholic or maybe just abuse drugs." Drugs and alcohol are forces that take over lives—they will eat you alive.

I'm not sure how to get through to kids who think they have it all figured out, but I can stand before them as someone who played the game and lost. I can tell horrific stories of thousands of people who "dabbled" as kids and were sucked up to their eyeballs. I've watched friends die because of drunk driving, overdose, suicide, and cirrhosis (liver disease from drinking too much).

I thought it was all a game. It's not.

Death may not come right away, but the substance abuser will be a physical mess, and emotionally this person will die slowly as depression takes over.

I can guarantee that drugs and alcohol will shorten your life span, leave you poor as dirt, and whittle away at your self-respect.

Still not convinced? Let the statistics speak for themselves:

ALCOHOL

- 2004—an estimated 16,694 people died in alcohol-related traffic crashes[5]
- approximately 40 percent of all crimes are committed under the influence of alcohol[6]
- drunk driving is the nation's most frequently committed violent crime—injuring one person every minute[7]
- 2003—drivers 21 to 24 years old were the most likely age group to be intoxicated in fatal crashes[8]
- 2004—motor vehicle crashes were the leading cause of death for people from two to 33 years old[9]

SMOKING

- between 80,000 and 100,000 kids start smoking every day[10]
- every eight seconds someone dies from tobacco use[11]
- One in 10 adult deaths are from smoking-related diseases—that's 4 million deaths a year[12]
- smoking-related illnesses claim more American lives than alcohol, car accidents, suicide, AIDS, homicide, and illegal drugs combined[13]
- teen smokers are more likely to use alcohol and other drugs[14]
- more than 4,700 chemical compounds have been found in cigarette smoke; 60 are known carcinogens (cause cancer)[15]
- cigarette smoking is responsible for more than 85 percent of lung cancers and is also associated with cancers of the mouth, larynx, esophagus, stomach, pancreas, uterus, kidney, bladder, and colon[16]
- every year cigarettes kill approximately 440,000 people[17]

DRUGS

- 1992—the overall cost of drug abuse to society was approximately $102 billion[18]
- Sept. 30, 2000—there were 73,389 drug offenders in federal prison. 99.2% (72,775) had committed a drug trafficking offense[19]
- 2001—there were 638,484 drug-related emergency room visits[20]

- 2001—1,586,902 drug arrests took place[21]
- 2000—186,000 people between ages 12-17 were in drug treatment[22]

Q. Religion seems so stuffy, and it doesn't seem relevant to me, an adolescent. Maybe I'll get into it later when I've become old—what's wrong with that?

A. First, I'd like to know how you are able to be sure you will make it to "old age." The fact is that every moment of every day, accidents happen. Did you know that in the year 2002 there were 106,742 accident-related deaths in the United States? Accidents are the fifth-leading cause of death.[23]

Only God knows how long a person will live. Are you willing to risk it?

Yes, I would prefer to wait till old age to become stuffy myself. "Religion" in one sense of the word can be boring. Who wants to listen to some monotone stuffed-shirt babble on about—whatever? But, that's not what it's all about. Thankfully!

It's a personal thing. You and God.

God created each person as an individual—with a unique personality and customized set of interests. That means that each one of us can enjoy Him right here and now, as we are made.

God is not stuffy. How could the Creator of the universe be stuffy? Think for a minute of some of the totally awesome things God created. A sense of humor—your sense of humor—God created that. Bubble-eyed goldfish . . . butterflies . . . waterfalls . . . your pet kitten or dog or horse. God put the love for music into our hearts, made our bodies so we could hike and climb mountains and sing and draw funny cartoons or beautiful pictures. No, God isn't stuffy at all.

I've met some stuffy "religious" people, and they've turned me off, too. But look beyond them to the others: See the Christian athletes who tell of their love for God; notice the joy in the face(s) of the singer or group who sings of the Lord; look closer at that schoolmate who goes to church and isn't afraid to talk about "religion." They know how to have fun, don't they?

I can't think of any better time in life to find, not "religion," but Christ Himself. No matter what the old people are doing, you can receive God's love for you—His perfect love—and discover that He's the best friend in the world.

Then you can serve God in your own way—the way in which He made you. You like music? Play your guitar and sing away. Be a Christian radio DJ. Is it adventure you crave? Get going—climb rocks or ride the rapids in a kayak as a camp counselor. Face paint, tell stories—be artistic as you help at summer vacation Bible school. You certainly don't have to be bored . . . or stuffy.

As an adolescent you have the energy, fresh outlook on life, and time to rock this world for Christ. What an incredible gift it is to be young. Remember, God loves passion. It's okay to be yourself when you're with your Creator.

Go for it!

Q. Do you have any lasting physical or emotional consequences from your years of wild living? Any effects upon your children?

A. Indeed!

Where do I begin? Physically, my body is worn. Many of my problems are direct results of my hard living. Chronic asthma was triggered (or at the least, greatly aggravated) by many years of smoking both cigarettes and marijuana. I have undergone two surgeries for severe sinusitis—again aggravated by inhaling damaging smoke through a nose broken by a live-in boyfriend. Ski accidents and fights I had while drunk have caused other breaks in my bones. I have cervical spine damage due to blows to the head. My immune system is so ineffective that in 2003 alone I made 51 trips to the doctor and had 71 prescriptions filled—most of them antibiotics and steroids for my lungs and sinuses.

Some physicians (including mine) feel that my immune depletion is a direct result of many years of marijuana smoking: "Marijuana use is associated with many detrimental health effects. These effects can include frequent respiratory infections, impaired memory and learning, increased heart rate, anxiety, [and] panic attacks."[24]

I certainly wasn't thinking beyond the thrill of the moment when I smoked and played around with drugs. I am reaping the consequences of that faulty thinking today. In my early 30s I ache so much that the hardest part of the day is simply getting out of bed.

But God is granting me strength each day, and with doctors' help, I believe my physical problems are improving.

God has done a miraculous amount of emotional healing in my soul. When I first came back to Christ, many times I found myself overwhelmed with the need to cry out in repentance.

One day, alone with God, I realized I needed to purge things of my old life from my personal belongings. I sorted through my raucous music tapes, photos taken during my wild life, and bunches of clothing (shirts emblazoned with bad messages, etc.), tossing them into a large trash can. I knew it was the right thing to do, but it was hard—almost like mourning the loss of part of my own self. But I've never looked back. Those "dark" things have now been replaced by things of "light" . . . things that don't bring dishonor to God.

More importantly, I also learned to forgive others. "I forgive you, ____________," I'd say out loud. "I know you are a lost soul without Christ, and I release you from bearing any responsibility for the hurt my life has endured." It worked, too! Occasionally I had to repeat the process, but God held my hand through every painful moment as I healed.

Some emotions linger still. *Will my husband come right home after he goes to the grocery store? I'm such a drippy faucet—I must annoy people.* The list could fill many pages. Feelings of inadequacy . . . reclusive tendencies . . . conversations replayed in my mind . . . lack of ambition—all are pitfalls I have to work hard to avoid. But once again, God has mercifully stepped in and surrounded me with people who are amazingly reaffirming. "I can do all things through Him who strengthens me" (Philippians 4:13). I have the power of Christ in my life, and He will provide the needed strength. When I am tired, I lean on

Him to hold me up.

So, yes—I have, by my actions, brought into my life a lot of physical pain and emotional suffering. But I don't spend time looking back. In writing this story, I have given my life back to God—every awful moment—praying that God will use my story in any way He so desires.

I will never have the opportunity to live my life over. No one does. However, there is a world full of young people who are right now making life-changing decisions for the first time. To them, and to the parents of floundering preteens and teens, I give my story.

In answer to the question regarding the effects of my waywardness upon my children (they are now teenagers), I must answer yes. They have had to struggle with some of the collateral damage resulting from the extremely difficult life I dragged them through. I pray for them, and most importantly, I strive to display Christ in my life for my children. In many ways I believe we are all growing up together.

I have not metamorphosed overnight into "Mother of the Year." I've come a long, long way though, and so have they.

Notes

Chapter 6

1. *New American Standard Bible*, 1973.

Chapter 10

1. Charles Spurgeon, quoted by Daniel Partner, ed., in *Heroes of the Faith* (Uhrichsville, Ohio: Barbour Publishing, 1998), p. 75.
2. Bill Bright, *Four Spiritual Laws* (Orlando: Campus Crusade for Christ, Inc., 1965).

Chapter 12

1. Katrina von Schlegel (p.d.), *Inspiring Hymns* (Grand Rapids, Mich.: Zondervan, 1951), p. 415.

Chapter 14

1. Words by Paul Steven Chapman, © Shepherd's Fold Music. All rights reserved. Used by permission.

Chapter 16

1. Dan Hayden, *When Life's a Wreck* (Wheaton, Ill.: Crossway, 2003), p. 21.
2. Helen H. Lemmel (p.d.), *Inspiring Hymn*, (Grand Rapids, Mich.: Zondervan, 1951), p. 379.
3. John Bunyan, *Pilgrim's Progress* (New York: Books, Inc., undated), p. 14. The complete reference says, "This miry Slough is such a place as cannot be mended; it is the descent whither the scum and filth that attend conviction for sin do continually run, and therefore it is called the Slough of Despond; for . . . there arise in his soul many fears, and doubts, and discouraging apprehensions, which all of them get together and settle in this place. This Slough kept one poor pilgrim, Mr. Fearing, from reaching his destination (the wicket gate) for a month (p. 240). Additionally a person can go through the Slough of Despair, leaving the Slough (event) behind, but still carrying the despairing debris with him. Mr. Fearing had "a Slough of despair in his mind, a slough that he carried everywhere with him" (p. 240).
4. For an excellent and uplifting study on the character of God, see Myrna Alexander, *Behold Your God* (Grand Rapids, Mich.: Zondervan, 1978).
5. Oswald Chambers, *My Utmost for His Highest* (Westwood, NJ: Barbour, published by permission of Dodd Mead, & Company, Inc., 1935), p. 2.

Chapter 18

1. Taken from *Fresh Wind, Fresh Fire* by Jim Cymbala; Dean Merrill. Copyright ©1997 by Jim Cymbala. Used by permission of The Zondervan Corporation (Grand Rapids, Mich.), front cover flap.

2. Cymbala, p. 65.
3. Cymbala, p. 61-62.

Chapter 20

1. "There Is a Way to Come Back Home Again." Words by Randy Vader. Music by Randy Vader and Jay Rouse. Copyright © 1991 PraiseGathering Music. All rights controlled by Gaither Copyright Management. Used by permission.
2. John Newton (p.d.), *Inspiring Hymms* (Grand Rapids, Mich.: Zondervan, 1951), p. 385.

Asking the Hard Questions

1. Sandy Lynam Clough, *And I Know He Watches Me* (Eugene, Ore.: Harvest House Publishers, 1999), p. 54.
2. Tim LaHaye, *Spirit-Controlled Temperament,* (Carol Stream, Ill.: Tyndale House Publishers, 1999), p. 54-55. For further insight into individual temperaments see also LaHaye's *Transformed Temperaments* (Tyndale) and Don and Katie Fortune, *Discover Your Children's Gifts* (Baker).
3. Kathy Troccoli, *Am I Not Still God?* (Nashville: W Publishing Group, 2002), p. 158.
4. Dr. James C. Dobson, *ADD/ADHD: Facts and Encouragement* (Part 1), booklet. (Colorado Springs: Focus on the Family, 1990).
5. MADD Online, "Total Traffic Fatalities vs. Alcohol Related Fatalities 1982–2004," http://www.madd.org/stats/0,1056,1298.00.html
6. MADD Online, "General Statistics," http://www.madd.org/stats/0,1056,1786,00.html
7. MADD Online, "Drunk Driving in the United States," http://www.madd.org/stats/0,1056,3726.00.html

8. MADD Online, "General Statistics," http://www.madd.org/stats/0,1056,1789.00.html
9. Ibid.
10. About, "Global Smoking Statistics for 2002," http://www.quitsmoking.about.com/cs/antismoking/a/statistics.htm
11. Ibid.
12. Ibid.
13. About, "Teen Smoking Facts for Parents and Teens," http://www.quitsmoking.about.com/cs/antismoking/a/statistics.htm
14. Ibid.
15. Stephen Mulcahy, CSN, "The Toxicology of Cigarette Smoke and Environmental Tobacco Smoke," http://www.csn.ul.ie/~stephen/reports/bc4927.html
16. PDRhealth, Thompson Healthcare, "Family Guide to Nutrition and Health," http://www.pdrhealth.com/content/nutrition_heath/chapters/fgnt30.shtml
17. National Institute of Drug Abuse (NIDA) "InfoFacts—Cigarettes and Other Nicotine Products," http://www.drugabuse.gov/infofacts/tobacco.html
18. Office of National Drug Control Policy (ONDCP) Drug Policy Clearinghouse Fact Sheet, "Drug Data Summary: March 2003," http://whitehousedrugpolicy.gov/publications/factsht/drugdata.index.html
19. Ibid.
20. Ibid.
21. Ibid.
22. National Survey on Drug Use & Health (NSDUH), "Drug Rehab," http://www.addiction-help-line.com/drug/rehab.html

23. National Center for Health Statistics, "Accidents/ Unintentional Injuries," http://www.cdc.gov/nchs/ fastats/acc-inj.htm
24. Drug Facts Office of National Drug Control Policy, "Marijuana," http://www.whitehousedrugpolicy.gov/ drugfact/marijuana/index.html

APPENDIX

Focus on the Family websites and phone number

http://troubledwith.com
http:www.family.org

For referrals to Christian counselors in your area or to speak with a Focus on the Family counselor, call weekdays (719) 531-3400, extension 2700.

Book resources for parents

A Woman's Guide to Getting Through Tough Times, Quin Sherrer and Ruthanne Garlock (Vine Books).

Angry Men and the Women Who Love Them: Breaking the Cycle of Physical and Emotional Abuse, Paul Hegstrom (Beacon Hill Press).

Blue Genes, Paul Meier (Tyndale).

Boundaries with Kids, Henry Cloud and John Townsend (Zondervan).

Caring for Sexually Abused Children: A Handbook for Families and Churches, R. Timothy Kearney (InterVarsity).

Fresh Wind, Fresh Fire, Jim Cymbala and Dean Merrill (Zondervan).

Mood Swings: Understanding Your Emotional Highs and Lows, Paul Meier (Nelson).

Parent's Guide to Top 10 Dangers Teens Face, Stephen Arterburn and Jim Burns (Focus on the Family).

Parenting the Wild Child: Hope for Those with an Out of Control Teenager, Miles McPherson (Bethany House).

Parents in Pain: Overcoming the Pain and Frustration of Problem Children, John White (InterVarsity).

Shattered Dreams: God's Unexpected Path to Joy, Larry Crabb (WaterBrook).

Stomping Out the Darkness, Neil T. Anderson and Dave Park (Regal).

Surviving the Prodigal Years: How to Love Your Wayward Child Without Ruining Your own Life, Marcia Mitchell (YWAM).

The Angry Child: Regaining Control When Your Child Is Out of Control, Timothy Murphy and Loriann Hoff Oberlin (Crown).

The New Strong-Willed Child: Birth Through Adolescence, James C. Dobson (Tyndale).

When God Doesn't Make Sense, James C. Dobson (Tyndale).

Why A.D.H.D. Doesn't Mean Disaster, Walt Larimore, Diane Passno, and Dennis Swanberg (Tyndale).

Why Christian Kids Rebel: Trading Heartache for Hope, Tim Kimmel (W Publishing Group).

Booklets by Focus on the Family (1-800-AFamily)

Help for Hurting Parents: Dealing with the Pain of Teen Pregnancy, Luther McIntyre (BD106).

How to Really Love Your Pregnant Teen (LK013).

Book resources for teens and young adults

Adolescence Isn't Terminal: It Just Feels Like It!, Kevin Leman and Steve Sever (Tyndale).

Boundaries in Dating, John Townsend and Henry Cloud (Zondervan).

He's HOT, She's HOT: What to Look for in the Opposite Sex, Jeramy and Jerusha Clark (WaterBrook).

I Have to Be Perfect: And Other Parsonage Heresies, Timothy L. Sanford (Llama Press).

Refuge: A Pathway Out of Domestic Violence and Abuse, Donald Stewart (Woman's Missionary Union).

The Search for Significance: Seeing Your True Worth Through God's Eyes, teen edition, Robert S. McGee (W Publishing Group).

Booklets for Teens and Young Adults from Focus on the Family (1-800-AFamily)

Alcohol and Drug Abuse: Resisting the Epidemic (LF236).

Dare2Dig Deeper/Friends: Developing Relationships that Last, Cheryl DeWitt (YC077).

Dare2Dig Deeper/Lethal Haze: The Vicious Truth About Drugs and Alcohol (YC028).

Five Reasons You Need the Piece of Paper (LF232).

FOCUS ON THE FAMILY®

Welcome to the family!

Whether you purchased this book, borrowed it, or received it as a gift, we're glad you're reading it. It's just one of the many helpful, encouraging, and biblically based resources produced by Focus on the Family for people in all stages of life.

Focus began in 1977 with the vision of one man, Dr. James Dobson, a licensed psychologist and author of numerous best-selling books on marriage, parenting, and family. Alarmed by the societal, political, and economic pressures that were threatening the existence of the American family, Dr. Dobson founded Focus on the Family with one employee and a once-a-week radio broadcast aired on 36 stations.

Now an international organization reaching millions of people daily, Focus on the Family is dedicated to preserving values and strengthening and encouraging families through the life-changing message of Jesus Christ.

Focus on the Family Magazines

These faith-building, character-developing publications address the interests, issues, concerns, and challenges faced by every member of your family from preschool through the senior years.

Focus on the Family **Citizen®** U.S. news issues

Focus on the Family **Clubhouse Jr.™** Ages 4 to 8

Focus on the Family **Clubhouse™** Ages 8 to 12

Breakaway® Teen guys

Brio® Teen girls 12 to 16

Brio & Beyond® Teen girls 16 to 19

Plugged In® Reviews movies, music, TV

FOR MORE INFORMATION

Online:
Log on to www.family.org
In Canada, log on to www.focusonthefamily.ca

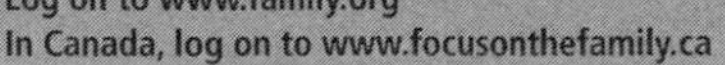

Phone:
Call toll free: (800) A-FAMILY (232-6459)
In Canada, call toll free: (800) 661-9800

BP06XFM

Find More Encouragement for Moms
from Focus on the Family®

Dreams of a Woman

Girlhood dreams shape almost every woman's life. But what happens when those dreams seem to be on hold — or denied? In Dreams of a Woman, *author Sharon Jaynes encourages women to reconsider their desires and allow God to surpass their dreams. Includes Bible study questions. Paperback.*

Give Them Wings

What can moms and dads do to prepare their kids for life as responsible young adults and themselves for the empty nest? Give Them Wings *provides practical insights to help teens choose the right college, embark on a career, and more. Best of all, it allows parents the freedom to look toward the future with hope. Paperback.*

Once a Parent, Always a Parent

What happens to a parent's role when all the kids have moved out? You'll find the expression true: Once a Parent, Always a Parent. *Chances are, your counsel will still be needed — perhaps more than ever! This book gives guidelines in establishing healthy boundaries, helping your son or daughter get off to a good start, and dealing with your new place in their lives. Paperback.*

• • •

Look for these special books in your Christian bookstore or request a copy by calling (800) A-FAMILY (232-6459). Friends in Canada may write Focus on the Family, PO Box 9800, Stn. Terminal, Vancouver, BC V6B 4G3 or call (800) 661-9800.

Visit our Web site (www.family.org) to learn more about the ministry or find out if there is a Focus on the Family office in your country.